AF581270

7/GALLERY OF THE ARTS/5 CONTINENTS

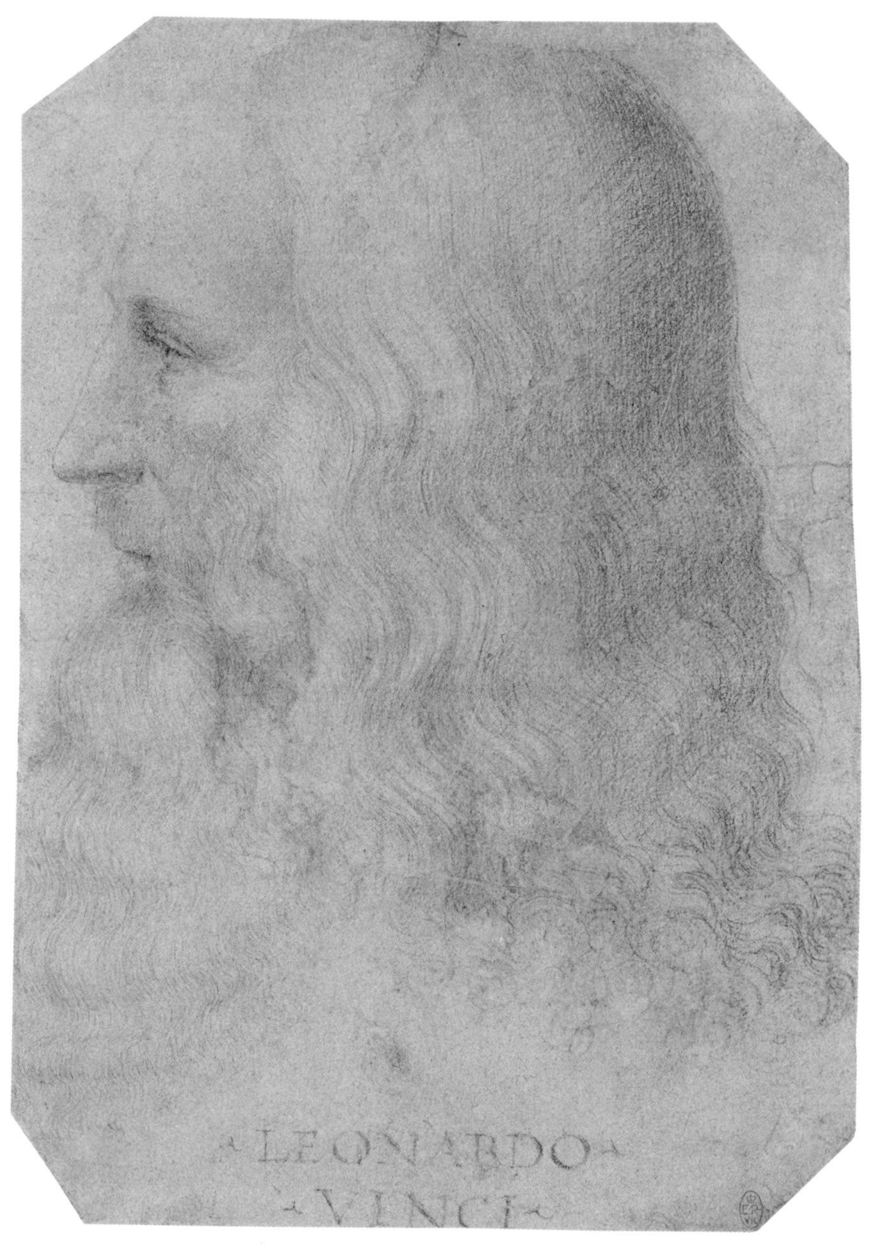
LEONARDO
VINCI

EDOARDO VILLATA

LEONARDO DA VINCI

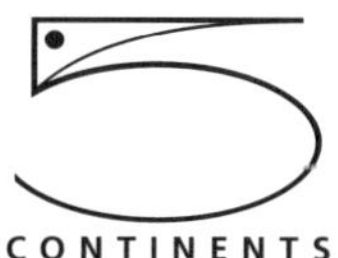

7/ GALLERY OF THE ARTS

Heartfelt thanks are due to Giovanni Agosti for his faith and helpfulness, and to Marco Albertario, Lia Bellingeri, Paola Gallerani, Pietro Marani, Jonathan Nelson and Cristina Passoni for their exceptionally friendly and patient attention and support.

PAGE 2
Francesco Melzi, *Leonardo da Vinci*, ca. 1515–18, Royal Library, Windsor Castle, inv. RL 12726.

EDITORIAL COORDINATOR
Paola Gallerani

TRANSLATION
Timothy Stroud

EDITING
Andrew Ellis

ICONOGRAPHIC RESEARCH
Alessandra Montini

CONSULTANT ART DIRECTOR
Orna Frommer-Dawson

GRAPHIC DESIGN
John and Orna Designs, London

LAYOUT
Virginia Maccagno

COLOUR SEPARATION
Digital Graphic (Milan)

PRINTED APRIL 2005
by Conti Tipocolor, Calenzano (Florence)

info@5continentseditions.com
ISBN 88-7439-126-9

PRINTED IN ITALY

CONTENTS

"MOTION AND BREATH"

BEGINNINGS

"But Italy's calamities [...] began with as much displeasure and fright in the spirits of the population as universal things were flourishing and happy. Because it is clear that since, more than a thousand years ago, the Roman Empire began to decline from the greatness to which it had risen with extraordinary ability [*virtù*] and fortune [*fortuna*], Italy had never been so prosperous, nor had found itself in so desirable a condition as the one that it enjoyed with tranquillity in 1490, and in the year previous and following. Because, with all at peace and serenity enjoyed by all, and no less cultivated in the mountainous and sterile areas than in the plains and more fertile regions, nor subjected to powers other than its own internal ones, it was not only abundant in inhabitants, goods and riches, but, made illustrious in the extreme by the magnificence of its many princes, the splendour of its many noble and beautiful cities, and the seat and majesty of its religion, it flourished with men skilled in public administration and great talents in the noble and useful sciences and arts; nor did it lack military glory, as this was understood then. Enhanced by so many adornments, it rightly enjoyed fame and a fine reputation amongst all nations."

However idealised, the image given by Francesco Guicciardini in his *Storia d'Italia* (1537–40) of a miraculous harmony in the Italy of the courts of 1490, which was destroyed by the ill-guided ambition of the lord of Milan, Ludovico Sforza, was the same for those who experienced that time directly. For example, the young Baldassar Castiglione, who spent a long period at the Sforza court to complete his education, and thus reflected the self-awareness of the court in some way, was an eye-witness to the entry of the French troops of Louis XII in Milan castle, which he commented upon in a letter of 8 October 1499: "In this parade the Majesty of the king of France entered the castle of Milan, formerly the receptacle of the flower of the men of the world, now filled with the basest taverns and perfumed with dung." We find the same nostalgic outlook in Bernardino Corio's *Historia Patria* (published in Milan in 1503), but at the start of the 1490s a Tuscan poet, Bernardo Bellincioni, described the Sforza court in substantially similar terms in a work published in 1493 that provided the first mention of Leonardo in print: "[Ludovico] has filled his court with virtuous men / [...] Only here is the sacred Mount Parnassus to be found, / and every learned man comes like a bee to honey; / [...] from Florence an Apelles was brought here [in the margin: "Magistro Lionardo da Vinci"]". Leonardo da Vinci had arrived in Milan at the age of thirty around 1482.

Born in 1452 the illegitimate son of a rising notary in Florence, Piero da Vinci, Leonardo probably followed his father to Florence soon after his infancy (he was still in Vinci in 1457) and, logically, would have begun his artistic career in the first half of the 1460s, probably between 1463 and 1465. This choice was probably not due so much to the resistance of the young Leonardo to becoming a notary, in accordance with the family tradition, but the desire of ser Piero to reserve that activity for his future legitimate sons (as in fact occurred, even though his eldest son was not born until 1476). Yet it was worth supporting the natural inclination of the boy to take up a profession able to offer fair possibilities of economic and social success for an illegitimate son of a member of the middle classes. Preference fell on the workshop of Andrea del Verrocchio, which, with that of the Pollaiuolo brothers, was the most prestigious in Florence. Perhaps personal friendship lent a hand in the choice, according to the account of Giorgio Vasari (1550 and 1568), but more important was the growing favour Andrea was finding in the circles of Giuliano and Lorenzo de' Medici, with whom the notary from Vinci had connections. Talented in particular as a sculptor, Verrocchio was also an expert jeweller, caster and painter. In the period of the late 1460s and early 1470s, youngsters like Botticelli and Perugino passed through his workshop, while in parallel with Leonardo painters like Francesco Botticini, Lorenzo di Credi, and sculptors and clay-modellers like Francesco di Simone Ferrucci, Agnolo di Polo and Gian Francesco Rustici, carried out their training. During his stay with Verrocchio (he was still documented there in 1476 though at the age of twenty, in 1472, he was already enrolled in the Compagnia di San Luca as an independent master able to accept individual commissions) Leonardo could have helped, and to some degree participated, in his master's more important commissions: the marble basin in the Sagrestia Vecchia in San Lorenzo, the tomb of Giovanni and Piero de' Medici in the same church (1469–72), the bronze group of the *Christ and Saint Thomas* for Orsanmichele (1466–83), the bronze *Putto with dolphin* executed for Lorenzo il Magnifico's Villa di Careggi (today in the Palazzo Vecchio), and even the placement of the great copper "ball" on the lantern of Santa Maria del Fiore (27 May 1472). Leonardo was definitely involved in this last operation and with great attentiveness: "Remember the soldering used to solder the ball of Santa Maria del Fiore. [...] Of copper impressed onto stone, like the triangles of this ball" (MS G, fol. 84v, ca. 1510). In Verrocchio's workshop Leonardo was able to receive training that was not only artistic but also technical, and this prompted him to study on his own behalf the operation of the equipment he had before him, including the especially spectacular and complex machinery designed by Filippo Brunelleschi to build the dome on the Florentine cathedral of Santa Maria del Fiore in Florence (copies and elaborations of this can be found in the *Codex Atlanticus*). Based on their style and writing, these drawings date from a period of around 1478–80, when Leonardo had long been active as a painter and sculptor and the first signs of dissatisfaction with his profession appear, to be replaced by the ambition to become a civil and military engineer.

Leonardo's debut as a painter is still debated, but his first known work seems convincingly to be the tiny *Dreyfus Madonna* in the National Gallery of Art in pl. 1 Washington, D.C. The uncertain proportions of the vacant Child and the still generic landscape are indicative of an immature painter, but one simply does not find in the enamelled finishes of Verrocchio's paintings, almost inlays of precious stones proudly displayed, and even less in the work of Lorenzo di Credi (who still contends with Leonardo the authorship of the small panel), the intense dialogue of looks between the two figures, which is given an almost embarrassing intimacy by the absence of secondary elements, and above all the wealth of lighting effects created by those bodies that are extraordinarily sensitive to the "natural" light filtered through the windows that open onto the countryside at dusk. The faint blush on the pallid flesh, the slightly disordered "lustres"—almost golden darts—in the hair (with above a diadem-halo created with virtuoso foreshortening), the concentric wraps of the drapes on the Madonna's shoulder, and most importantly the soft gathering of the red dress, on whose liquid-crystalline consistency the light performs continuous evolutions, all argue for the hand of the young Leonardo in this sort of miniature on panel. In the absence of certain chronological data, it seems probable that this can be dated to around 1469–70, when a small work destined for private worship might be diverted to a good pupil. This painting has been associated with a silverpoint drawing in the Gemäldegalerie in Dresden, which is also variously attributed to Leonardo, Lorenzo di Credi, and generically to Verrocchio's workshop, but I consider it a part of Leonardo's graphic corpus, in spite of the various cleanings it has undergone, not necessarily of restoration (they might signify the repeated use of drawings inside the workshop, the passage of an idea to that of an approved model, perhaps for works like the *Madonna and Child* in the monastery at Camaldoli, for which the attribution to Leonardo should not even be considered). Leaving aside the uncertainty of the pose of the Madonna's left arm, this drawing reveals a degree of doubt in the position of the Child (standing or seated), a more elaborate hairstyle for the Virgin and, above all, a less ethereal physical consistency, in which the shoulder is solid and round rather than slender and sloping, and her prominent breasts swell her dress. These are all elements seen in a later version of the same theme, the so-called *Madonna of the* pl. 3 *Carnation* in the Alte Pinakothek in Munich. Leonardo continued to work on the same basic idea though on a larger scale, embellishing the scene with secondary elements (the simple windows are turned into magnificent two-light versions, and Mary's highly elaborate hairstyle exploits Verrocchio's ideas seen in drawing 1895-9-15-785 in the British Museum, London), but attempting to resolve the problems that the Washington panel had, so to speak, left undecided. The fat, toddling Child moves clumsily and disconnectedly though quite naturally compared to his predecessor (it was an idea that was to appeal to Filippino Lippi), and the ambitious foreshortening of the Madonna's left hand seems much more convincing, both in the solidity of the design and the permeable and sophisticated relationship between light and shade. The elaborate drapery seems almost to have a life of its own and multiplies the instances of intricate lighting effects timidly suggested in the *Dreyfus Madonna*. The comparison that is sometimes advanced with the sculptural work carried out in Verrocchio's workshop, with which several sources and Leonardo himself admitted to being involved (though no attempt to identify sculptural work by Leonardo has so far been convincing), serves to emphasise Leonardo's already mentioned development in the representation of space and volume. His understanding of the three dimensions is translated into a more pervasive hollowing of surfaces, and therefore in a denser and more extensive presence of shadows. Though this effect today appears accentuated by the condition of the painting, which in general has a damaged coat and exasperating curls on the pictorial film of the complexions—perhaps caused by an overly oily binder—we see the effort to soften the surfaces and make them porous to the shadows, programmatically avoiding excessively dry and delineated outlines. This was a process that Leonardo followed throughout his career and which he theorised around 1490–92: "When you represent in your work shadows which you can only discern with difficulty, and of which you cannot distinguish the edges so that you apprehend them confusedly, you must not make them sharp or definite lest your work should have a wooden effect", and again: "Take care that the shadows cast upon the surface of the bodies by different objects must undulate according to the various curves of the limbs which cast the shadows, and of the objects on which they are cast" (MS A, respectively fols 94v and 101v). Very often (we will see it again), Leonardo described in words a concept *after* he had tested it in painting, which for him was always a preferred method of study and understanding. In addition to the appearance of a damp, cold mountainous landscape beyond the windows in the Munich *Madonna*, through which a thin stream trickles on the left, this work has about it a character of some Flemish *tabuleto* (small panel), which was in high fashion in Florence in the 1470s (unlike, for example, Ghirlandaio, northern painting seemed to Leonardo not infinite clarity but an infinity of degrees of light): we see it in the brown tones of the surroundings, in which the evening light creates strong contrasts, and in the virtuosity of the carnation the Madonna holds, in her brooch and especially in the vase at the bottom right, which faithfully reflects the refined taste of Verrocchio. Many elements in the poetics of this small painting produced for private devotion are repeated, though for other purposes, in the large *Annunciation* in the Uffizi. This came pl. 2 from the monastery of San Bartolomeo in Monteoliveto, and was perhaps painted for an Olivetan church in a setting that may not have been very much different, though on a smaller scale, to the *Annunciation* painted by Alesso Baldovinetti in the chapel of the cardinal of Portugal in San Miniato al Monte (though the idea of a private commission that was then bequeathed to San Bartolomeo cannot be excluded). If so, this would provide the basis for a different assessment of the perspective, which has often been criticised but which is instead of surprising mastery, even in the overly dazzling display of virtuosity. The almost marble-like consistency given to the panel by its recent restoration does not impede recognition of the resemblances to the more problematic *Madonna* in Munich: the face of the Virgin is almost the same (though slightly younger in the *Annunciation*), as are her almost plant-like locks of hair, the lily held by the angel and the illustrated botanical treatise represented by the ground-cum-carpet on which the dark shadow of the heavenly messenger lays, almost as though brushing it. In the background we see an indication of the mountainous landscapes so dear to Leonardo, in which the peaks blur and almost evaporate in the indistinct misty greyness of a port in early autumn. It is a prelude, though still empirical and uncertain, of the principle of "aerial perspective" which he put into words after many painting, at the start of the 1490s (MS A, fol. 105v): "You know that in an atmosphere of equal density the remotest objects seen through it, as mountains, in consequence of the great quantity of atmosphere between your eye and them—appear blue and almost of the same hue as the atmosphere itself when the sun is in the East." The greater smoothness of this painting, which is still unable to renounce completely the sharp outlines (*termini spediti*), could indicate a slight precedence compared to the more carefully treated *Madonna* in Munich. Above all it denotes great effort and was probably for viewing by the public, therefore it was entrusted to Leonardo as an independent master. The traditional dating of 1472–73 seems credible, which would suggest the Munich work was from 1473–74. Moreover, the work is typical of the Verrocchiesque milieu, for example, the Madonna's highly ornate bookrest, which is correctly related to the tomb of Piero and Giovanni de' Medici completed in 1472, and the fall of the drapery. A pen study exists in Christ Church, Oxford (no. 0036) for the sleeve of the angel, and the cloak that shrouds the legs of the Virgin is in some way related to the one in the *Fortezza* painted by Botticelli around 1470 for the Arte della Mercanzia. But typical, in particular, of the workshop of Verrocchio (and, to a lesser degree, of Ghirlandaio), are the brush-on-linen studies of drapery. The two studies—nos. 2256 and RF 41904 in the Louvre—are especially close to the period of the Uffizi *Annunciation*, as seen in the firm and somewhat dry lines in which the light administered with traces of lead white plays an important role; this last touch influenced Marco d'Oggiono and perhaps Giovanni Agostino da Lodi in

Milan, which demonstrates that Leonardo took these works with him to Lombardy. On the other hand, study no. 2255 in the Louvre [fig. 1] seems softer and more atmospheric. It is apparently linked to the position of the Madonna's legs but, rather, it is close in conception to the panel in Munich if not to the successive *Benois Madonna.* These works were not therefore just a trial run for the young painter but a continual exercise for Verrocchio's collaborators. Of this last small canvas there exists a second, almost identical, version by Lorenzo di Credi (Fondation Custodia, Paris, no. 2491) that seems to have been executed side by side with Leonardo, and which explains the tangible origin of some of Leonardo's didactic precepts: "I say and insist that drawing in company is much better than alone, for many reasons. The first is that you would be ashamed to be seen behindhand among the students [...]. Another is that you can learn from the drawings of others who do better than yourself; and if you are better than they, you can profit by your contempt for their defects, while the praise of others will incite you to farther merits" (MS A, fol. 106v, ca. 1490–92). From this point on, we are in the recorded period of Leonardo's work, with his first known dated drawing: the famous landscape, folio 8P recto, in the Uffizi, annotated "on the 5th day of August 1473, the day of Saint Mary of the Snow" ["addì 5 d'agossto 1473 dì di sancta Maria della Neve"] [fig. 2]. To consider it "the first modern landscape" is undoubtedly an exaggeration linked to the old conditioned reflex to consider Leonardo the inventor of more or less everything (and therefore also of landscape painting), nor is it of much interest to go hunting for the precise spot from which Leonardo made his drawing. It should be considered as a completely finalised study for a painting, specifically for the execution of a landscape in Flemish taste, for example, the background to the *Martyrdom of Saint Sebastian* (National Gallery, London, originally in the church of the Santissima Annunziata) by Piero Pollaiuolo, circa 1475. Above all this drawing should be assessed against the output of Verrocchio's workshop, and we see that there are features of the landscape and nature that are very similar to early works by Leonardo. The most intriguing claim is that Leonardo's hand is seen in certain sections of *Tobias and the Angel* in the National Gallery, London, more probably in the lovely fish than the little dog.

A no less enchanting landscape, which has no mountains but a horizon that dissolves into the blue air (indeed, the air is not at all "heavy", so clear it can almost be
pl. 5 measured), is seen behind the figure of *Ginevra Benci* in the damaged panel in the National Gallery of Art in Washington, D.C. The work dates almost certainly from 1475–76, when the nobleman Bernardo Bembo, the father of Pietro (author of *Asolani* and *Prose della volgar lingua*) and Venice's ambassador to Florence, began an affair with Ginevra, dedicating her verses that were read in the Medici circle (participating in the game were other literati associated with Il Magnifico such as Cristoforo Landino and Alessandro Braccesi, besides Lorenzo himself). The link is unquestionable, given the

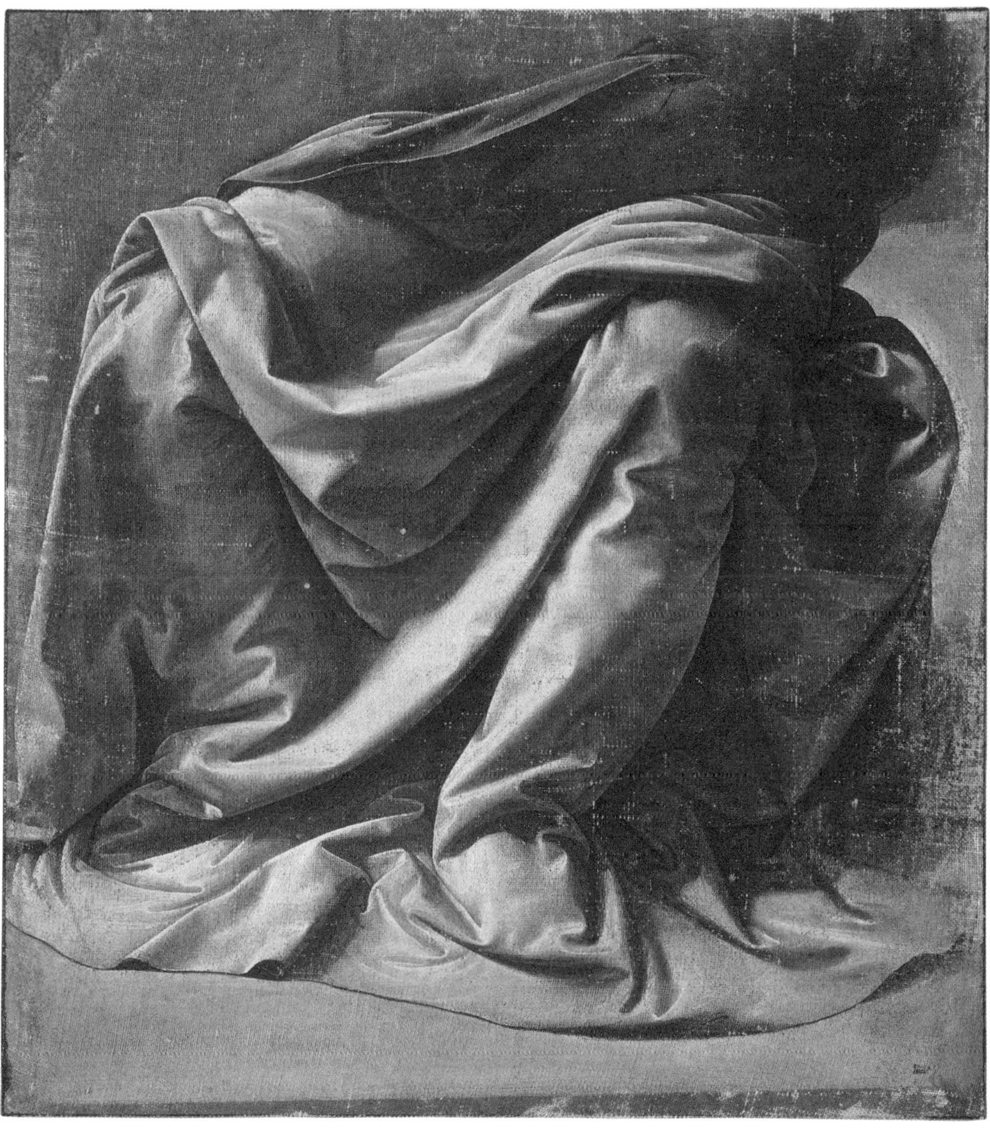

Fig. 1. *Drapery for a seated figure*, brush and grey tempera, white heightening, on grey prepared linen cloth, 26.6 x 23.3 cm, Département des Arts Graphiques, Musée du Louvre, Paris, inv. 2255.

motto painted on the back, the first version of which, VIRTUS ET HONOR, read by infrared, was Bembo's and was altered by Leonardo himself to VIRTUTEM FORMA DECORAT. The painting is still strongly considered to be related to Verrocchio's work, particularly the famous *Lady with a Bunch of Flowers*, a marble bust in the Bargello, of which the facial features, hairstyle and dress make it almost a three-dimensional twin to Leonardo's portrait. In addition to the almost competitive relationship it has with the sculpture—which is also evident in the torsion of the model that makes her pl. 4

delicately bend her neck—Leonardo's work has other elements typical of his painting in the long term, for example, the highlighting of her pale face against a dark background (in this case *ginepro*, meaning juniper in Italian, and an evident reference to the name Ginevra), the secondary shadows thrown by the scarf and the hardly suggested strings of her bodice, and the trembling of the reflection of the trees in the river in the background.

The recent graphic reconstruction of the original *facies*, with the restoration of the crossed arms lost when the lower part of the panel was cut off, has no basis in reality as it derives from a drawing made in 1488–90 (RL 12558, Windsor). The painting of Ginevra remained in Florence (it is mentioned by sources like Vasari and the *Libro di Antonio Billi*; and anyway, if it had been passed from Bernardo to his son Pietro, we would certainly have known about it) and may have provided the opportunity for Leonardo to establish a long-lasting relationship with the Benci family, to which he was still close in the early Cinquecento. The renown of the client made Leonardo one of the most highly visible painters in the mid-1470s, and the extreme care he took in the production of the portrait (the outlines were partly given using pouncing, and perhaps for the first time Leonardo attempted to soften the shifts between tones by blurring and mixing colours directly with the tip of his fingers) seems to suggest that he was the first to understand the importance of the work. On the other hand, in 1476 Leonardo was in the company of a member of another family close to the Medici, Lionardo Tornabuoni, and also of a brigade of jewellers, models and doublet-makers who were all accused anonymously of sodomy on 9 April and confirmed on 7 June. Despite being absolved of the charge, which might have been dictated by political prudence, it should be noted that this was another connection between Leonardo and the circle of the Medici (according to the Anonimo Gaddiano and Vasari, Leonardo also frequented the famous "garden of San Marco" that was fundamental to the young Michelangelo), and that the anonymous report informs us that Leonardo was "with Andrea Verrocchio". This last comment refers of course to the fact that Leonardo, as an independent master, was Verrocchio's collaborator and as such able to accept independent commissions. This episode cannot have damaged Leonardo's reputation so much considering that, at the start of 1478, he was given the prestigious commission for the altarpiece for San Bernardo's Chapel in the Palazzo della Signoria. Although he may have sketched this work, Leonardo never completed it.

Towards the end of 1478, Leonardo began to paint two Madonnas, as he jotted down on a sheet in the Uffizi (446 Er): "[...]ber 1478 I began the two Virgin Marys". The
pl. 7 style makes it probable that one of these was the *Benois Madonna*, now in the Hermitage in Saint Petersburg. This version of the theme is no longer comparable to previous ones, as they were as static and based on a silent game of eye contact as this

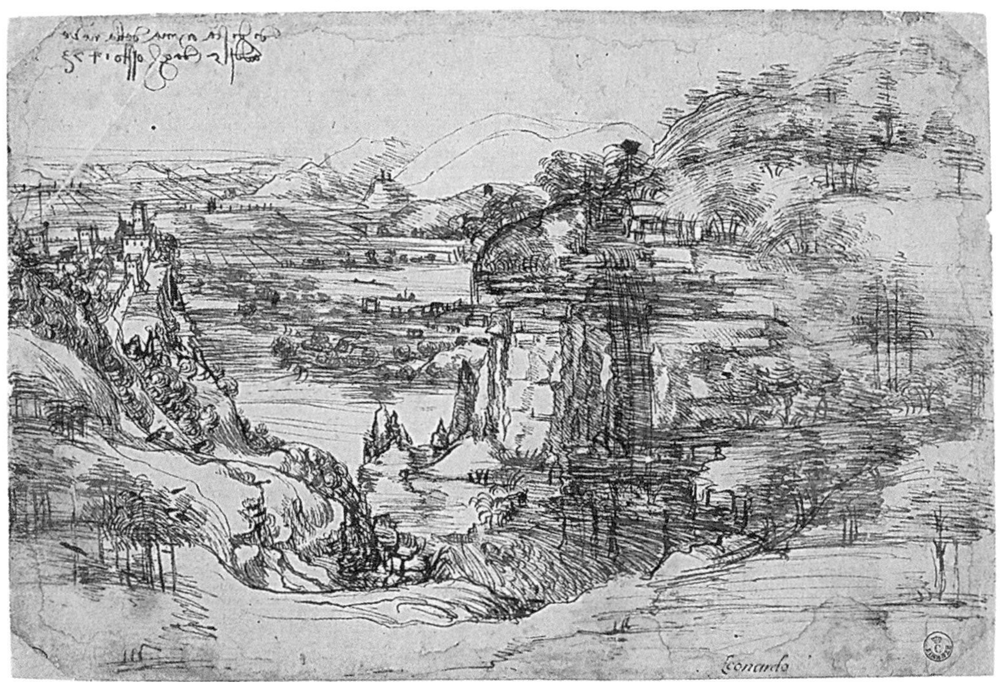

Fig. 2. *Drawing of a landscape*, 5 August 1473, pen and ink, 19 x 28.5 cm, Gabinetto Disegni e Stampe, Galleria degli Uffizi, Florence, 8P recto.

one is dynamic, almost energised, with the burst of infantile hilarity from the Madonna countered by the equally infantile seriousness of the Child as he observes the flowers his mother holds between her fingers. The shade is more enveloping, the graduated levels of the characters and their spatial arrangement is more definite and solid, and the liquid light on the sleeve of the mother-child Mary is more oil-like, than had yet been seen. Even the Virgin's pose—with her left leg bent and right one straight, and between the latter and her bent arm the puff of her dress that suggests one of the diagonals of the painting, though deriving from a marble relief attributed to Donatello (the *Dudley Madonna* in the Victoria and Albert Museum, London)—is an anticipation of the figure of Mary seen in the much later *Virgin and Child with Saint Anne* in the Louvre. As far as the physical condition of the painting allows a judgement to be made, it seems that the softer consistency is analogous to that in the small *Annunciation* in the Louvre, which is a small format variant of the painting of pl. 6
the same subject in the Uffizi. The authorship of this work too is contested between Leonardo and Lorenzo di Credi, but is attributed to the former because of its compositional rigour, the delicacy of the chiaroscuro passages and the exceptionally mature and refined use of "aerial perspective". In addition, there are several points of high refinement, for example, the hems of Mary's cloak are extraordinarily powerful despite the small dimensions of the painting, which seem embraced or captured by

the shadows thrown by the bookrest and benches on the right. This painting has traditionally been thought to be part of the predella for the altarpiece commissioned from Verrocchio for the Duomo in Pistoia, which was painted almost entirely by Credi between 1478 and 1486. The link is possible even though it has not been demonstrated, and comparison with a painting that we know was part of the predella (the *Saint Donatus with the Tax Collector* in Worcester Art Museum) is enough to recognise straight away the same artistic vocabulary, but also the substantial difference in quality. In taking up once again the ideas he had exploited in the first *Annunciation*, Leonardo made use of a design, though simplified, which the rather pedantic style showed to be somewhat earlier (428 Er, Uffizi). It was one that had been produced for the Florentine panel but then set aside (though it remained the common property of Verrocchio's workshop; the young Perugino used it for the hanged man on the right in the small *Miracle of Saint Jerome* in the Louvre). Continual comparison with sculptural practices led Leonardo to tackle increasingly the problem of the spatial positioning of his figures, which by this time he was able to portray in a masterful manner either at the culmination of a movement or in meditative suspension. The many drawings of the Madonna in the late 1470s and early 1480s (associated with the painting in the Hermitage, the other "Virgin Mary" begun in 1478 and perhaps never painted, and the San Bernardo altarpiece, unless the last two are the same painting) demonstrate Leonardo's genuine persistence in varying the pose of the figures on the same sheet; for instance, the beautiful sketch on folio 12276 recto in Windsor [fig. 3]. The Madonna, whose bust is almost a mirror image of the *Benois Madonna*, turns towards the Child, who is suckling intently or gazing into space with an air of melancholy. The lower part of her body is traced in sketchily and displays a rotation of great effect. The infant Baptist is seen below, another idea that occupied Leonardo for a long period. Conceptually, this drawing has many points of contact with the famous angel that the artist added—with the landscape on the left and other elements—in
pl. 8 Verrocchio's *Baptism of Christ*, which was previously in San Salvi in Florence and today is in the Uffizi. Unlike what one usually thinks, this contribution by Leonardo to an earlier painting, which remained in the workshop for a long period, should date from a later period of his career, perhaps around 1480. Compared to the half figure of Ginevra Benci, when Leonardo was just setting out on the path of understanding of
pl. 9 the use of space, the pose of the angel is too complex and affected for a work of 1475, being set around three different axes (one each for the head, back and legs), and the face too heavily charged with a new melancholic hypersensibility. Not to mention the mastery of the pictorial execution with which Leonardo softens and modernises the rough painting of Verrocchio, with the tremulous landscape created with air and veils of colour, and with the water of the Jordan that sparkles as it bathes the legs of Christ, whose body loses its nervous leanness and is softened to the point of flaccidity.

On the folio in Windsor mentioned above, next to the sacred group we see a number

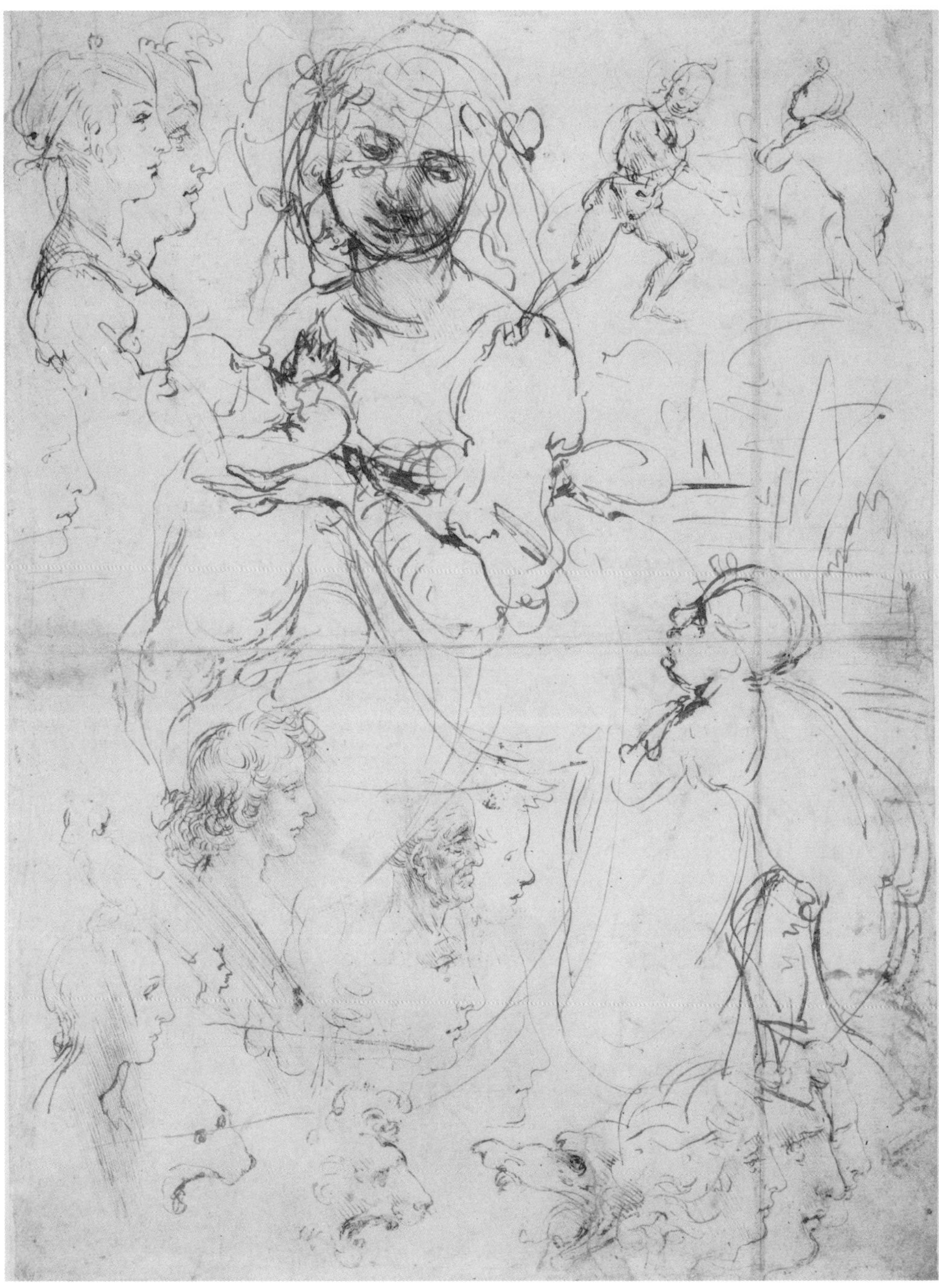

Fig. 3. *Madonna nursing and other studies*, ca. 1478–80, pen and ink, 23.2 x 19 cm, Royal Library, Windsor Castle, inv. RL 12276 recto.

of rather banal human profiles, and the more interesting ones of a lion and dragon facing one another (the fight between which Leonardo drew on other sheets around 1480) and a soldier (?) running at the top right. These elements in some way relate to
pls. 11-13 the background scene in the uncompleted *Adoration of the Magi* (Uffizi) that was commissioned by the Augustinian canons for the high altar in San Donato a Scopeto in March 1481 (the documents continue to the end of September, which marks the last known reference to Leonardo in Florence). The almost square format was not new for this subject in Florence (Botticelli had already used it, and Filippino Lippi would do the same when he completed the San Donato altarpiece), but what was radically new was the layout of the composition, which did away with the Magi's sumptuous retinue and cut the scene cleanly into two planes. The background, for which the perspective was carefully studied, demonstrates the juxtaposition of builders constructing a building (probably a temple) and a brawl between horseback soldiers that was almost certainly inspired by classical sculpture. For the first time we see in a painting the contemporary presence of two elements that were literally to obsess Leonardo from this time on: the organisation of collective work, with men often reduced to teeming mechanised ants in his sketches, and the outbreak of ugly, uncontrolled though typically human violence. And the foreground—in which arranged in a chorus around the timeless group of the Madonna and Child we see reverent, ecstatic, meditative, distracted and dancing men and angels (the kneeling mago in the left foreground seems a close relation to the angel in the *Baptism of Christ*)—depicts the instant of harmony of a group that at any moment will break up. It is not easy to explain the sudden appearance in Leonardo's world of this extreme tendency to pathos that was often to re-emerge in his work as an instinct to be dominated. Till this time he had been a follower of Verrocchio specialised in virtuoso work on lighting effects, clothing and a realism typical of Flemish painting. One possible suggestion is that he made a trip to Rome to see the antiquities but, without excluding *a priori* this hypothesis, it seems more economical to explain his development with the above-mentioned garden of San Marco in which, besides studying collections of ancient works of art, the sculptor Bertoldo di Giovanni, older than Leonardo by a little over ten years, offered continuity with the more tragic aspect of Donatello's work (perhaps encouraging a different reflection on the sculptor's work which was anyway daily in view in Florence, like the relief of *Saint George with the Princess*, ca. 1417, in Orsanmichele and now in the Bargello). For that matter, Verrocchio himself tended to favour pathos in his sculptures from the 1480s. It is not even overly strange that twenty years were required before Leonardo's *Adoration of the Magi*—which the young Raphael studied during his stay in Florence around 1505, and whose composition lies at the base of both the latter's *Disputa* and the *School of Athens* which he frescoed in the Stanze in the Vatican—revealed all its potential for the sixteenth-century "modern style" through study of its variety of expressions,

foreshortening, references to ancient art and lofty formulation. Leonardo himself did not take much less (between the *Last Supper* and the *Battle of Anghiari*) to master, on a proportionate scale, the inventions heralded by Donatello's work, and this might be the real reason why the *Adoration of the Magi* remained uncompleted. Leonardo was ahead of himself, still not having the technical ability to master these inventions which, in 1481–82 were objectively inconceivable (and not even suggested by those surviving preparatory drawings, which are highly remote in terms of novelty and pl. 10
intensity). If we tried to complete the extraordinary sketch with the pictorial surface of the Angel in the *Baptism*, or the *Benois Madonna* or the first *Virgin of the Rocks*, we would fail utterly because the attempt would be too ambitious.

Leaving behind him this defeat (Vasari says it remained in the Benci household), Leonardo moved to Milan at an imprecise date in either 1481 or 1482. This move may have been related to Lorenzo il Magnifico's public relations policy (at the same time the best painters in Florence were heading to Rome to fresco the Sistine Chapel); at the time, Lorenzo was on the best of terms with Ludovico Sforza (Il Moro), who, in turn, was administering power as tutor to his nephew Duke Gian Galeazzo. Leonardo, "a man without letters" (as he controversially defined himself), of technical but no humanistic background, was unable to be part of the Neo-Platonic culture as this was the preserve of the intellectual elite in Florence, though as a member of the Medici circle he might have picked up something on the subject. However, his interests were increasingly veering towards engineering and mechanics, and in Milan, where the Aristotelian leanings prevalent in Pavia University (and the resultant more "material" ideology) were stronger, Leonardo felt he must have been able to establish himself in this field rather more than as an artist. This attitude is reflected in the famous letter he dictated to an amanuensis that was to be sent to Ludovico Sforza but which was never sent (*Codex Atlanticus*, fol. 1082r) in which he gives a detailed description of his skills in military engineering and then briefly presents himself as a civil architect, sculptor and painter, emphasising Ludovico's project to build a bronze equestrian monument to his father Francesco, the first Sforza duke of Milan.

MATURITY IN MILAN

As far as we are aware, Leonardo's first commission in Milan came from the Scuola della Immacolata Concezione at the church of San Francesco Grande (the contract was signed on 25 April 1483 and represents the earliest proof of Leonardo's presence in Milan). In the company of the brothers Evangelista and Giovanni Ambrogio de Predis—painters linked to the Sforza court—he was to paint the wooden ancona produced from 1480 by the sculptor Giacomo Del Maino (but formerly

commissioned to Pietro Bussolo), and to embellish it with panels of "Our Lady" and four angels on each side dressed in Greek style, "a painting in which they sing and the other in which they play [instruments]". The extensive archive documentation on this commission is extremely complex and difficult to understand. Leonardo painted two versions of the subject (commonly known as the *Virgin of the Rocks*), the first of which
pls. 14, 23 is in the Louvre and the second, painted later, in the National Gallery in London. The second is the only one that is known to have been placed on the altar of the Immacolata Concezione. The Paris work is still entirely linked to Florence: Leonardo used a pyramidal composition based on a clear, sharp and linear drawing, and on a continuous and very calligraphic series of reflections of light (which today are difficult to recognise due to the general blackening of the painting). This approach reveals Leonardo experimenting with coloured light reflecting from one body onto another much earlier than his writings deal with the problem "scientifically". Though everything is set in the semi-darkness of a cave, Leonardo succeeds in bringing out the threadlike highlights of the hem of the Madonna's dress and the cloak of the angel, or allows the angel's transparent sleeve to be tinged delicately by the red reflected by the gown. The scene is somewhat different to what the contract required, which refers to "our lady with her son and angels", and develops the theme explored by Leonardo in various drawings around 1480 (one of which, P II 14 in the Ashmolean Museum, Oxford, has a perspective sketch on the verso that may have also been a first idea for the background in the *Adoration of the Magi*) of the Madonna of Humility, in other words seated or kneeling on the ground, with the infant Baptist. I believe that the iconological reading based on the visions of the Portuguese Jew, Amedeo Mendes da Silva—who converted to become a Franciscan and died in the odour of sanctity but also heresy in 1481 in Milan—has received too much attention, with the hypothesis that the "book of Amadio" that Leonardo recorded among his own books around 1503–04 (MS Madrid II, fols 2v-3r) was in fact Mendes's *Apocalypsis Nova* (when it seems very probable that it was *La Bella Camilla* by Piero da Siena, which was also referred to in manuscript tradition as the *Libro d'Amadìo*, a work close to the popular taste from which Leonardo never turned away, and mixed with other titles such as *Geta a Biriae Birria*, *Novellino* and *Guerin Meschino*). Following this lead there have been some extraordinary suggestions, like the interpretation of the angel as a harpy, whose right foot seems disproportionate and almost monstrous. But as the *Virgin of the Rocks* was meant to fill the central space in the upper register of the ancona, it was clearly painted to be seen from below, and this explains any apparent incongruent proportions. This is deduced from the contract, which refers twice to "our lady in the middle" (i.e., in the central panel), the first indicating the sculpture to be coloured and the second to the "panel [...] painted on the flat", each of which occupies the "middle" of its register; also indicative is comparison with another wooden ancona dedicated to the Immaculate Conception by Giacomo Del Maino, executed for San

Maurizio in Ponte in Valtellina. In this the statue of the worshipping Madonna fills the central niche of the lower register and seems very similar to what the document in Milan seems to suggest. It should be said, though, that a very recently discovered document, though later (1579), and subsequent to early alterations and movements, explicitly affirms that the sculpture was on the upper register.

The similarity of style with Leonardo's Florentine works indicates that the Parisian version of the *Virgin of the Rocks* was produced in a fairly short period, and its reception, which was rather limited and only by particularly intelligent painters, seemed over shortly after 1485. In addition to having an influence of the early career of Boltraffio, who was attracted into Leonardo's orbit at an early age (see the *Madonna* in the Museo Poldi Pezzoli in Milan, ca. 1485), echoes of Leonardo's painting may be seen in the misty landscape of the *Madonna* by the young Bramantino in the Museum of Fine Arts in Boston, and, more externally, in the head of the Magdalen on the right in the small *Deposition* (Szépmüvészeti Múzeum, Budapest) painted at the same time by Ambrogio Bergognone.

Also linked to Florentine sculptural models and stylistically close to the Parisian version of the *Virgin of the Rocks* is the so-called *Lady with an Ermine* (Czartoryski pl. 16
Muzeum, Kraków), which is probably a portrait of the Milanese noblewoman, Cecilia Gallerani. That it should be her is also suggested by the Greek name for an ermine, *galè*, which is also a symbol of chastity. A slightly later date—around 1485, at most 1486—can be hypothesised for this first appearance of solutions that Leonardo was to experiment with widely: these included the more mobile portrayal of the sitter, who is given an expression that is both ingenuous and knowing, the primary shadows that eat away at the figure, and the secondary ones of the necklace on the lady's neckline, a colder and thicker chromatic tone emphasised by the greyish-blue of the mantle that rests over her left shoulder, and the introduction of the uniformly dark background—entirely repainted to make it duller and monotone—so as to accentuate the figure of the lady. But though this work was unquestionably daring and experimental, there is also something forced about it: the resolution of the virtuoso use of chiaroscuro is too evident, as is the sculptural rotation which makes it seem like an extreme version of the earlier *Lady with a Bunch of Flowers* by Verrocchio. Some years later this painting must have been known at the court in Mantua, since a clear echo of it is seen in a portrait, perhaps of the Marchesa Isabella d'Este, painted by Lorenzo Costa in the early Cinquecento (in the royal collections at Hampton Court), and all modern experts concur that the Kraków portrait of Cecilia Gallerani is the painting Isabella asked to borrow from Cecilia on 26 April 1498 so that she might compare it to a painting by Giovanni Bellini. Naturally the loan was made and, in her courteous reply, Cecilia specified that:

"I would send it very willingly, if it resembled me. But do not think that this was the fault of the painter, of whom I truthfully believe there is no other like him: but only because this portrait was painted when I was very young, and I have completely changed appearance to the point that nobody, seeing the painting and me together, believes that it is my portrait."

It was therefore a portrait painted during early adolescence, as is confirmed by the childlike face and the almost flat chest. Today we know that Cecilia was born around 1473, and that would seem to confirm the date proposed on the basis of style. It would also follow that the painting was not commissioned by Ludovico il Moro in person (who became her lover around 1489 and remained so at least until the political marriage he made with Beatrice d'Este in 1491), and diplomatic sources inform us that in 1490 (when she was about seventeen years old), Cecilia was pregnant by Ludovico and as "beautiful as a flower". It should be mentioned that at the end of 1483 a marriage contract was signed between the Gallerani family and Stefano Visconti, which was annulled in 1487. Given the date of 1485–86, the portrait in Kraków might have been painted as a "marriage portrait" for the groom, which was returned to Cecilia when the planned marriage was definitively called off.

pl. 18 The *Portrait of a Musician* (Pinacoteca Ambrosiana, Milan) seems very advanced in conception even more so than in real execution. Apart from the powerful structure of the man's face (which reflects the anatomical studies of the human skeleton Leonardo began around 1487, in which the skull is analysed in impressive pen drawings like an architectural structure [fig. 4]), the observer is struck by the much more imposing physical and spatial presence of the sitter (perhaps the *maestro di cappella* in the cathedral of Milan, Franchino Gaffurio, though other proposals have been made) despite the fact that the format is less affected and forced. The expressive tone concentrates on the face at the moment the figure's voice is heard. At first Leonardo had thought of not painting the hands that hold the sheet of music, but then they were added, perhaps to make clear what the musician was doing. He had therefore already considered the possibility of expressing the *moti mentali* (motions of the mind) of the musician without accompanying them with physical gestures, but both his theorising on the matter and the full success of the notion only came in future years: "There are several *moti mentali* [expressed] without movement of the body, and others with movements of the body. The *moti mentali* without movements of the body leaves out the arms, hands and other part of the body that indicates life" (*Libro di Pittura*, 370, a passage that was probably written in the 1490s). The interval between the *Lady with an Ermine* and the *Portrait of a Musician* may have been months rather than years, as is revealed by the subtle blurring of the chiaroscuro sections with the tip of a pen and sometimes with the fingertip. These were months in which a mutual antagonism

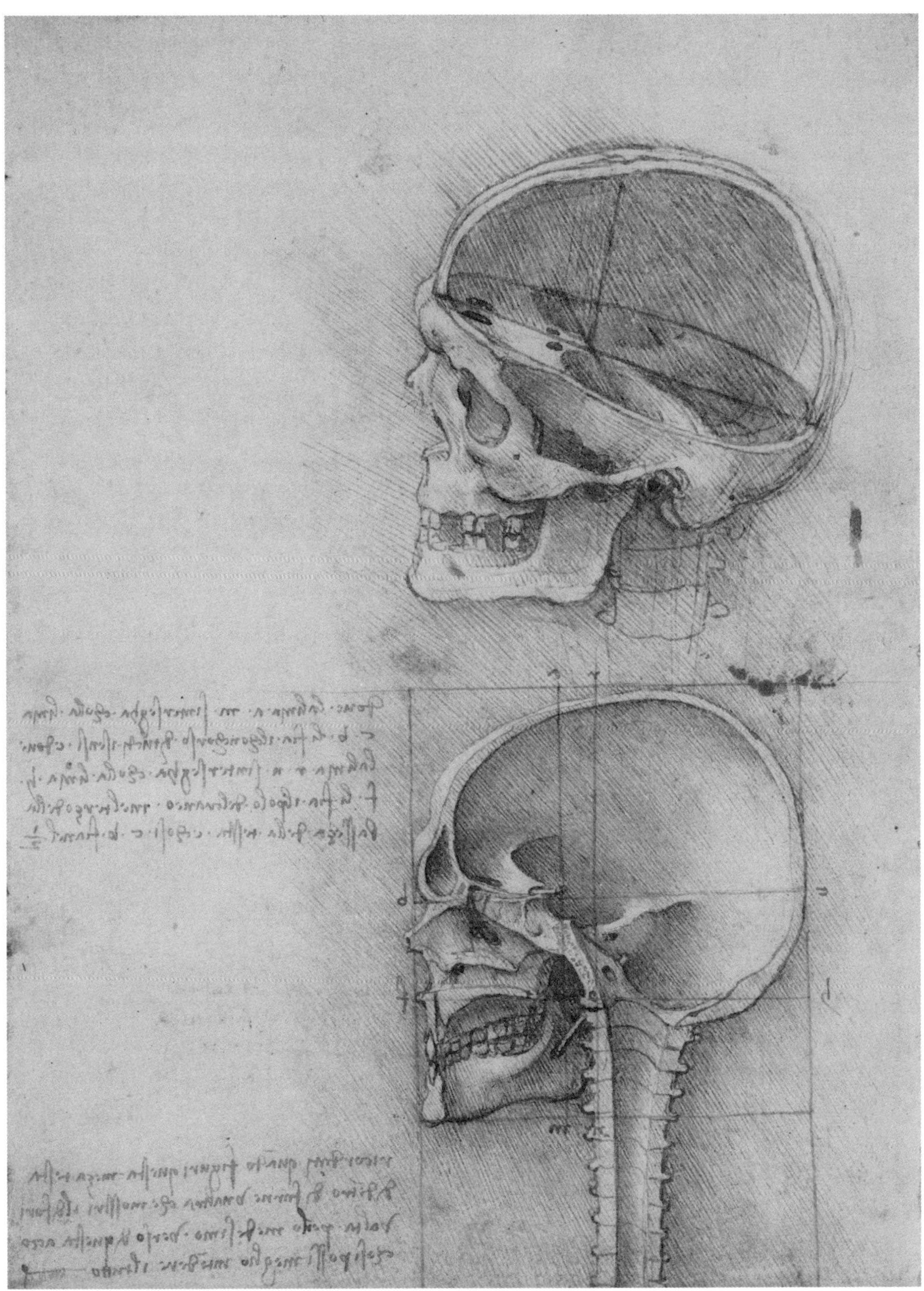

Fig. 4. *Study of skulls in section*, ca. 1489, pen and ink, 18.1 x 12.9 cm, Royal Library, Windsor Castle, inv. RL 19057 recto.

arose between Leonardo and Bramantino, and the fact that Bramantino was aware of the *Musician* and other of Leonardo's paintings is shown by the frescoes for Casa Visconti in Milan, which were probably painted, as is believed today, from a design by Bramante (particularly the *Heraclitus*) and, above all, the *Christ at the Column* formerly in Chiaravalle (all these works are now in the Brera). Leonardo's focus on anatomical definition and the perfection of his treatment of *moto mentale* (though more forceful)
pl. 17 is seen in the unfinished *Saint Jerome* in the Pinacoteca Vaticana. The theatrical gesture of the penitent saint is a dramatic development of an idea created for one of his Madonnas, perhaps the *Virgin of the Rocks* (as suggested by fol. RL 12560 in Windsor) and which he renewed for his figure of Matthew in the *Last Supper*; but what is new in the *Saint Jerome* is the monumental grandeur of the saint, with his arched bust and, one would say, the density and stagnancy of the luminous highlights visible on his shoulders. We are also aware of Leonardo's increasing dissatisfaction with linear perspective, which, in Milan—as seen in Butinone, Zenale, Bramante, and Bramantino—had convinced brilliant followers. We see him mature the conviction (or perhaps it would be better to say the feeling) characteristic of his scientific studies that the world is a continuous, organic and living space that the painter better than anyone else can, and must, understand and explore in its generative processes, and then repeat it in the sense of a phenomenal imitation unlinked either to excessive schematism (painting "is the only imitator of all works seen in nature [...] which, with philosophy and subtle speculation, considers all the qualities of form, air and sites, plants, animals, grasses and flowers, which are girdled by shadow and light. And truly this is science and the legitimate daughter of nature, because painting was born of nature": MS A, fol. 100r, ca. 1490–92) or in the sense of new creation, even beyond what exists in nature though in accordance with nature's laws ("the deity that possesses the knowledge of the painter ensures that the mind of the painter is transmuted into a reflection of the divine mind, since with this freely wielded power he proceeds to the generation of various species of animals, plants, flowers, landscapes" (*Libro di Pittura*, 68, early 1490s).

The theme of a half-length portrait against a dark background was taken to its
pl. 21 completion in the *Belle Ferronnière* (Louvre) in which all the elements with which Leonardo had been experimenting in earlier works reached a balance that we might call definitive. The torsion and dominance of space are rendered with sovereign nonchalance, without the effort seen in the pose of the *Lady with an Ermine* or the rigidity of the setup of the *Musician*; he creates effects of chiaroscuro with an organic unity that was lacking in earlier works (this was the period of, or maybe just before, the writing of MS C, ca. 1490–91, which widely focused on the study of optics and the refraction of light), revealing marvellous effects like the shaft of light that bathes the woman's alabaster jaw. The psychological suspension—never so fleeting and

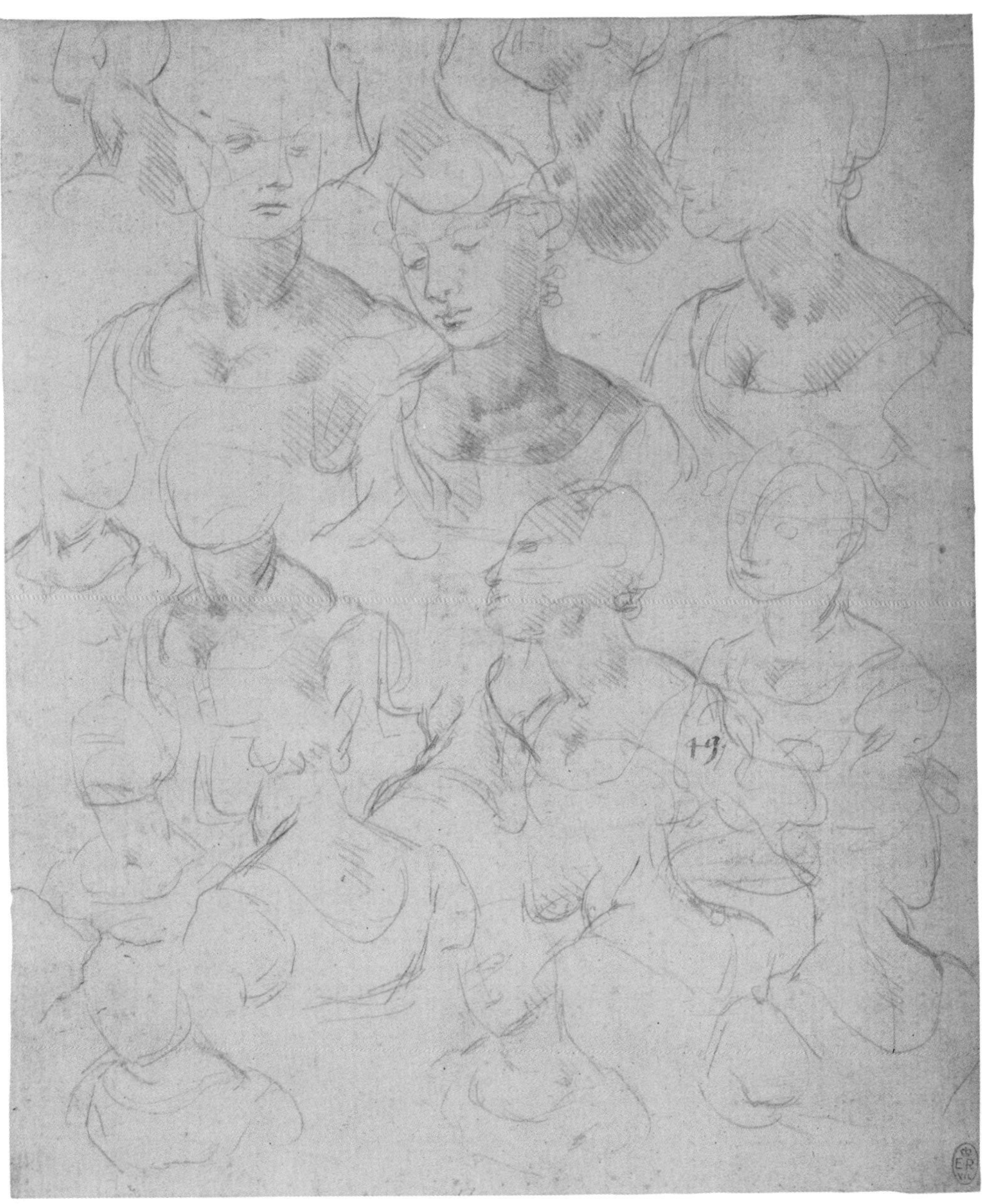

Fig. 5. *Seventeen studies of a female bust*, ca. 1486–87, metalpoint on pale pink prepared paper, 23.2 x 19 cm, Royal Library, Windsor Castle, inv. RL 12513.

instantaneous (and here radically "without hands" as the *Musician* could never have been)—takes us into a world of sentimental sensitivity typical of court culture at the end of the Quattrocento, which Leonardo had by then entered fully. The sudden, hardly perceptible flash of the glance of the lady to her left is revealed in the amazing quivering coda of tiny white dots of light on the darting pupils of her brown eyes, which illustrates with amazing economy the turning movement of her entire figure. I get the impression that, for Leonardo, the appearance in Milan of a work by Antonello da Messina (similar or identical to the *Ecce Homo* in the Collegio Alberoni in Piacenza) may have been decisive; indeed, Bramantino also seems to have been aware of it, as a painting almost contemporary with Leonardo's portrait (the *Compianto* formerly on the facade of San Sepolcro and now in the Pinacoteca Ambrosiana, ca. 1488–89) underlines not its refinement but its pathos, which is taken to its extreme in the pained expression of the weeping Saint John. Purely as hypothesis, I wonder if it were not the *Belle Ferronnière* that was the portrait of Cecilia Gallerani that Leonardo painted for Ludovico il Moro (evidently before the marriage to Beatrice d'Este at the start of 1491), for which Bernardo Bellincioni (who died in 1492) composed a sonnet that is usually associated with the *Lady with an Ermine*, but which seems equally suited to the portrait in the Louvre ("with his painting / he portrays her as she seems to be listening, and does not speak"). Considering the difference between a young girl of twelve or thirteen and a seventeen-year-old "as beautiful as a flower" and perhaps pregnant (Cecilia bore Ludovico a son in May 1491), comparison of the ladies' facial features in the portraits in Kraków and Paris does not seem impossible, however non-determinant.

Leonardo's persistent study of how best to present a the bust in a half-length portrait is shown by a metalpoint drawing in the Royal Library in Windsor [fig. 5], in which Leonardo made seventeen variations of the pose of a young model. One of these is the solution he adopted in the *Lady* in Kraków, but that of the *Belle Ferronnière* is not included. A closer design is seen in another famous drawing made using the same
pl. 20 technique (inv. 15572 D.C., Biblioteca Reale, Turin) in which there are striking resemblances in the delicate caresses of the light surfaces, here created using lead-white highlights, and above all in the fleeting moment expressed by the sitter's
pl. 23 expression. This drawing is often considered preparatory for the angel in the *Virgin of the Rocks*, but it was probably a life study that did not actually make it to a painting, even though there are resemblances with the angel—but with the angel in the London version of the painting rather than the one in Paris. An extraordinarily difficult work to study, the London panel seems to date from around 1490 for reasons of internal coherence and the huge influence it had on painters in Milan during the last decade of the century: for example, Boltraffio, Francesco Galli (called Francesco Napoletano), Zenale, the "Maestro of the Sforza Altarpiece", and perhaps even

Bramantino. We are referring, moreover, to the painting on the altar of the Immacolata Concezione in San Francesco Grande (the fate of the first version remains obscure, which only reappeared around 1610 in the royal collections in France, but perhaps is the same "altar panel in which there was a Nativity that was sent by the duke to the emperor" referred to by Vasari, even though there are some clues to suggest it was exhibited in the Milanese church of San Gottardo in Corte). A recently discovered document refers to a payment of 730 imperial lire (the overall remuneration, according to the 1483 contract was 800 lire) made to Leonardo and to the de Predis brothers on 23 December 1489, which would seem to be for the painting in the National Gallery that was supposed to be delivered a short while later. Having received an offer for the panel much larger than that agreed in 1483, Leonardo and Ambrogio de Predis wrote an entreaty to Ludovico Sforza (undated, but seeming to be from the period 1491–93) asking for arbitration to decide either a supplementary payment or that the "scholars" renounce the panel in favour of the painters so that the latter might sell it. This might indicate that the panel had not yet been delivered, but in 1503 Ambrogio (alone as Leonardo had left Milan some time earlier) returned to the attack, asking once again for either the settlement or the return of the altarpiece, which was now in the church. The idea cannot be excluded that the painting had already been inserted in the large wooden frame by the time of the first entreaty (in which case the painters asked either for economic satisfaction, or that the brothers of the confraternity "return" the painting).

Iconographically there is little difference between the two versions (the gesture of indication made by the angel was removed, while the haloes and reed cross in the London painting were added at a later date) but everything changed in the style and intentions. The dazzling golden light in the half-darkness of the Paris painting gives way to a diffused and pervasive lunar light that thickens oil-like on the surfaces it touches, emphasising the cold, clear range of colours. More evident, the volume of the figures has increased so that they appear monumental and statuesque, and amplify the effect of looking upwards with respect to the earlier version (this is also the case of the panels with the two musician angels that are also in London, but painted by Leonardo's collaborators; one of these might have been Francesco Napoletano, who seems responsible for the green angel and perhaps also for the podgy, quivering Jesus). And then there is the dreaming angel—with the rather dazed, glassy gaze and vaporous starched lace garment, like the decorations on the shoulder of the *Belle Ferronnière*—which argues that the sketch in the Pinacoteca in Parma known as *La Scapiliata* is from the same period (1490–91). The imperceptible excess of melancholy pl. 25
characteristic of high society, a minimum of residual gauntness and the use of lead white to create an almost mother-of-peal effect, mean that this work cannot be referred to the first decade of the Cinquecento, when Leonardo's humanity was made

manifest in his handling of the soft and abundant flesh of his figures, and in the magnification of figurative volumes to statuesque proportions from the *Last Supper* onwards. But the difficult moment at which the second *Virgin of the Rocks* was handed over was substantially the one in which he, after years of studies that led to nothing—and perhaps piqued by Francesco Puteolano's preface to the vulgarisation of *De gestis Francisci Sphortiae* by Giovanni Simonetta, published in Milan in 1490, in which he claimed that only poetry leads to perpetual fame, but not painting or sculpture—Leonardo took seriously the work he had agreed to on the equestrian monument dedicated to Francesco Sforza. "On the 23rd day of April I began this book and started anew on the horse" (MS C, fol. 15v). This fact is important not only because it documents Leonardo's definitive involvement in the plans of the court (confirmed by his organisation of a festival to celebrate Gian Galeazzo Sforza's marriage to Isabella of Aragon at the start of 1490, and which won great admiration from his contemporaries), but also because it confirms several dates for us. Since those surviving plans for the gigantic clay model to be used in the casting show that Leonardo decided to create the horse at walking pace rather than trampling a fallen
pl. 22 enemy, we have a certain date (within 1489) for a famous drawing on blue prepared paper (RL 12358, Windsor) that shows just this design. The silverpoint on prepared paper technique used for the drawing, and the modelling created using parallel, left-to-right lines, is analogous to the Turin folio referred to above. This was the exact moment that Leonardo laid aside his Florentine drawing tradition (which was certainly still in use in his workshop in the early 1490s, when his followers, with Boltraffio at the head, continued to study the more virtuoso potential of delicate chiaroscuro and soft modelling) in favour of coloured chalks, which he also used for writing on some sheets of MS C (1490–91).

Using red and grey chalks (including red ones on red prepared paper to create effects of more vibrant mobility and a more volatile luminism), in addition to exercises of deliberate melancholy, like the famous head of a woman in the Louvre [fig. 6], Leonardo executed the drawings for the heads of the apostles in the *Last Supper* (Windsor, except for one of the head of Christ that is in poor condition and not universally accepted by all as being by Leonardo; Brera). These were studies of heads, hands, feet and drapery in which the artist managed to abandon the gauntness typical of Florentine art, with forms seeming to expand, the drapery come alive, and the faces, which were idealised in terms of classical beauty, venerable old age and even in the baseness of Judas, becoming absolute. The earliest drawing, which was almost
pl. 19 certainly linked only indirectly to the *Last Supper*, is the Windsor folio RL 12552 in which the red chalk gives a quick outline of a musician singing. Overlapping this is an architectural sketch made with a pen that is highly unlikely to be later than 1490 (following comparison with similar drawings in MS B), which means that the

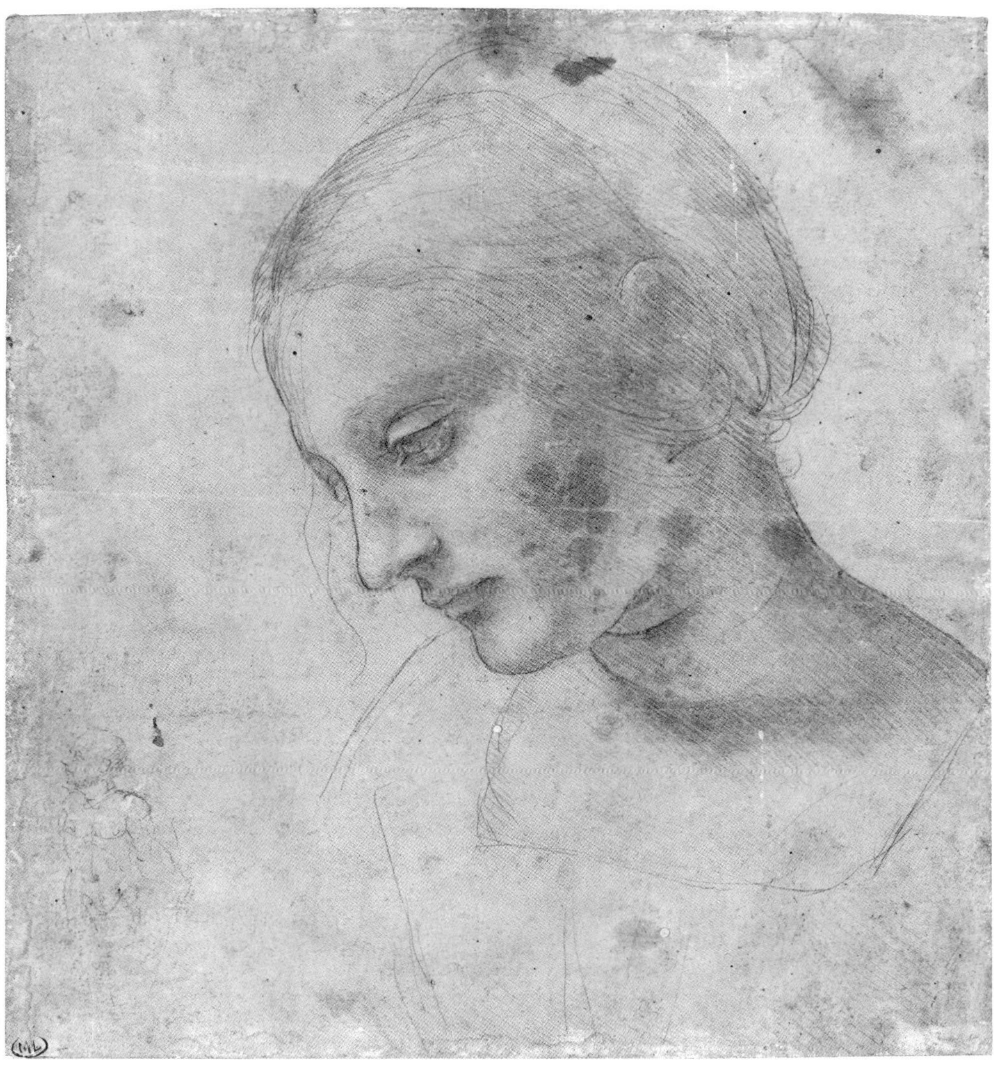

Fig. 7. *Head of a woman in half-profile*, ca. 1490, metalpoint on prepared light blue paper, white heightening, 17.9 x 16.8 cm, Département des Arts Graphiques, Musée du Louvre, Paris, inv. 2376.

drawing was from the late 1480s and among Leonardo's first experiments with this graphic technique. Earlier studies from those that have survived for *The Last Supper* are in dark chalk on white paper (RL 12551 and 12546, Windsor, which are respectively pl. 26
for Philip's face and Peter's arm). Drawings 12547, 12548 and 12550 from the same pl. 27
collection (studies for the heads of Bartholomew, Judas, and Simon) were probably a little later, around 1495, perhaps following a contact in 1494 with the French painter Jean Perréal, from whom Leonardo claimed to learn "the way to colour *a secco*, and the white salt method and to make kneaded paper [...] and his box of colours"

(*Codex Atlanticus*, fol. 669r). For these drawings he used red pencil on red prepared paper, creating striking images of a heroic and more than ideal humanity.

But when was the *Last Supper* painted? The painting fills the north wall of the refectory in Santa Maria delle Grazie, a Dominican convent that was particularly dear to Ludovico il Moro. We know from documents and sources that the works must have come to an end towards the end of 1497, but it is less easy to establish when they began. An idea still far from the final solution is seen in a couple of pen sketches on folio RL 12542 in Windsor [fig. 7]. This contains slightly earlier geometrical studies that refer to the construction of an octagon and its possible architectural uses. They have equivalents in MSS B and A (ca. 1487–90 and 1490–92) and also in the ideas seen in folios in the *Codex Atlanticus* and *Codex Trivulzianus* (ca. 1487–88) linked to the project that Leonardo had entered in 1487–90 for the competition for the construction of the crossing tower for Milan Cathedral (this was won by Giovanni Antonio Amadeo). If we consider that it was only in 1488 that the refectory at Santa Maria delle Grazie was completed, then it seems likely that Leonardo's commission (which is not documented but probably supported by Ludovico, if not actually his idea) occurred very soon after. A confirmation of this is given by the sixteenth-century literary tradition on Leonardo's slowness and the exasperation of the brothers, particularly the famous writer Matteo Bandello, who was nephew to the prior of the convent and studying there in the 1490s. In the introduction to a tale in his most important book, Bandello described Leonardo at work on the *Last Supper*:

"I have also seen him, according to the whim or caprice that took hold of him, leave at midday, when the sun is at its zenith, leave from *Corte vechia* [the ducal palace, now the Palazzo Reale] where he was building that amazing earth horse, and come straight to the Grazie and climb the scaffolding, take the brush and give one or two brushstrokes to one of the figures, and straightway leave and go somewhere else."

The "earth horse", which was started, or better "restarted", around 1490 was completed at the end of 1493 and may have been unveiled for the festivities surrounding the wedding of Bianca Maria Sforza (Ludovico's daughter) to the emperor, Maximilian Habsburg (who opened the way for Ludovico to attain the ducal title).

If we consider Bandello a reliable witness, we have to conclude that Leonardo had
pls. 28-31 already completed the preparatory stages of the *Last Supper* at the latest in 1493 and had begun to paint. The large wall painting in fact inaugurated the Cinquecento, with the following elements in particular making an impact on the more intelligent artists: the theatrical and dynamic focusing of the *moti mentali*, the classical and ideal character of these superhuman figures, the masterly illusive use of perspective and

almost icy light (studied in relation to the false windows in the background but in particular to the real ones in the refectory) which reveals preciousness and clearness of the surfaces and brings out the physical aspect of things and people, and, above all, the monumental scale that even Michelangelo only adopted halfway through the Sistine Chapel. For an execution of such length it is probably not impossible to glimpse some progress within the painting, for example, in the sharply expanded and colossal proportions of the last three apostles on the right (Matthew, Thaddaeus, and Simon), who were almost certainly painted last. Another consideration that emerged with regard to the *Adoration of the Magi*, but which here is still more apparent, is how different Leonardo's magnificent drawings are from the final versions of his most important pictures (just compare the drawing for the head of Philip with the incomparable reality, which aptly embodies the sentimental nobility that so pervaded courtly culture in the early Cinquecento). The drawings were more pervasive and provided an easy, structured means of divulging artistic ideas, but it was the second that were decisive for the ensuing development of Italian art.

Although Leonardo—ever busy organising festivals and being involved in a court dispute on the primacy of the arts or poetry—had witnessed the supply of raw bronze destined for the casting of his "horse" rerouted to Ferrara to make cannons (the model remained however, splendid and fragile, just like the Sforza dukedom of which it was the emblem—both of which were toppled by the French in 1499), he could in recompense enjoy the favour of Ludovico as a painter. Besides the proposed decoration of several rooms in Porta Giovia castle in Milan with "twenty-four Roman stories" (a project perhaps never actually carried out), and the long-dreamed of plan of commissioning him to paint the wall opposite the *Last Supper*, upon which Giovanni Donato da Montorfano, typically Milanese in the style of Foppa and Butinone, had only recently in 1495 frescoed a large *Crucifixion* (it may have been Leonardo or one of his collaborators that overpainted the now completely illegible ducal portraits in tempera at the sides of the fresco), Leonardo certainly decorated a ground-floor room in the north-west tower of Porta Giovia castle, called the Sala pl. 32 delle Asse. Executed in 1498–99, this work cannot be properly appraised from the existing vault, which was entirely repainted during restoration work to the castle in the late Ottocento; it can however be appreciated from large monochrome fragments (a probable sign of incompletion, perhaps due to the crushing of the Sforza troops in August 1499). In these frescoes, the plant decoration with celebratory significances (an idea already used with less heterodox results in the lunettes above the *Last Supper*) became a cogent display of disturbed vitalism, in which extraordinarily organic new growth ravages rocks and bricks. Leonardo's long-standing botanical studies became the basis for a celebration of the simultaneously creative and destructive power of nature in a context that, as far as is suggested, represented the definitive abandonment by Leonardo of the "legitimately constructed" perspective seen in the *Virgin of the Rocks* and repeated in the *Resurrection of Christ with Saints Leonard and Lucy* (today in Berlin), which was commissioned from Boltraffio and Marco d'Oggiono in 1491 and was still to be painted—either in part or whole—in 1494. The decoration marked the beginning of a story of "continuous space" that was later seen in the domes of Parma by Correggio, the Calvary Chapel at the Monte Sacro at Varallo by Gaudenzio Ferrari, the Sala dei Giganti by Giulio Romano at the Palazzo Te in Mantua and, even earlier in some ways, the vault of the Sistine Chapel by Michelangelo. But what a difference there is between this and the enchanting, luminous drawings from more or less the same period that Leonardo made of undergrowth in red pencil on the two sides of folio RL 12431 at Windsor.

INSIDE THE "MANIERA MODERNA"

The French invasion of Milan, its brief recapture by the Sforza troops, and then Ludovico's definitive overthrow at the Battle of Novara in 1500, created a chaotic situation that induced Leonardo to repair to Mantua, where in the winter of 1499/1500 he produced two versions of the cartoon with the portrait of Isabella
pl. 33 d'Este (one remains, in the Louvre. It was prepared for pouncing but never reached the painting stage despite Isabella's insistence). The resorting to a medal by Gian Cristoforo Romano for Isabella's image, rather than the *marchesa* herself, meant that Leonardo's attempt to provide a psychological portrait was rather hampered, but we can see the development that the artist had gained on the scaffolding of Santa Maria delle Grazie, in the spatial mastery of the simple but imposing bust. It was in this period of travels that Leonardo went to Venice to offer his opinion on military engineering matters to the government of the Serenissima (but the one who profited most from his presence and works was perhaps the young Giorgione), and probably thence to Rome and Tivoli, though why is not known, where he studied Roman statues (perhaps the damaged *Muses* in Hadrian's Villa which a few months later fired the imagination of Bramantino, who reinvented them when frescoing the castle in Voghera). However, it was perhaps also during this period that Leonardo deceived himself with the decision that he would give up painting as a profession and devote himself to engineering. The fact is that when he returned to Florence in
pl. 36 1501 he immediately created a sensation with the cartoon of the *Virgin and Child with Saint Anne and Saint John the Baptist* (National Gallery, London). Here, Leonardo had taken a subject dear to the Florentines, particularly at a moment when republican values were being lauded (on Saint Anne's Day—26 July 1343—the revolt against the tyrant Gualtieri di Brienne began; the cartoon had such an impact that "for two days his room was filled with men and women, young and old, going as to a solemn festival to see Leonardo's marvels", according to Vasari, in an event that was perhaps

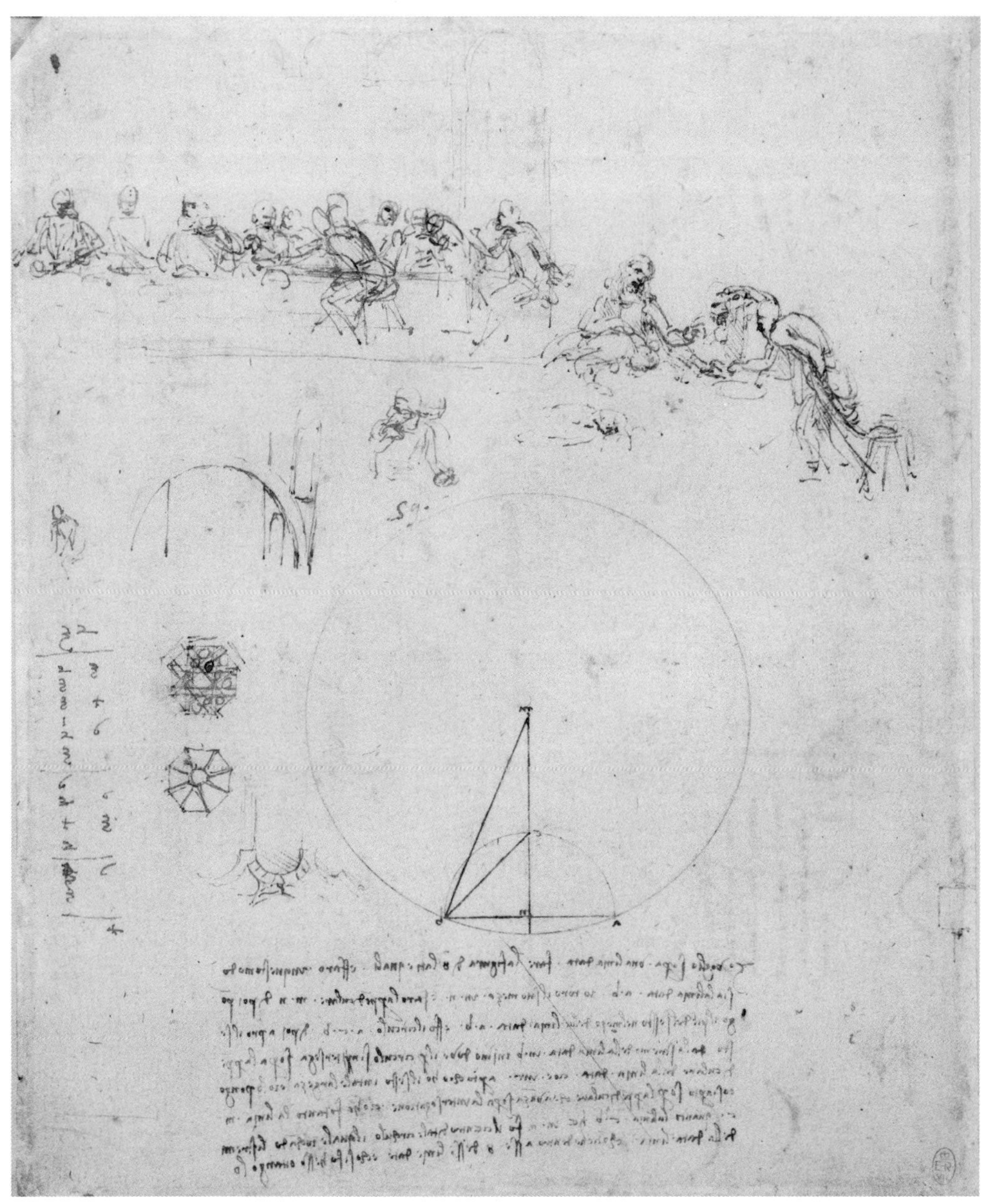

Fig. 7. *Study for the Last Supper, and geometric and architectural drawings*, ca. 1488–89, pen and two types of ink, 26.6 x 21.4 cm, Royal Library, Windsor Castle, inv. RL 12542.

more political than aesthetic, even though the writer from Arezzo, who had been a courtier to Grand Duke Cosimo I, was not in a position to allude to this), and in the cartoon developed ideas he had harboured for over twenty years. Despite the fact that the cartoon is closely linked to means of expression Leonardo used in the *Last Supper*, though in an undramatic context that provides an almost marmoreal definition of the figures, the version translated to panel and now in the Louvre —the invention of which must have been created in parallel, perhaps as a tribute to Anne of Brittany, queen of France, with which Florence was at that time allied (a description of it may exist in a letter by one of Isabella d'Este's informers in 1501)— brought back into use ideas formed in the late 1470s and early 1480s and seen in the *Benois Madonna* and first *Virgin of the Rocks*, though rendered monumentally to match his later vision.

The same informer, Brother Pietro da Novellara, tells that Leonardo was "highly impatient with the paintbrush", curbing himself to occasionally "putting his hand" to pictures painted by his assistants who, with the exception of the evasive Gian Giacomo Caprotti, were no longer those he had in Milan. The workshop paintings include versions in private collections (one formerly in the Reford Collection, and one belonging to the Duke of Buccleuch that was recently stolen) of the so-called *Madonna of the Yarnwinder* (another composition seen by Novellara and therefore datable to 1501), which Leonardo may have supervised but provided little or nothing of his own work.

In June 1502 he went to Piombino as a military engineer for Cesare Borgia and left his easel and brushes to one side. The time he spent there was probably backed by the Florentine republic, which was formally allied to France, and France was an ally of Duke Valentino (Cesare Borgia); for company Leonardo had Nicolò Machiavelli constantly at his side. Leonardo remained in Piombino, travelling around the Marches and Romagna, till 1503 when he reappeared in Florence. The most spectacular outcomes of this technical period are the map of Imola and the map of the
pl. 35 Valdichiana, both of which are in Windsor Castle (RL 12284r, 12278r). Both maps striking in their detail and accuracy, but also disturbing from the standpoint of the living, organic vitalism they express. Back in Florence and with the support of Machiavelli, Leonardo was once more involved in engineering tasks, like the diverting of the river Arno in order to help Florence in its war against Pisa. The ambitious plan was begun but set aside due to excessive difficulties after an enormous financial outlay. In spite of everything, Leonardo's fame in Florence was linked to painting, and to this he returned with unsuspected energy. We can imagine the shock on his contemporaries of a sketch of a wall painting (with which Leonardo tried to revive the Roman technique of encaustic painting) of the *Battle of Anghiari* he began in 1503

for the *gonfaloniere* Piero Soderini in the Sala del Gran Consiglio in the Palazzo Vecchio. Although it was never finished, its impact is discernible in the many (though poor) copies and in the literary references to the work in connection with the equally unfortunate cartoon by Michelangelo of the *Battle of Cascina*; Benvenuto Cellini referred to this pair of works as "the school of the world". Echoes of it are also seen in the works of Piero di Cosimo, Raphael, Pontormo, Sodoma, and Gaudenzio Ferrari. There are also several excellent drawings in terms of general composition (especially those in the Gallerie dell'Accademia in Venice, nos. 215 and 216) and the heads pls. 37, 38
of the warriors (Szépművészeti Múzeum, Budapest), but to understand how this masterpiece at the extreme limit of the *maniera moderna* (High Renaissance style) occupies a space in the Italian Cinquecento that could not be filled by any other work, it is sufficient to consider how we would have imagined the *Last Supper* to be if all that had remained were a few preparatory studies and their copies. We can only say that its colossal scale, the portrayal of extreme physical effort in the men and animals, and the variety of poses and foreshortening of the soldiers and horses—seemingly sucked in by the central vortex of the fight for the standard—appeared then (and indeed were) utterly new and unusual; equally so, probably, was the richness of colour seen in the armed soldiers in extravagant uniforms. In certain drawings connected with this ill-fated project—which was brought to a halt after a technical problem (another but more upsetting smack in the face than the failed diversion of the Arno) and never restarted, despite the insistence of the Republic—and in those of powerful, agitated horses, solutions were experimented with for a painting of Leda, one of Jove's most famous loves, who is at times portrayed standing and at others crouching, with clear references to the more sensual Roman statuary. The *Leda* was another work that has disappeared, though it is known from copies and drawings, particularly of the head. Leonardo made trials of Leda's head in pen drawings pl. 42
(RL 12516 and 12518, Windsor Castle) in which the shading, which had now gone beyond the linearity of the sheets he filled in Milan, is created with curves that follow the lines of the body, emphasising its rotundity, but also creating an effect of instability, changeability and uninterrupted vibration. Following the explosion of bestial, Dionysiac fury in the *Battle of Anghiari* (which had a follow-up in the drawing of *Neptune*), in light of his new progress, Leonardo returned to the elegant, courtly pl. 43
portraiture of the 1490s. The soft curve of Leda's neck is clearly a development of the ideas at the base of the so-called *Scapiliata* in Parma and of Saint John in the *Last Supper*.

This is particularly apparent in the half-length *Saint John the Baptist* dated to 1505–06, pl. 41
which is a dynamic development of an idea created for an *Annunciating angel* known of through copies. Fifteen years afterwards, Leonardo's *Baptist* once more took up the theme of a turning figure (here this is especially accentuated: his writings of

this period also dwell greatly on the illusion of the *rilevo*, or relief, as the principal point of painting) against a dark ground. In fact the delicate bust of this young man is literally immersed in darkness, and only half emerges from it, thereby concentrating the observer's attention on the face and its direct gaze—perhaps the first time that Leonardo used this expedient in his painted works—and the open, almost laughing smile. The figure is created using an intertwining of thin, almost monochrome applications of paint that display skill in the handling of the transition between sections of light and shade. In the meantime, Leonardo began to test himself with a
pl. 39 portrait *a lume universale*, in other words "outdoors", of Mona Lisa del Giocondo (close examination of ancient sources makes the traditional identification of the *Mona Lisa* with the painting in the Louvre self-evident). The format was not a small innovation for Leonardo (who knows, he may have been influenced by certain paintings that could be seen in Florence, like the marvellous *Francesco delle Opere* of 1494 by Pietro Perugino, now in the Uffizi), who had always placed his portraits against a dark background or used more convenient expedients, like the juniper bush behind the figure of *Ginevra Benci* (Washington, D.C.). To a certain extent, the
pl. 5 painting's slow development was probably due to just this, and the radically unnatural landscape, which remained unfinished in parts, was perhaps altered to its current
pl. 40 appearance some years later in parallel with the geological studies seen in the *Codex Leicester* (presently in the Gates Collection in Seattle, but often on the move from one temporary exhibition to another) compiled in 1508, or with his later drawings
pl. 44 of rocks in Lombardy. But there are also other tangible elements that support such a conclusion: apart from Vasari's essay, according to which "having spent four years upon it, [Leonardo] left it unfinished" (and it was four years, from 1503 to 1506, that he stayed in Florence), we see clear references to the *Mona Lisa*'s format in the portrait of *Maddalena Doni* (Pitti Palace, Florence), in the *Lady with a Unicorn* (Galleria Borghese, Rome), and in the face of the *Portrait of a Young Man* (Budapest), all of which were painted by Raphael. What is unusual is that Raphael made use of a much more highly emphasised bust in torsion than seen in the apparent calm of the *Mona Lisa*. It is as though he had seen a *Gioconda* without her transparent veils that fall from her forehead and shoulder, thereby attenuating the slightly drooping effect. Confirmation is given by a "snapshot" of the *Mona Lisa* taken by Fernando Yañez de Almedina, the Spanish painter employed by Leonardo as an assistant on the *Battle of Anghiari*, and who returned to Spain in 1506. In a panel representing the *Pentecost* he painted from 1506 with Fernando de Llanos for the monumental polyptych in the cathedral of Valencia, there is a rather alienated countrywoman at bottom right who has the exact face, hair and shoulder of the *Mona Lisa*, but without her accessories (whereas the Madonna has the face seen in the *Saint John* in the Louvre). We see her at the moment her smile begins and her glance becomes distracted, the spatial authoritativeness of a blooming body, the rosy flesh-tones on which the shadow

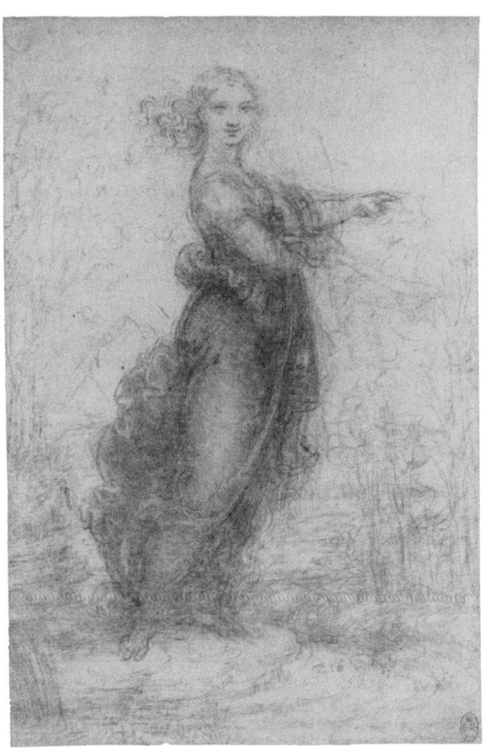

Fig. 8. *Female figure* (presumed to be Dante's Matelda), 1517–18 ca., black chalk, 21 x 13.5 cm, Royal Library, Windsor Castle, inv. RL 12581.

breaks, then almost disappears and reappears in minute transitions which Leonardo achieved using the technique he favoured in this late stage of his painting career: successive layers of paint with different doses of colour.

After this work, never fully completed, Leonardo's activity as a painter became less frequent (he returned to Milan in 1506 and remained there till 1513, except for a brief visit to Florence in 1508, when he moved to Rome. During that seven-year period he concentrated on hydraulics, architecture, sculpture, and anatomy, and spent little time on painting), and his ideal seems to become one of a timeless, almost unreal style, epitomised by the *Virgin and Child* pl. 36
with Saint Anne (Louvre). This was a late execution (certainly earlier than 1517, though perhaps not very much so), considered "perfectissimo" by the secretary to Cardinal Luigi of Aragon, of a cartoon dating, as has been seen, from 1501. This too was a protracted work and today not in good condition: the two women portrayed already have something about them that is different to the *Mona Lisa*, like an excess of sweetness on the one hand, and a more diaphanous and less physically corruptible flesh on the other. Everything in this work is aimed at a definitive though mental stylization, from the lovely stones at the bottom to the sparkling fleece of the lamb, from the practically insubstantial drapery to the spectral pl. 45
landscape in the background, which is one of the oddest and most disquieting in western painting. Leonardo had already arrived, though perhaps unknowingly, at this forbidding and cerebral poetry—though yet poetry—in several lovely drawings that should really have been schematic: from diagrams of circa 1505 on bird flight in the *Codex on Bird Flight* (Biblioteca Reale, Turin), to the pen diagram on the *lumen cinereum* on folio 2r in the *Codex Leicester*.

On the other hand, Leonardo was very aware of the unleashing of natural forces he depicted in the famous drawings of the *Deluge* (ca. 1513–16, Windsor). He imagined a pl. 47
terrestrial apocalypse based purely on the laws of mechanics and hydraulics, without

any divine intervention to give it sense, unless it was the purely formal one of hurricanes and floods portrayed in elegant, almost neo-Verrocchiesque curls; this was the same technique he used contemporaneously when he repainted an earlier and simpler version of the draping of the red garment that ties behind the Virgin's back in the *Saint Anne* in the Louvre. During these disappointing years spent in Rome (1513–16) in the service of Giuliano de' Medici, the brother of Pope Leo X, on studies of curved mirrors and various eccentric ideas, little remains of Leonardo's painting beyond what has been mentioned, except for a possible portrait of a woman painted for Giuliano but anyway lost (perhaps a nude version of the *Mona Lisa* that is referred to in derivations, the best of which is the cartoon in the Musée Condé in Chantilly)
pl. 46 and *Saint John the Baptist in the Desert* (transformed into a *Bacchus* in the Seicento) in the Louvre. This work, weakened by many attempts at restoration and repainting, seems to be an dubious attempt to restore warmth and gentleness (overly so) to the Herculean nudes painted by Michelangelo on the vault of the Sistine Chapel (completed in 1512).

Leonardo's last years (he died in 1519) were spent in France in service to the king, François I, who was the artist's sincere admirer. Between supervising festivities, the desire to reorder his writings so that they might perhaps be printed, and paralysis of the right hand, he almost certainly painted no more. Even the lines in his drawings were hesitant and almost evanescent, for instance, the famous *Lady pointing* in Windsor [fig. 8], which is sometimes thought to be Dante's Matelda but may simply have been a fashion plate to decorate a private party.

Leonardo's greatest contribution to the history of art was completed between the *Adoration of the Magi* and the works produced during his stay in Florence between 1503 and 1506. Some of his writings were cited, sometimes indirectly, in the debate on the arts in the Cinquecento and Seicento, whereas his scientific and technological studies only became universally known from the late Ottocento, with a more comprehensive knowledge of his work and the growth of the Leonardo myth, fuelled by the profitable industry of mass culture that trades on his name. But Leonardo's historical importance is as the painter who opened the way to the "modern style" of Michelangelo and Raphael and the Cinquecento, something that Vasari understood better than anyone:

"Lionardo da Vinci [...] began the third style, which I will call the modern, notable for boldness of design, the subtlest imitation of Nature in trifling details, good rule, better order, correct proportion, perfect design and divine grace, prolific and diving to the depths of art, endowing his figures with motion and breath."

LIST OF PLATES

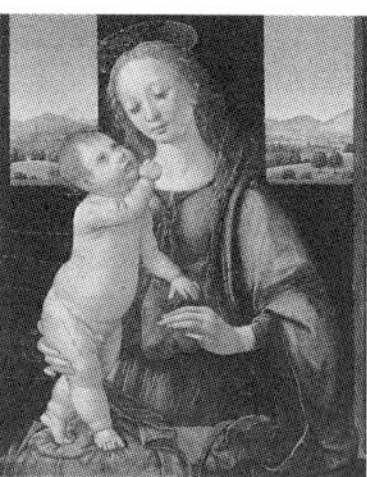

Pl. 1. *Madonna and Child (Dreyfus Madonna)*, ca. 1469–70, oil on wood, 15.7 x 12.8 cm, Kress Collection, National Gallery of Art, Washington, D.C., inv. 1952.5.65. Previously in the collection belonging to Gustave Dreyfus, then belonging to the art dealer Duveen in New York (1930), it entered the collection of Samuel Kress in 1951 and was given to the Washington museum the following year. The attribution to Leonardo is not unanimous.

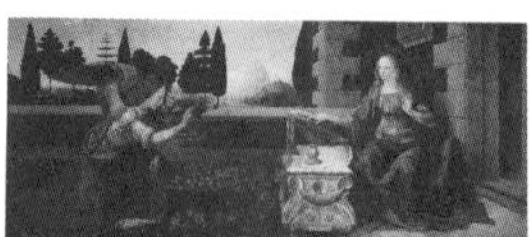

Pl. 2. *The Annunciation*, ca. 1472–73, tempera and oil on wood, 98 x 217 cm, Galleria degli Uffizi, Florence, inv. 1618. The painting, attributed to Domenico Ghirlandaio, arrived in the Uffizi in 1867 from the church of San Bartolomeo di Monteoliveto in Florence. It may have been one of the first important commissions received by Leonardo, who had been an independent master since at least 1472. It was restored by Alfio del Serra in 2000.

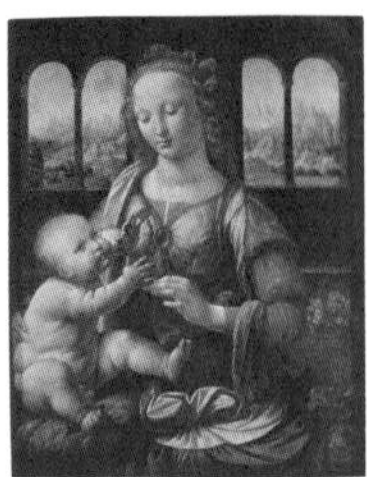

Pl. 3. *Madonna and Child (Madonna of the Carnation)*, ca. 1473–74, oil on wood, 62 x 47.5 cm, Alte Pinakothek, Munich, inv. 7779. The history of the painting remains unknown before it was acquired by the museum from the Haug di Günzburg Collection in 1886, already attributed to Leonardo at the time. Its identification as a "Madonna della caraffa"—which Vasari claims belonged to Pope Clement VII—is entirely hypothetical.

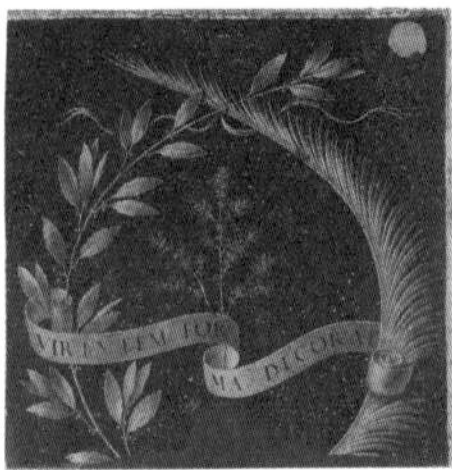

Pl. 4. *Portrait of Ginevra Benci*, verso, 1475–76, tempera and oil on wood, 38.8 x 36.7 cm, Ailsa Mellon Bruce Fund, National Gallery of Art, Washington, D.C., inv. 1967.6.1a-b. The retro, painted on false porphyry with a scroll ("VIRTUTEM FORMA DECORAT") between branches of laurel and juniper, has suffered particularly from its undocumented reduction in format. Reflectography has revealed an earlier version with the motto "VIRTUS ET AMOR", which was that of the Venetian ambassador Bernardo Bembo.

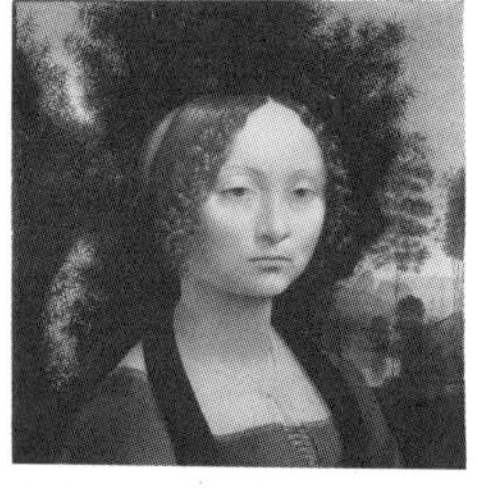

Pl. 5. *Portrait of Ginevra Benci*, 1475–76, tempera and oil on wood, 38.8 x 36.7 cm, Ailsa Mellon Bruce Fund, National Gallery of Art, Washington, D.C., inv. 1967.6.1a-b. The work has been trimmed at the bottom and to the right (originally it would have shown the hands of the lady portrayed). It entered the collections of Prince Joseph Wenzel of Liechtenstein in 1733 attributed to Cranach, then it was transferred from Vienna to Vaduz during World War II. It was purchased by the National Gallery of Art in 1967.

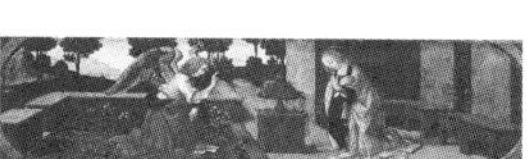

Pl. 6. *The Annunciation*, ca. 1478–79, tempera on wood, 16.2 x 60.6 cm, Musée du Louvre, Paris, inv. M.I. 598. Recorded in the Campana Collection in Rome in 1858 as a work by Domenico Ghirlandaio, this small painting was purchased by Napoleon III in 1861 and arrived in the Louvre two years later. The style and its size make possible the traditional hypothesis that it comes from the predella in the altarpiece commissioned from Verrocchio in 1478 for the Duomo of Pistoia (the main panel is still *in loco*) but there is no confirmatory evidence to support this.

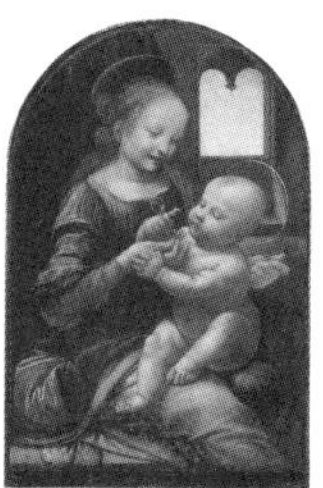

Pl. 7. *Madonna and Child (Benois Madonna)*, ca. 1478–80, oil on wood transferred to canvas, 48 x 31 cm, Hermitage, Saint Petersburg, inv. T E 2773. Information on the provenance of this painting is uncertain. It may have been bought in 1824 in Astrakhan by the dealer Sapoznikov, whose niece married the painter Léon Benois. His family was the owner until it was purchased by the Hermitage in 1914 (another version says that it belonged to the Kurakini princes in the nineteenth century). It was transferred to canvas from wood in 1824.

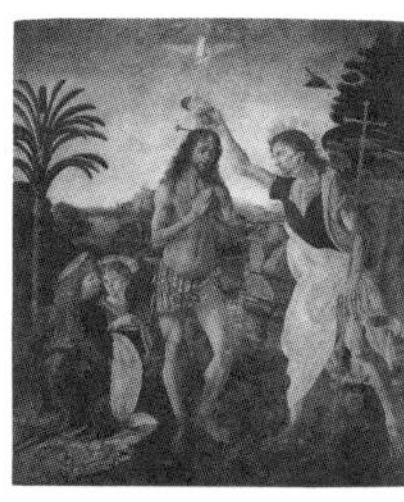

Pl. 8. Andrea del Verrocchio and Leonardo da Vinci, *The Baptism of Christ*, ca. 1475–80, tempera and oil on wood, 180 x 152.5 cm, Galleria degli Uffizi, Florence, inv. 8358. The work arrived in the Accademia di Belle Arti in Florence in 1810 from the Vallombrosano convent of Santa Verdiana. It was passed to the Uffizi in 1914. This should be the *Baptism of Christ* painted by Verrocchio, to which Leonardo added an angel, as recorded by Vasari in the San Salvi monastery that in 1564 passed to the congregation of Vallombrosa. It was restored by Alfio Del Serra in 1999.

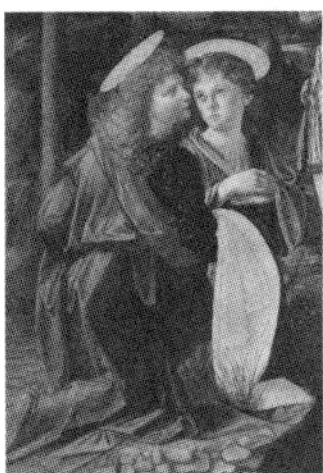

Pl. 9. Andrea del Verrocchio and Leonardo da Vinci, *The Baptism of Christ*, detail, ca. 1475–80, tempera and oil on wood, 180 x 152.5 cm, Galleria degli Uffizi, Florence, inv. 8358. Francesco Albertini (1510) also recorded "an angel by Leonardo da Vinci" in San Salvi. The advanced dating—towards 1480—could support Vasari's anecdote that once Verrocchio had seen this addition, he gave up painting. It would certainly not have been in a huff "because a boy knew more than him", but because his late career seems to have been dedicated entirely to sculpture.

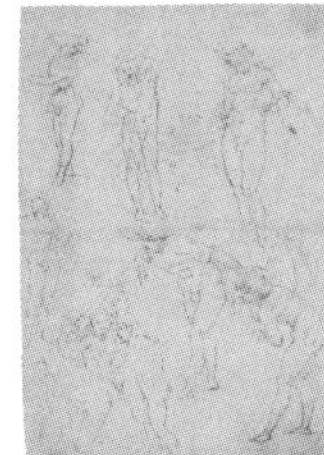

Pl. 10. *Study of grouped figures*, ca. 1481, pen on traces of metalpoint and pencil, 27.4 x 18 cm, Graphische Sammlung, Wallraf-Richartz Museum-Fondation Corboud, Cologne, inv. Z 2003. This drawing was almost certainly part of the collections belonging to Ferdinand Franz Wallraf. The study was probably for the *Adoration of the Magi*. Despite the dynamic nature of the drawings and a hint of ancient art, the result remains far from the formal solidity of the panel.

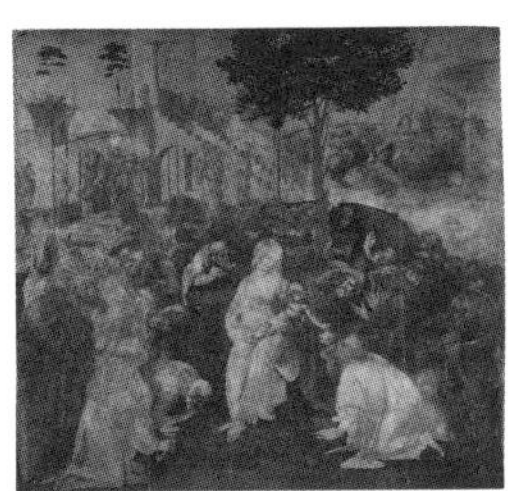

Pl. 11. *The Adoration of the Magi*, 1481–82, oil on wood, 243 x 246 cm, Galleria degli Uffizi, Florence, inv. 1594. Commissioned by the Augustinian monks of San Donato a Scopeto in 1481, according to Vasari the work was left uncompleted by Leonardo with the Benci family when he left Florence for Milan about 1482. It reached the Galleria Medicea in 1670 from the collection of Antonio and Giulio de' Medici; it was then transferred to Villa di Castello before returning permanently to the Uffizi in 1794.

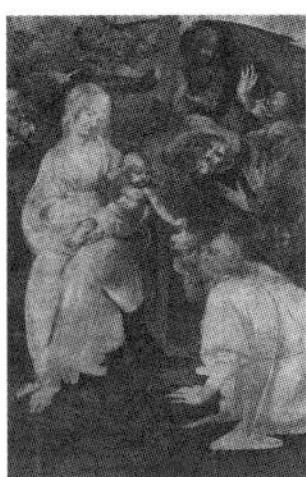

Pl. 12. *The Adoration of the Magi*, detail, 1481–82, oil on wood, 243 x 246 cm, Galleria degli Uffizi, Florence, inv. 1594. In spite of early retouches and a thick layer of dirt and oxidised paint, there is no doubt that the different degrees of completion (with parts that, though devoid of colour, have thin coatings of paint, while others are hardly sketched) are the responsibility of Leonardo himself. They may also be an indication of his concern regarding the impossibility of giving a fifteenth-century perfection to a composition whose invention —seen in its compositional balance, plasticity and pathos—already heralded the new century.

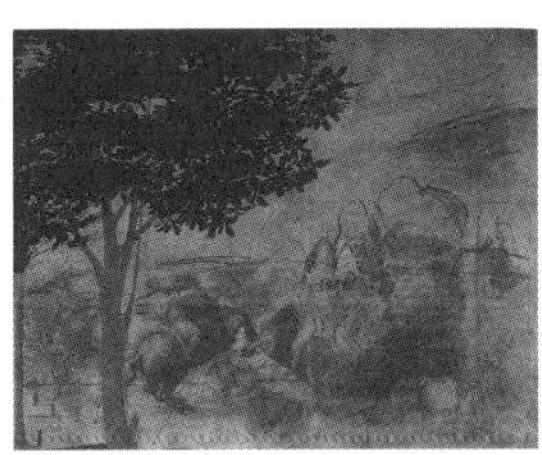

Pl. 13. *The Adoration of the Magi*, detail, 1481–82, oil on wood, 243 x 246 cm, Galleria degli Uffizi, Florence, inv. 1594. With affinities to classical models (perhaps taking its cue from a cameo belonging to the Medici and already known to Donatello), this furious brawl between horsemen and foot soldiers only just remains in the scanty space of the background of the panel. It remained in the back of Leonardo's mind and exploded again on a colossal scale in the central scene of the *Battle of Anghiari*.

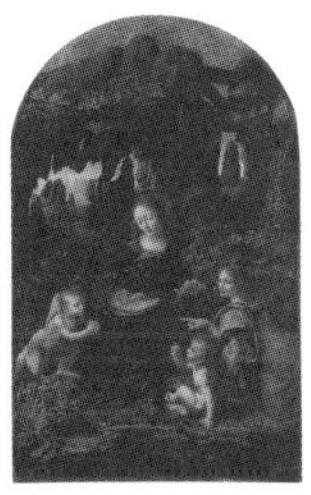

Pl. 14. *The Virgin of the Rocks*, ca. 1483–84, oil on wood transferred to canvas, 199 x 122 cm, Musée du Louvre, Paris, inv. 777. Documented in the royal collections of France in the 1608–10 inventory made by Rascas de Bagarris as simply "Une Nre Dame", it remained there until the creation of the Louvre in 1793, to which it has always belonged. It was transferred from wood to canvas by François Hacquin in 1805.

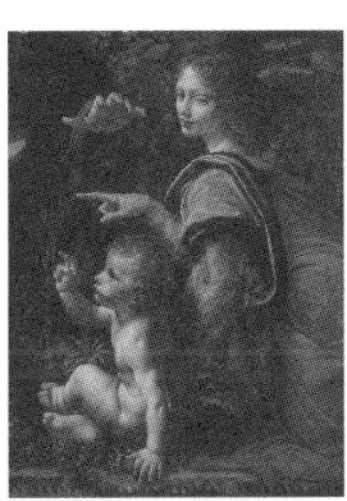

Pl. 15. *The Virgin of the Rocks*, detail, ca. 1483–84, oil on wood transferred to canvas, 199 x 122 cm, Musée du Louvre, Paris, inv. 777. This painting is closely linked to Leonardo's last Florentine works by its careful composition, use of colour and keen, almost calligraphic design. Yet it is apparent that the master had already begun—much earlier than occurs in his theoretical writings—to experiment with the reflections from one coloured mass onto another, as we see in the angel's transparent sleeve slightly tinged with the reflected red of the cloak.

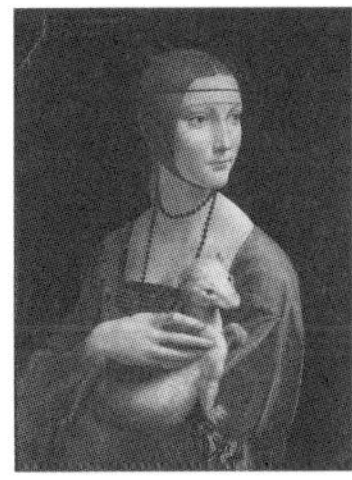

Pl. 16. *Lady with an Ermine*, ca. 1485–86, oil on wood, 55 x 40.5 cm, Czartoryski Muzeum, Kraków, inv. 134. Lent by Cecilia Gallerani to Isabella d'Este, marchesa of Mantua, in 1498, the portrait only reappeared with certainty in 1809. It was exhibited in Puławy Castle in Kraków as the property of Princess Czartoryski, having been given to her by her son Adam following his purchase of it in Italy almost certainly between 1799 and 1801. It moved several times between Paris, Dresden, and Berlin but was returned to Kraków in 1946.

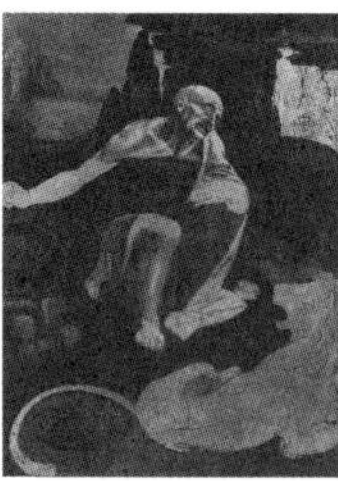

Pl. 17. *Saint Jerome Penitent*, **ca. 1485–86, oil on wood, 103 x 75 cm, Pinacoteca Vaticana, Vatican City, inv. 337.**
The panel is mentioned in the will made in 1803 by the painter Angelica Kaufmann, and in 1839 in the *post mortem* inventory of Cardinal Fesch, the uncle of Napoleon, whose collection was dispersed in 1845. The painting was purchased by the Vatican before 1857. The head of the saint was cut out and then recomposed at an uncertain date: it may have been an attempt to cut the painting up for commercial purposes.

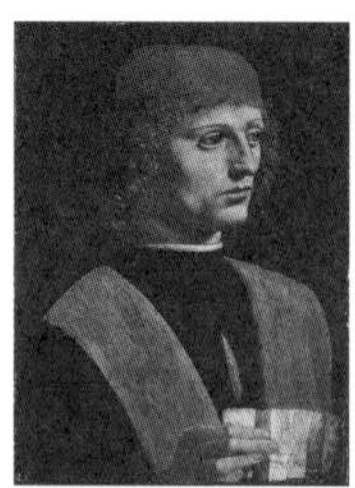

Pl. 18. *Portrait of a Musician*, **ca. 1485–86, oil on wood, 44.7 x 32 cm, Pinacoteca Ambrosiana, Milan, inv. 99.**
Documented at the Ambrosiana possibly from 1672 and without doubt from 1685, attributed to Leonardo but then altered to Luini, the work was painted over thereby concealing the hand and scroll (supporting the hypothesis that the subject was Ludovico il Moro). This layer of paint was removed by Luigi Cavenaghi in 1904. The long jacket has been left incomplete in its reddish preparative state, while the man's garment beneath, which was originally red, has been repainted.

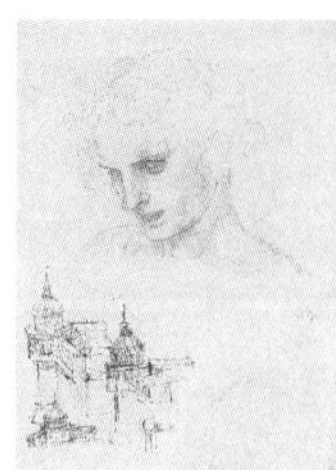

Pl. 19. *Bust of a musician and architectural sketches*, **ca. 1487–88, red pencil and brown ink on paper, 251 x 171 mm, Royal Library, Windsor Castle, inv. RL 12552.**
Like all Leonardo's drawings at Windsor, this one belonged to Pompeo Leoni (who died in Madrid in 1609). He had made a volume of them that entered the possession of Thomas Howard, earl of Arundel, around 1630, and entered the royal collections in 1690. The volume was divided into sections either in the late Ottocento or early Novecento.

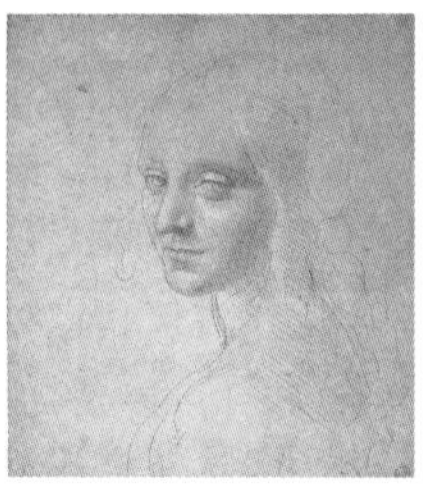

Pl. 20. *Bust of a young woman*, **ca. 1488, metalpoint and lead white on ochre prepared paper, 18.1 x 15.9 cm, Biblioteca Reale, Turin, inv. 15572 D.C.**
Thsi work entered the collections of Carlo Alberto of Savoy between 1831 and 1840, like the other drawings by Leonardo in Turin purchased with the rest of Giovanni Volpato's collection. Its earlier history is unknown. It seems to have preceded shortly the *Belle Ferronnière*, to which it may have been related.

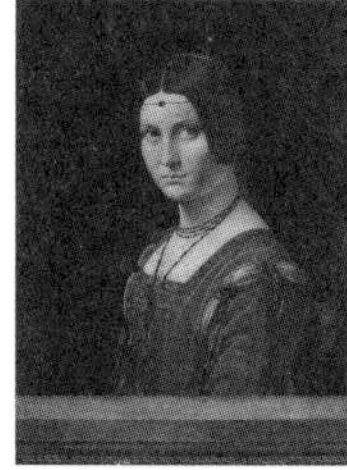

Pl. 21. *Portrait of a Woman (La Belle Ferronnière)*, **ca. 1489–90, oil on wood, 63 x 45 cm, Musée du Louvre, Paris, inv. 778.**
Recorded in the royal collections in Fontainebleau in 1642 as the "duchesse [sic] de Mantoue", it has been suggested that this was the portrait on wood "d'une femme de fasson ytalienne" mentioned in 1500, with portraits of the Sforza (war booty?), as part of the property of Anne of Brittany, wife of Louis XII, and with a portrait of "a certain lady of Lombardy", seen by Luigi de Beatis in October 1517, in the castle of Blois, along with books that had belonged to Ludovico Sforza.

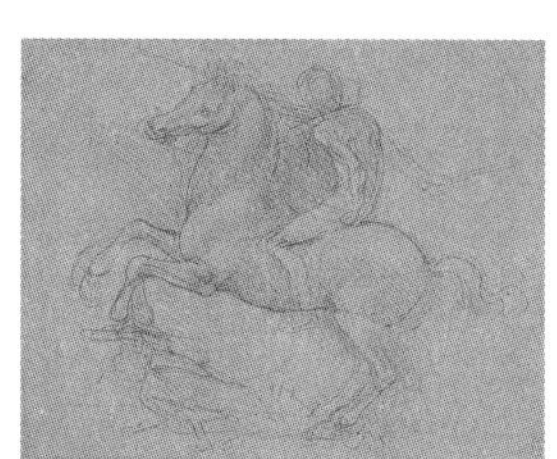

Pl. 22. *Study for the Monument to Francesco Sforza*, **ca. 1488–89, silver point on blue prepared paper, 15.2 x 18.8 cm, Royal Library, Windsor Castle, inv. RL 12358.**
One of the most famous silverpoint drawings from Leonardo's years in Milan, this relates to the monument devoted to Francesco Sforza before the solution was chosen of the horse at walking pace (1490–93): the continuous alterations in the image reveal how little Leonardo based the theme on the statue's technical requirements.

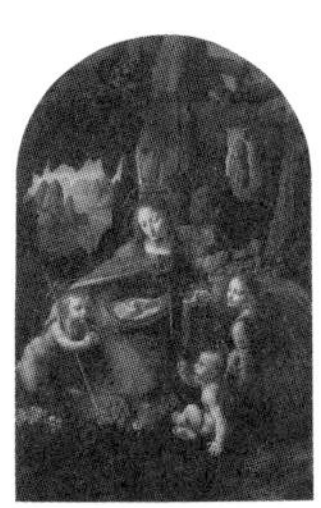

Pl. 23. *The Virgin of the Rocks*, **ca. 1489–91 (with possible retouches in 1506–08), oil on wood, 189.5 x 120 cm, National Gallery, London, inv. 1093.**
This was the central panel (perhaps in the upper register) of the ancona of the Immacolata Concezione in San Francesco in Milan. The confraternity of the same name was annexed in 1781 to the Ospedale di Santa Caterina alla Ruota, and it was here that the English painter, Gavin Hamilton, purchased it in 1785. He resold it to Lord Lansdowne the following year, it passed to Lord Suffolk's collection in 1817, and from there to the National Gallery in 1880.

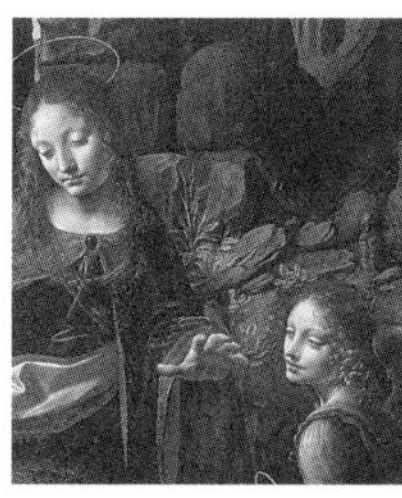

Pl. 24. *The Virgin of the Rocks*, **detail, ca. 1489–91 (with possible retouches in 1506–08), oil on wood, 189.5 x 120 cm, National Gallery, London, inv. 1093.**
According to notarial documents, the work was still incomplete in 1506 despite having been placed on the altar. Even today the back of the Child, and the hands and part of the angel's wings seem unfinished. It is difficult to say whether brushstrokes were added between 1506 and 1508, whether by Leonardo or anyone else.
It was given a rather too vigorous cleaning in 1948–49 by the Gallery's restorers.

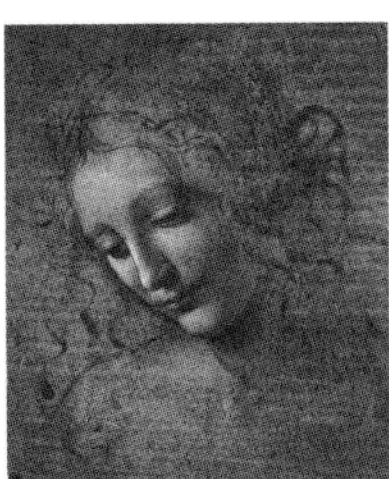

Pl. 25. *Head of a young woman (La Scapiliata)*, ca. 1490, raw umber, green umber , and lead white on wood, 24.6 x 21 cm, Pinacoteca Nazionale, Parma, inv. 362.
In 1826 Giuseppe Callani, the son of the painter Gaetano Callani, proposed its purchase to the Accademia di Belle Arti in Parma, but it was bought instead in 1839 by the Galleria Palatina, which formed the nucleus of the modern art gallery. The reference to the "head of a dishevelled woman, sketched" by Leonardo in an inventory of the Gonzaga collections in 1627 is hypothetical.

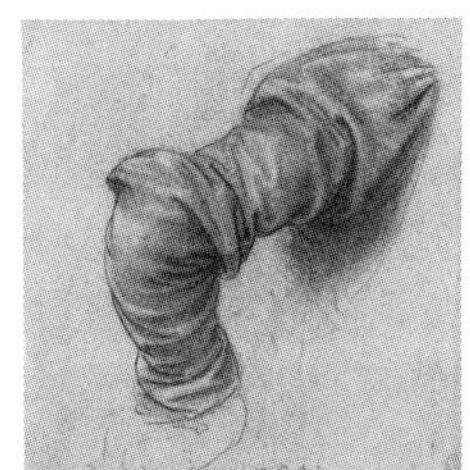

Pl. 26. *Study for the drapery of a right arm*, ca. 1493, black chalk with highlights in lead white and pen on paper, 16.6 x 15.4 cm, Royal Library, Windsor Castle, inv. RL 12546.
This is a preparatory study for the right arm of Peter in the *Last Supper*. It is extraordinarily complex in the changes of tones but still without the monumental aspect of the studies made in red pencil on red paper. A similar solution is seen in the woodcut that adorns the frontispiece of the *Rime* by Bernardo Bellincioni published in 1493, which may have been based on a drawing by Leonardo.

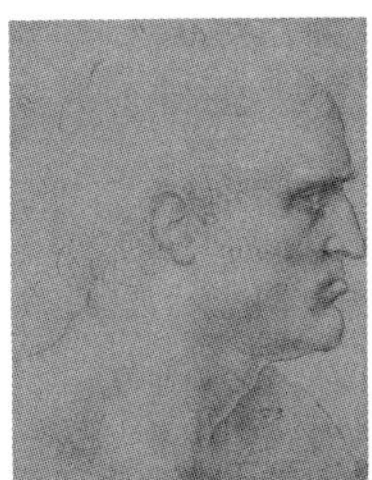

Pl. 27. *Man in profile looking right*, ca. 1495, red chalk on red prepared paper, 19 x 14.6 cm, Royal Library, Windsor Castle, inv. RL 12548.
Some of the most outstanding graphical works by Leonardo da Vinci are the figure in profile used for Bartholomew in the *Last Supper* and other sheets linked to the mural. It may have been preceded by such folios as RL 12552 (Windsor, here pl. 19) and the so-called *Self-portrait* in the Biblioteca Reale in Turin, which was also executed on white paper.

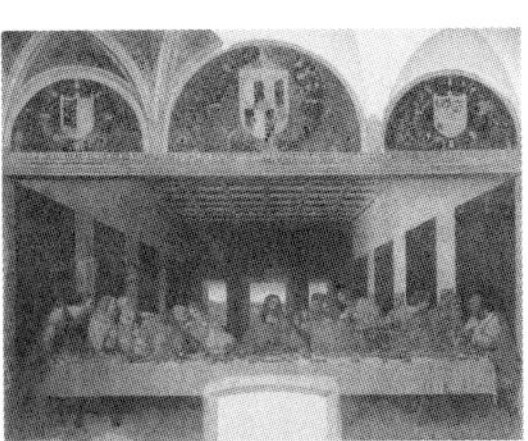

Pl. 28. *The Last Supper (Cenacolo)*, ca. 1491–97, tempera and oil on two states of preparation, 660 x 880 cm, north wall, refectory, convent of Santa Maria delle Grazie, Milan.
Completed around the end of 1497, the wall painting has undergone a number of restorations: in the 1900s alone there were those by Cavenaghi (1908), Silvestri (1924), Pellicioli (1951–54, following serious war damage), and Brambilla Barcilon (1979–99). From the left the figures are as follows: Bartholomew, James Minor, Andrew, Peter, Judas, John, Christ, Thomas, James Major, Philip, Matthew, Thaddaeus, and Simon.

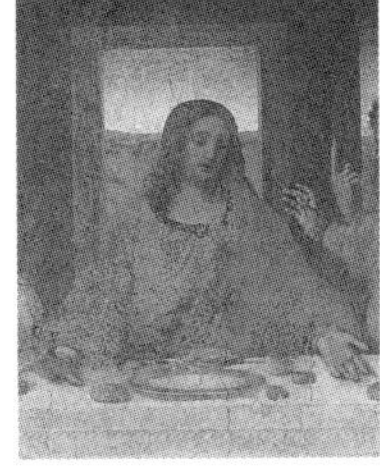

Pl. 29. *The Last Supper (Cenacolo)*, detail, ca. 1491–97, tempera and oil on two states of preparation, 660 x 880 cm, north wall, refectory, convent of Santa Maria delle Grazie, Milan.
Only since the last restoration —though still seriously impeded by the disastrous state of decay of the painting—is it possible to appreciate the cool range of colours Leonardo chose, and the mental state of many of those portrayed. One of these is Christ, who is shown at the moment of announcing the betrayal, and in an pose that suggests the medieval iconography of Christ the Judge in the scene of the Last Judgement.

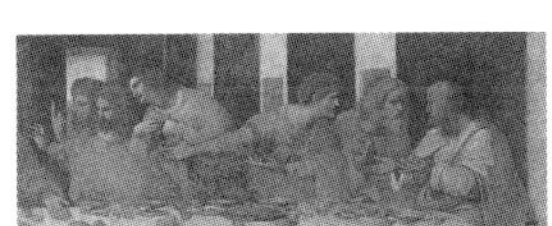

Pl. 30. *The Last Supper (Cenacolo)*, detail, ca. 1491–97, tempera and oil on two states of preparation, 660 x 880 cm, north wall, refectory, convent of Santa Maria delle Grazie, Milan.
The right side of the painting is generally in better condition, and has allowed a greater quantity of original pigment to be revealed. Note the attempt to show consecutive moments from a single action in the movements of the apostles, with Philip representing a point of extreme idealisation. Exceptional for its colossal size, heroic dignity (not without classical references in the pure profile of Matthew), delicacy of colouration and formal synthesis, this group was perhaps the last to be painted.

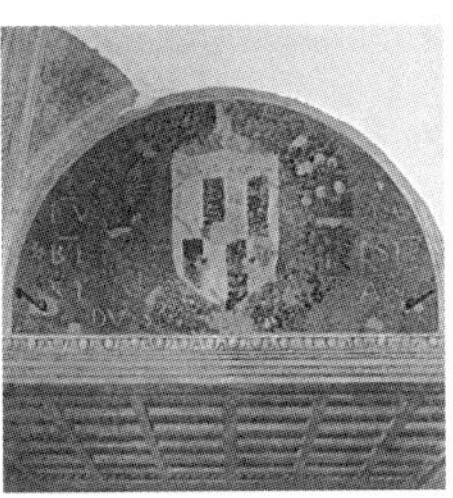

Pl. 31. *The Last Supper (Cenacolo)*, detail, ca. 1491–97, tempera and oil on two states of preparation, 660 x 880 cm, north wall, refectory, convent of Santa Maria delle Grazie, Milan.
Rediscovered only in 1854, the three lunettes with coat of arms, inscriptions and plant motifs are an integral part of the construction of the *Last Supper,* and were probably painted before the central scene. The gold letters—perhaps added at a later moment, though very shortly afterwards; and restoration has revealed a repeat of the lunettes—allude to Ludovico il Moro, Beatrice d'Este, and their sons Massimiliano and Francesco, born in 1493 and 1495; they stand out against a blue ground that has almost completely disappeared, leaving the red preparation visible.

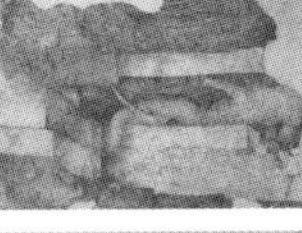

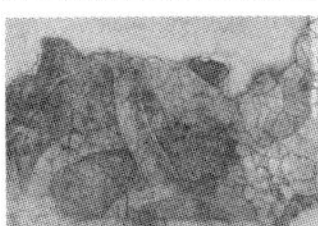

Pl. 32. *Decoration with plant motifs*, 1498–99, tempera on wall, northeast wall, Sala delle Asse, Castello Sforzesco, Milan.
Rather than from the vault—which was completely repainted in 1901–02 by Ettore Rusca on the basis of the few original traces—Leonardo's intentions can be intuited from the two surviving monochrome fragments that were salvaged in 1954. It seems probable that these two were to be painted, which therefore indicates that the work was not completed following the abandonment of the castle by the Sforza in summer 1499.
Of Leonardo's many original and surprising inventions, this decoration is useful for understanding the technique he adopted in mural painting: a careful monochromatic definition before applying the colours.

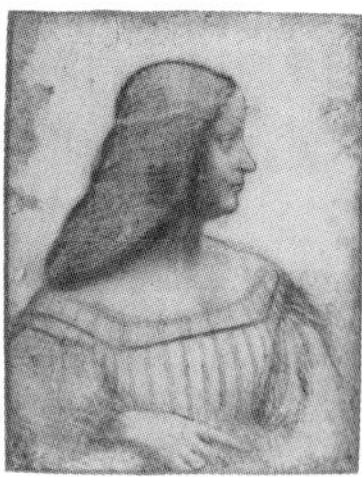

Pl. 33. *Portrait of Isabella d'Este*, **1499–1500, black chalk, red chalk and stump, ochre chalk, white heightening; a first black chalk drawing is visible in several areas; light white preparation of the paper on upper right and left parts, 61 x 46.5 cm, Musée du Louvre, Paris, inv. 753.**
Completed by March 1500, the cartoon is pricked for pouncing but almost certainly it was never transferred. It moved from the Calderara to Vallardi Collection in 1829, from where it was sold in 1856 to the Louvre.

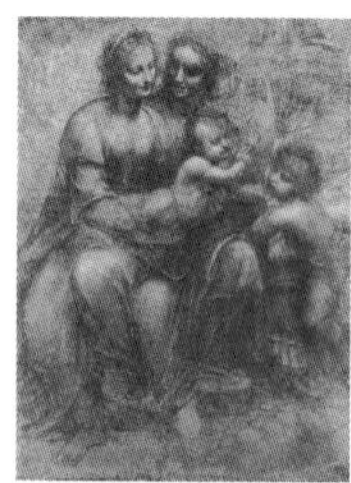

Pl. 34. *Virgin and Child with Saint Anne and Saint John the Baptist*, **1501, black chalk and lead white on paper, 141.5 x 104 cm, National Gallery, London, inv. 6337.**
Documented by Lomazzo in 1584 in the house of Aurelio Luini (whose father, Bernardino, made the copy now in the Pinacoteca Ambrosiana, Milan), and subsequently by Sebastiano Resta (before 1696) in the Arconati Collection in Milan, in 1721 the cartoon reached the Marchesi Casnedi. From there it moved to the Sagredo Collection in Venice (before 1749), where it was purchased in 1763 by the consul Robert Udny. It moved to the Royal Academy in London in 1791, which ceded it to the National Gallery in 1966.

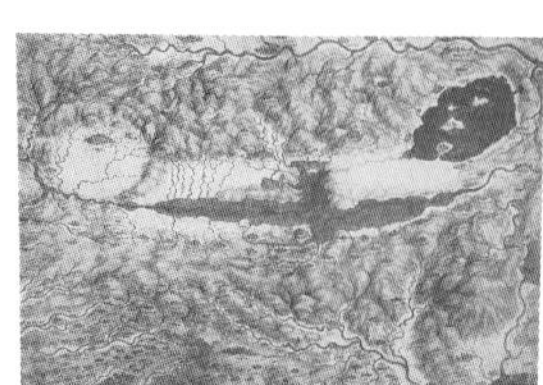

Pl. 35. *Map of Valdichiana*, **1503, pen, ink and watercolours on paper, 33.8 x 48.8 cm, Royal Library, Windsor Castle, inv. RL 12278 recto.**
This work dates to the early months of 1503, towards the end of his service with Cesare Borgia. As the refinement shows (an elaboration of previous partial surveys) and the left-to-right handwriting, this was a drawing for presentation. It is an impressive example of the organic unity of Leonardo's conception of the world: the water conduits branch out like veins in his anatomic drawings, and Lake Chiana resembles the birds in flight that he drew shortly after in the Turin *Codex on the Birds' flight*.

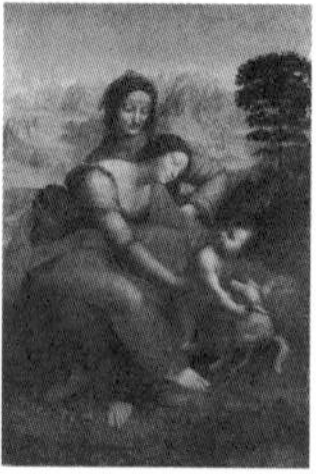

Pl. 36. *Virgin and Child with Saint Anne*, **ca. 1501–15, oil on wood, 168 x 129 cm, Musée du Louvre, Paris, inv. 776.**
Perhaps conceived as early as 1501, the painting was a long time in execution. Leonardo still had it with him in Amboise in 1517 but its subsequent movements are uncertain (it was either brought back to Milan by his pupil Caprotti—known as Salai—or purchased by François I). It was probably the work in the French royal collections mentioned by Giovio (ca. 1529) and other sixteenth-century sources. Recorded as being in Richelieu's palace in 1651, it was given to Louis XIII and registered as being in Fontainebleau in 1654.

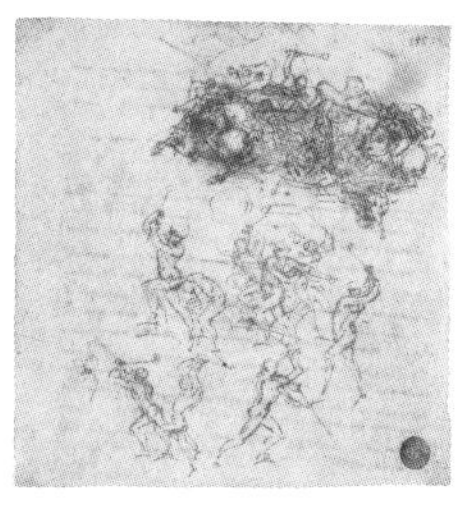

Pl. 37. *Study for the Battle of Anghiari*, **ca. 1503–04, ink on traces of black chalk, 16.4 x 15.2 cm, Gallerie dell'Accademia, Venice, inv. 215 recto.**
This study shared the same fate as almost all Leonardo's works in Venice: at the end of the Seicento it belonged to Cardinal Monti in Milan, from whom heirs it passed to Venanzio de Pagave (where we know it was in 1784) and his son Gaudenzio; it was purchased by the painter Giuseppe Bossi in 1807 and, after his death, by Abbot Celotti in 1818. Celotti deposited it with the Venetian galleries for which it was purchased by Emperor Francis I in 1822.

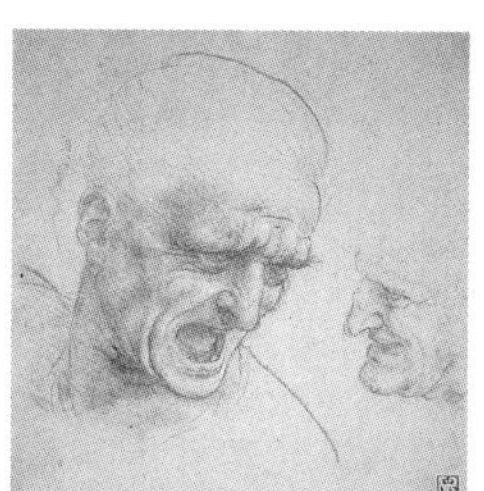

Pl. 38. *Head of a warrior for the Battle of Anghiari*, **ca. 1504, black chalk and traces of red chalk on paper, 19.2 x 18.8 cm, Szépmüvészeti Múzeum, Budapest, inv. 1775.**
At one time belonging to the Esterházy family, it was bought from Paul Esterházy by the Hungarian government in 1870. Having decided upon the composition of the central struggle for the standard, Leonardo moved on to study the details of the faces of the main characters—the *condottieri* Nicolò Piccinino and Pier Giampaolo Orsini.

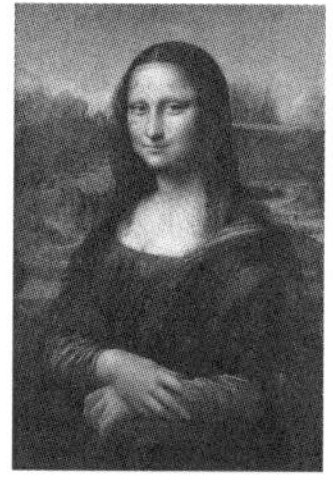

Pl. 39. *Portrait of Lisa del Giocondo (Mona Lisa)*, **ca. 1503–12, oil on wood, 77 x 53 cm, Musée du Louvre, Paris, inv. 779.**
Begun in Florence around 1503, the portrait of Lisa Gherardini, the wife of the silk merchant Francesco del Giocondo, it is not certain that the painting was with Leonardo in Amboise in 1517. Perhaps brought back to Milan by Salai or purchased by François I in 1518, it certainly entered the collection of the French king, who died in 1547.

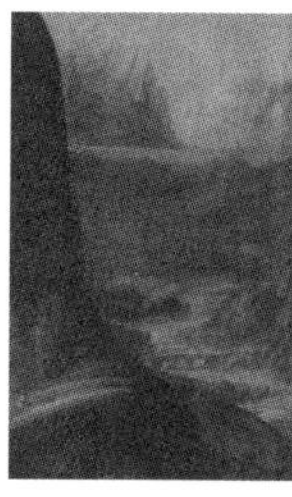

Pl. 40. *Portrait of Lisa del Giocondo (Mona Lisa)*, **detail, ca. 1503–12, oil on wood, 77 x 53 cm, Musée du Louvre, Paris, inv. 779.**
According to Pierre Dan (1642), François I paid the astronomical sum of 4,000 gold *scudi* for the painting. The intellectualistic landscape, which contrasts strongly with the natural manner of the figure, is in turn covered by the woman's transparent veil, which falls from her head to her shoulders and over her arms, thereby creating a sense of expansion and rotundity that were not part of the original scheme.

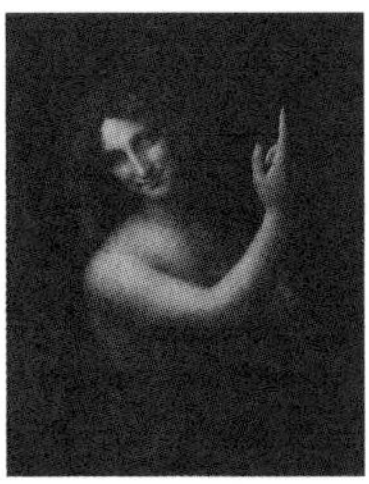

Pl. 41. *Saint John the Baptist*, ca. 1505–06, oil on wood, 69 x 57 cm, Musée du Louvre, Paris, inv. 775.
Also with Leonardo at Amboise in 1517, it reappeared in 1637 when Louis XIII's chamberlain, Roger Duplessis de Liancourt, gave it to Charles I of England. When Charles' collection was sold in 1649, the painting was purchased by the French dealers Cruso and Térence, who sold it in 1651 to the banker Evérard Jabach. It moved to Louis XIV in 1662. Transferred to Versailles around 1691, it remained there until it entered (1801) the Muséum central des arts, later named the Louvre.

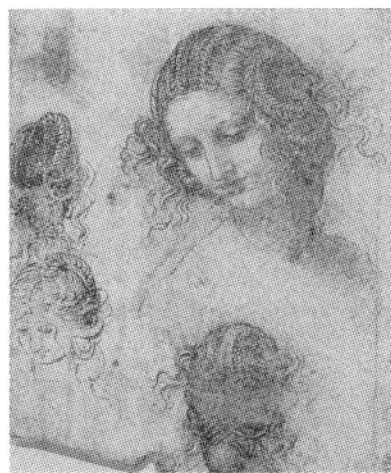

Pl. 42. *Studies for the head and hairstyle of Leda*, ca. 1505–06, black chalk retouched with ink on paper, 20 x 16.2 cm, Royal Library, Windsor Castle, inv. RL 12516.
Executed during the same period as the *Saint John the Baptist* and the lost *Annunciating Angel*, Leonardo experimented with the theme of a young, twisted nude body (here in particular harking back to antique art) in the also lost *Leda*, of which copies and some preparatory drawings remain. The shading is made using curved and continuous lines, whose almost plant-like woven texture create the delicate lighting effects with extraordinary lightness.

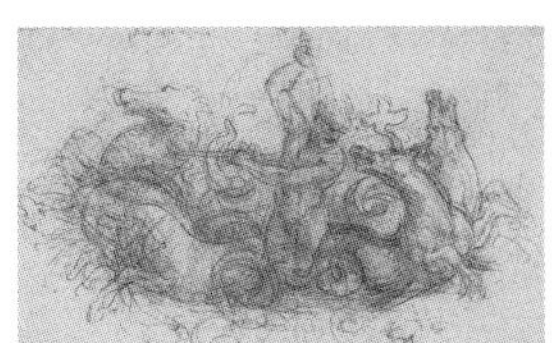

Pl. 43. *Neptune on his sea chariot*, ca. 1508, black chalk on paper, 25.2 x 38.9 cm, Royal Library, Windsor Castle, inv. RL 12570.
This monumentally structured drawing (which owes something to Michelangelo's *Battle of Cascina*) has a force similar to that seen in the equestrian *Battle of Anghiari*, though it is perhaps without the formal control seen in pls. 37 and 38. It would seem to fit the information given by Vasari relating to a drawing of Neptune that Leonardo gave to the Florentine Antonio Segni.

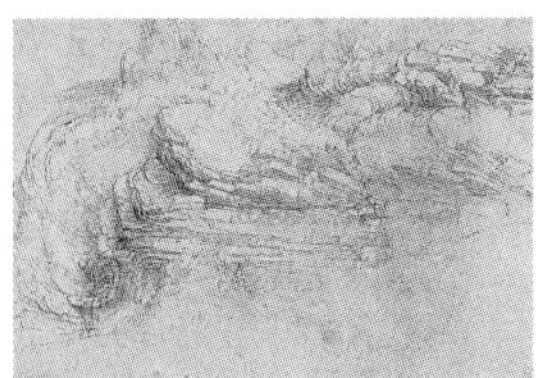

Pl. 44. *Rocky formation*, ca. 1510–13, black chalk retouched with pen on paper, 18.5 x 26.8 cm, Royal Library, Windsor Castle, inv. RL 12394.
Almost unintentionally, the scientific nature of the drawing gives way to Leonardo's sense of vitalism, with these (probably) Lombard rocks being transformed into living beings. It was from drawings like this one (or the 12397 from the same collection) that the landscapes in the *Mona Lisa* and *Virgin and Child with Saint Anne* [pls. 40 and 36] in the Louvre were developed.

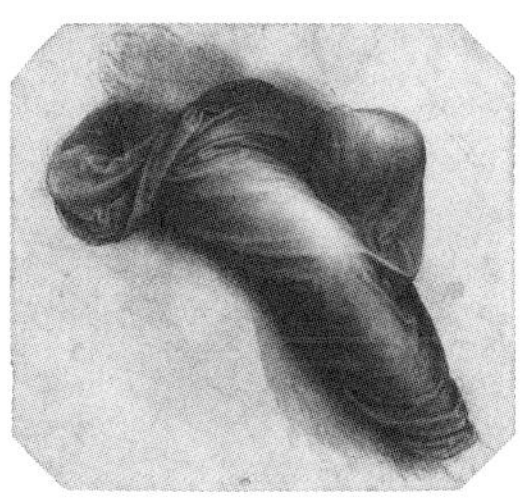

Pl. 45. *Drapery enveloping the legs of a seated figure*, ca. 1513–15, first sketch in black chalk and black chalk wash, white and black pigments applied in distemper, 23 x 24.5 cm, Musée du Louvre, Paris, inv. 2257.
This study was clearly made as a preparation for the Paris version of *St Anne*. It belongs to the final phase of Leonardo's graphic activity. The unstable, crumbling consistency of the lines and the powdery quality of the colours are related to folios such as the *Female figure* from Windsor [fig. 8]. The fact that above the bluish mantle Leonardo dashed in the drapery of the Virgin's dress—which in the painting was a late addition—suggests a late date, probably during the master's stay in Rome.

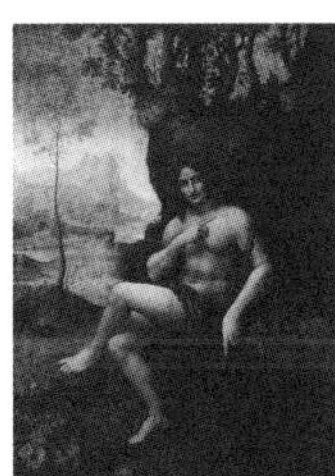

Pl. 46. *Saint John the Baptist in the Desert*, ca. 1514–16, oil on wood transferred to canvas, 177 x 115 cm, Musée du Louvre, Paris, inv. 780.
Hypothetically related to a commission from Pope Leo X (Giovanni de' Medici), as referred to by Vasari, the painting was recorded as being in the French royal collections around 1610. Transformed into a *Bacchus* between 1683 and 1695, it was transferred to canvas by François Hacquin in 1794–95.

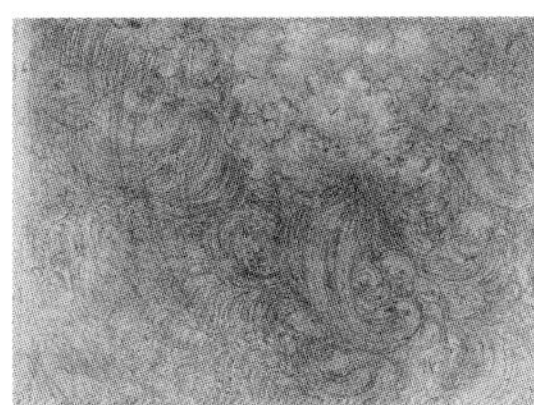

Pl. 47. *Drawing of the Deluge*, ca. 1516–17, black chalk on paper, 15.8 x 21 cm, Royal Library, Windsor Castle, inv. RL 12383.
In a series of eleven folios (RL 12377–86, and 12401, Windsor), the drawing represents Leonardo's graphic work taken to the extreme. His knowledge of hydraulics and geology led Leonardo to imagine an "end of the world" without any religious conception and dominated entirely by the laws of nature. The decorative elegance only contributes further to the sense of estrangement and anguish.

PLATES

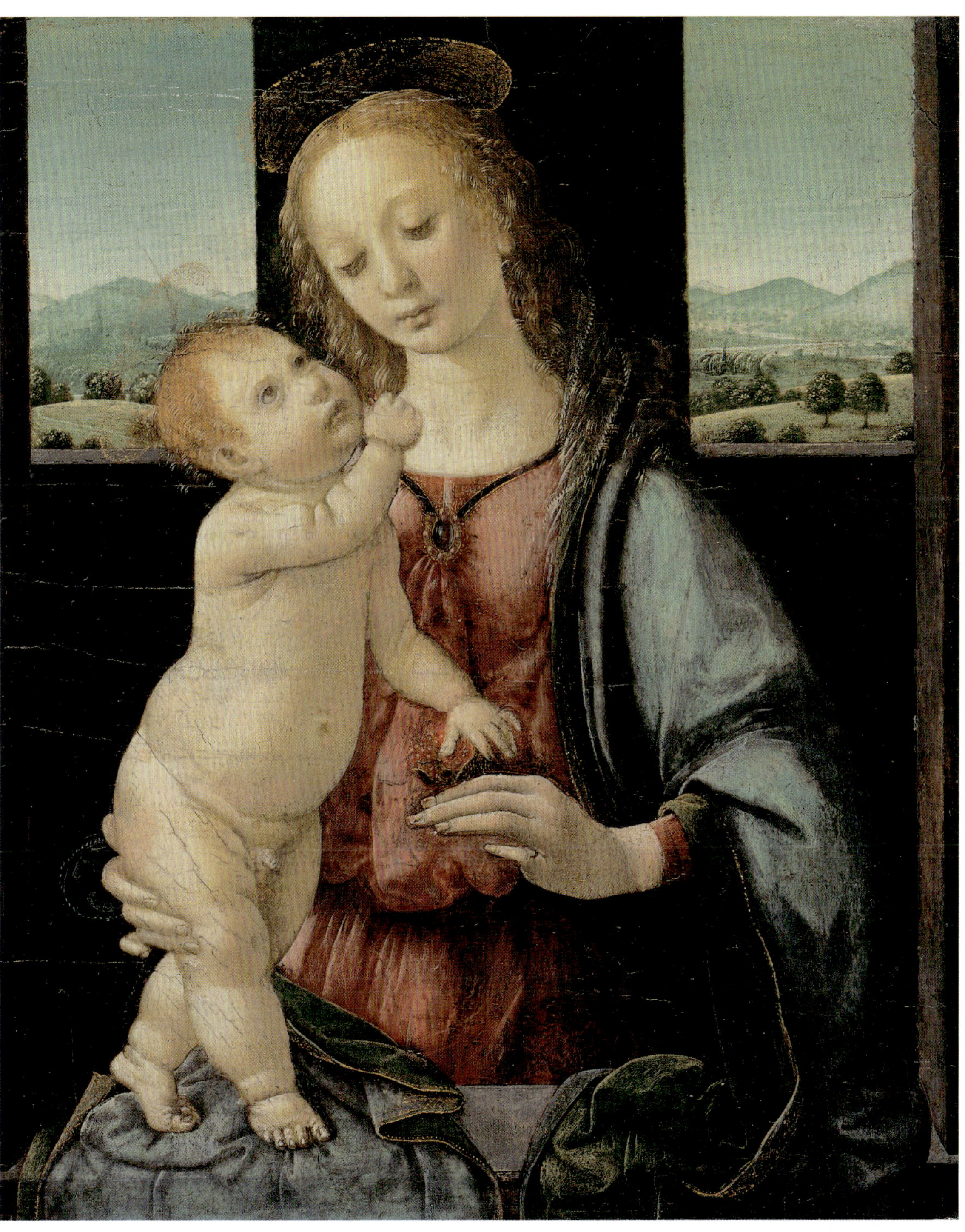

1

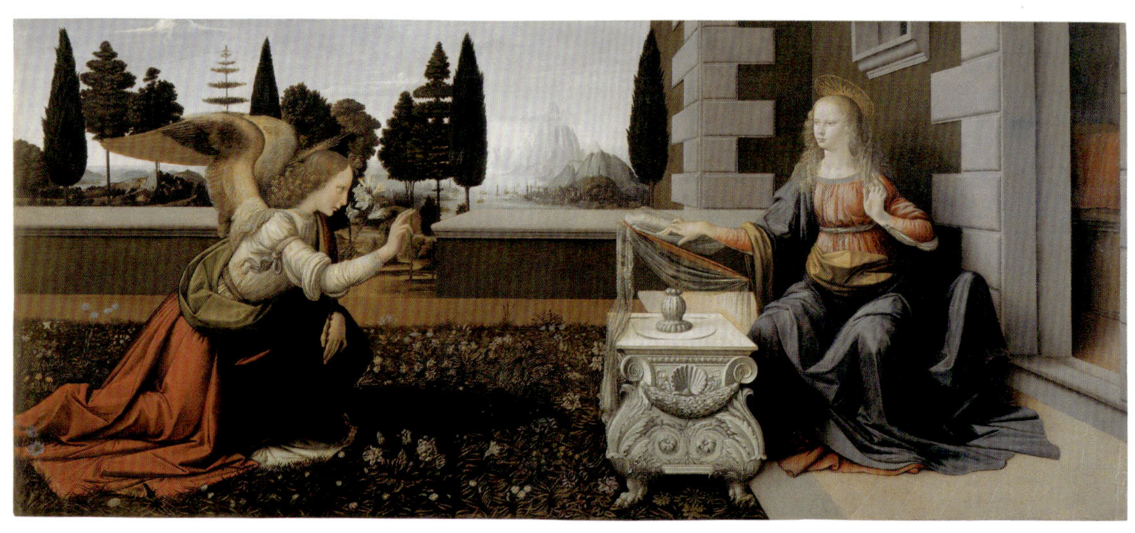

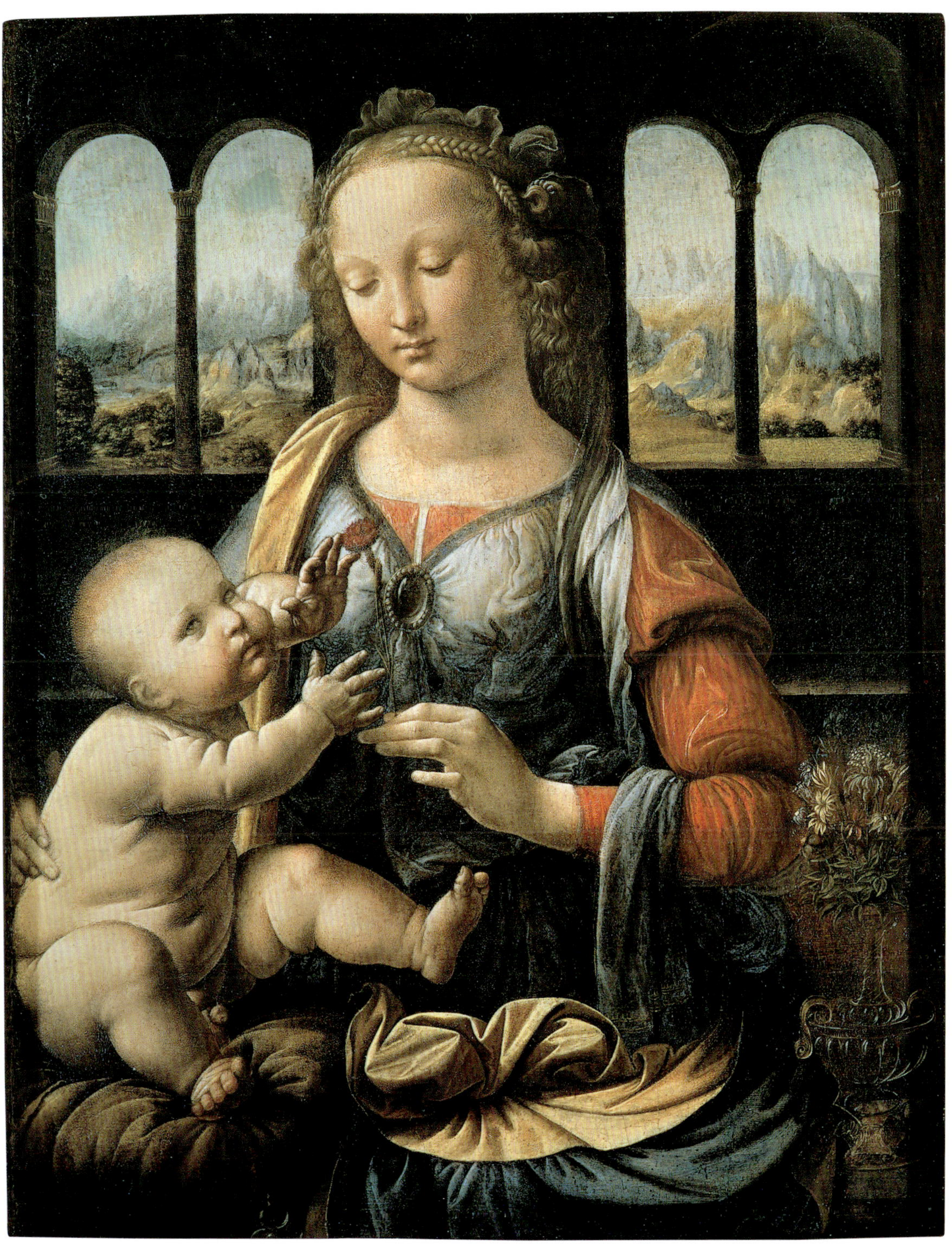

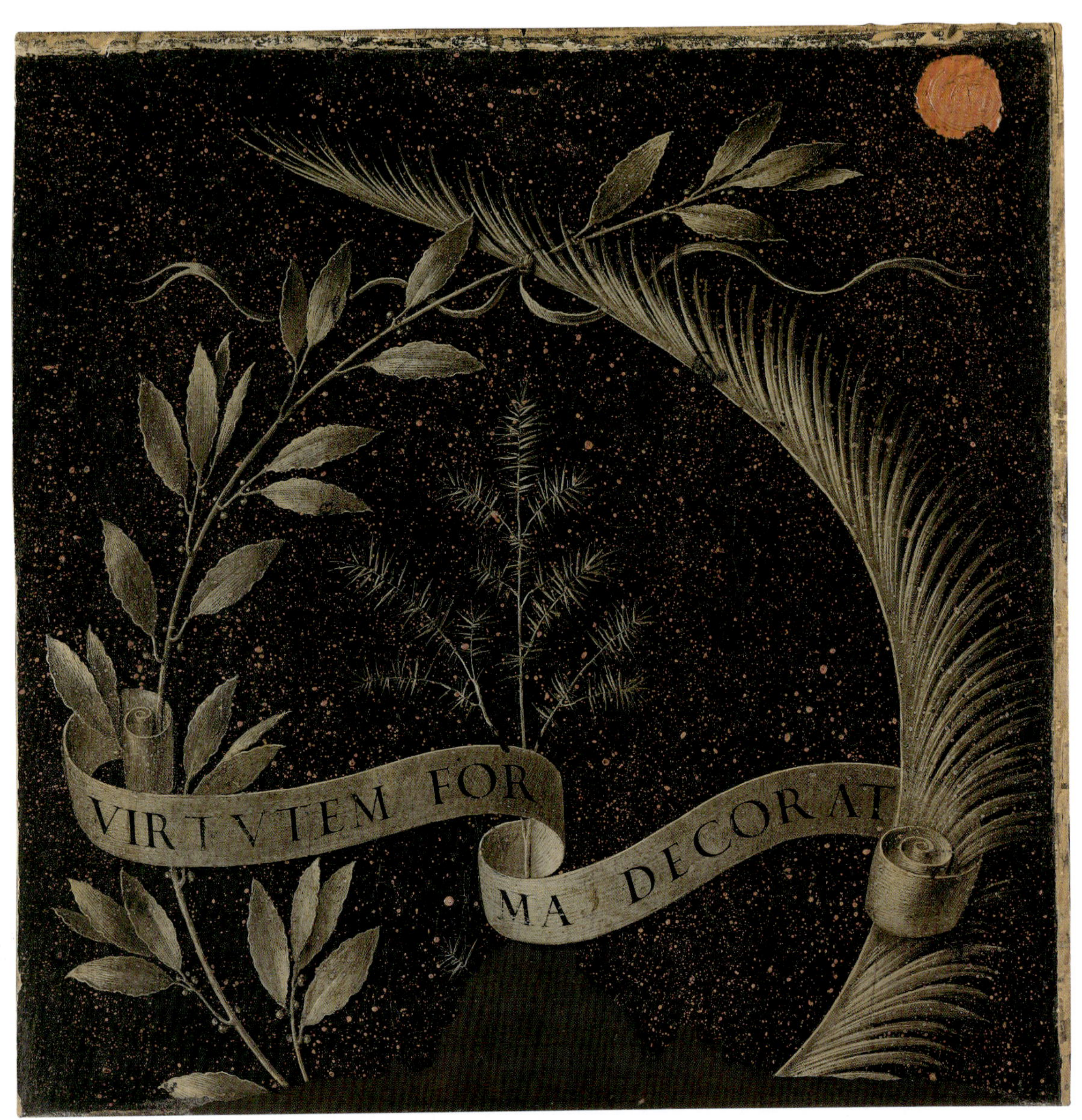
VIRTVTEM FORMA DECORAT

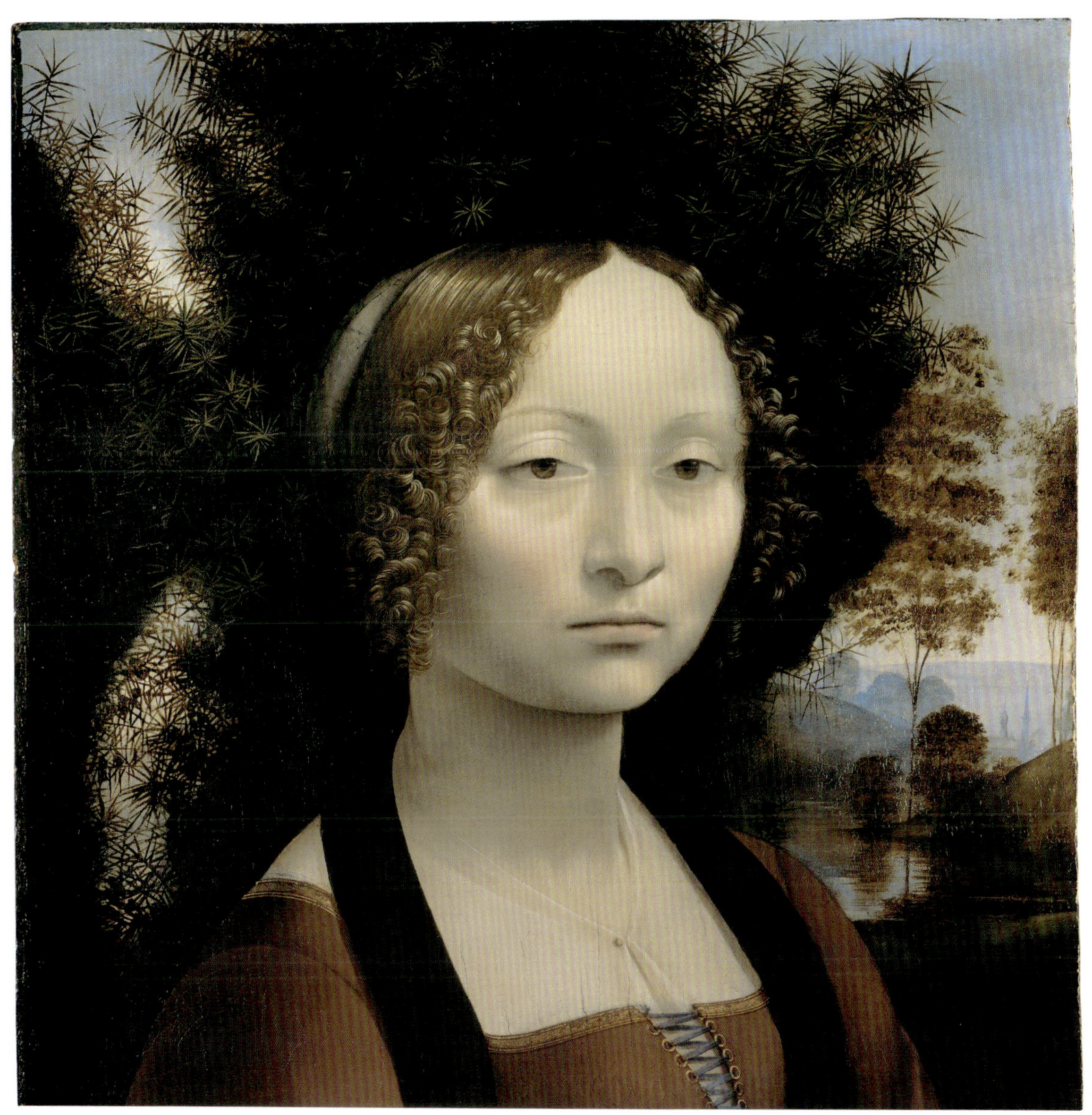

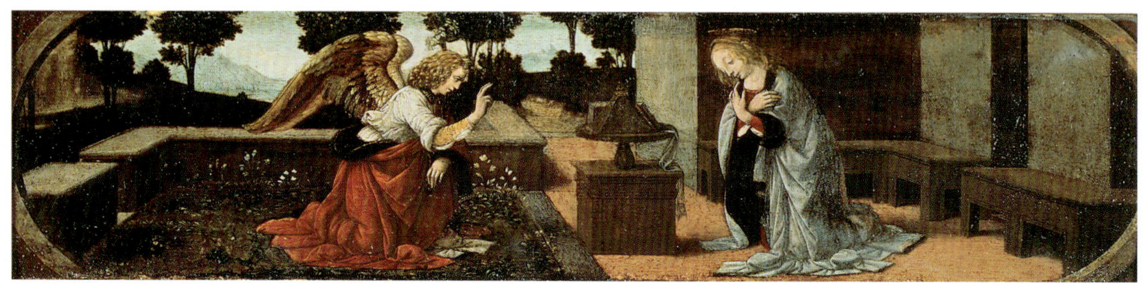

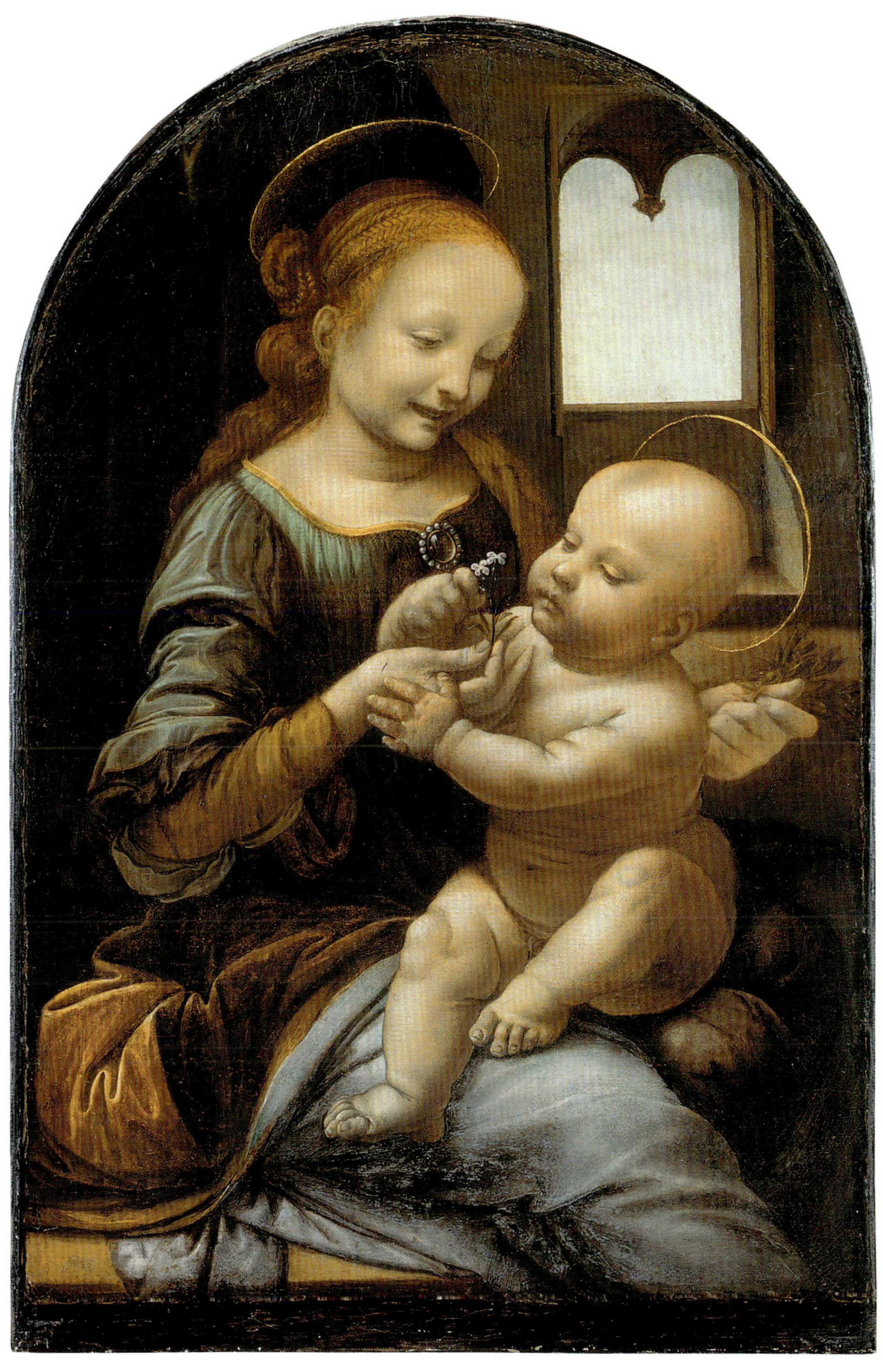

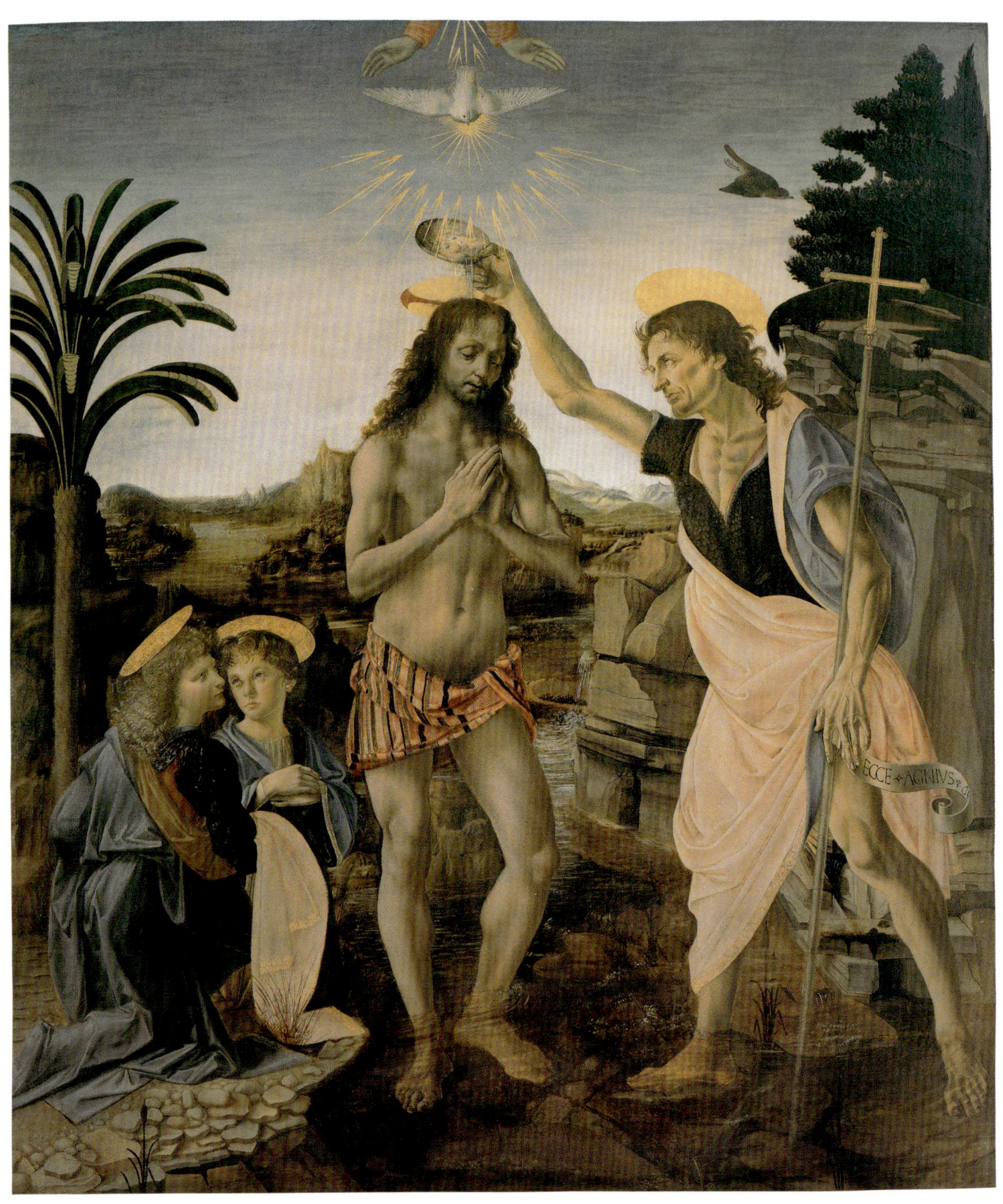
ECCE AGNIVS

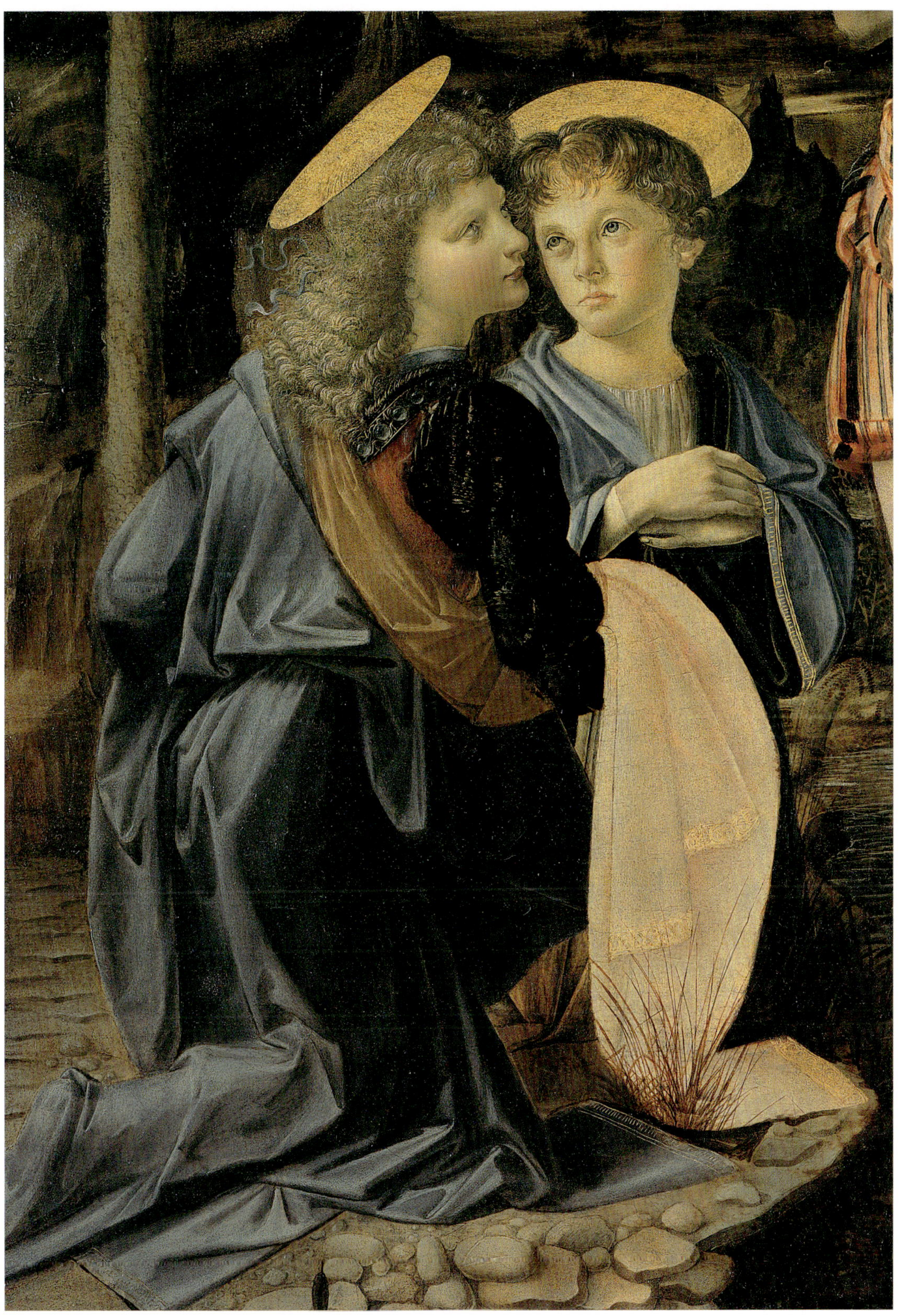

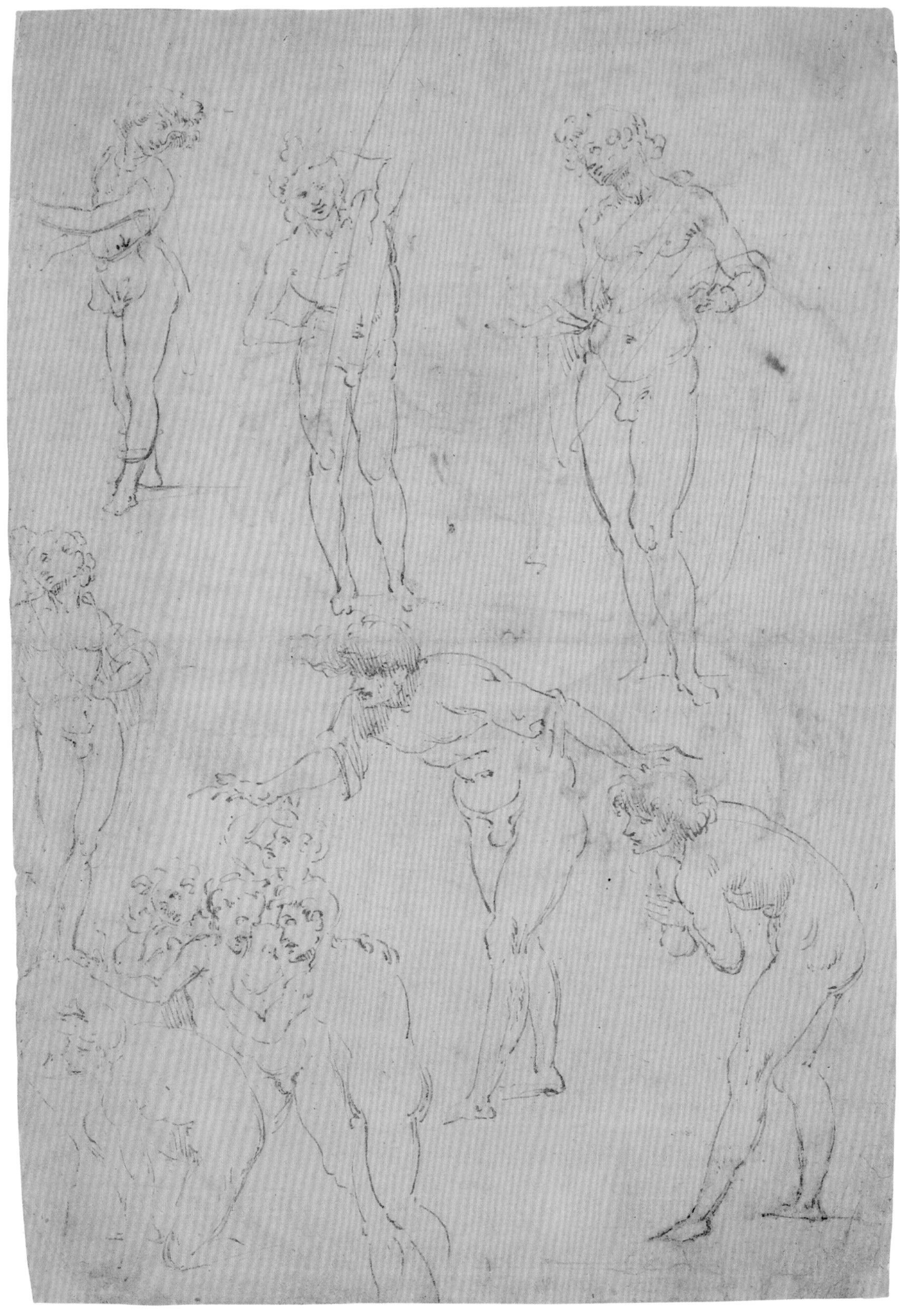

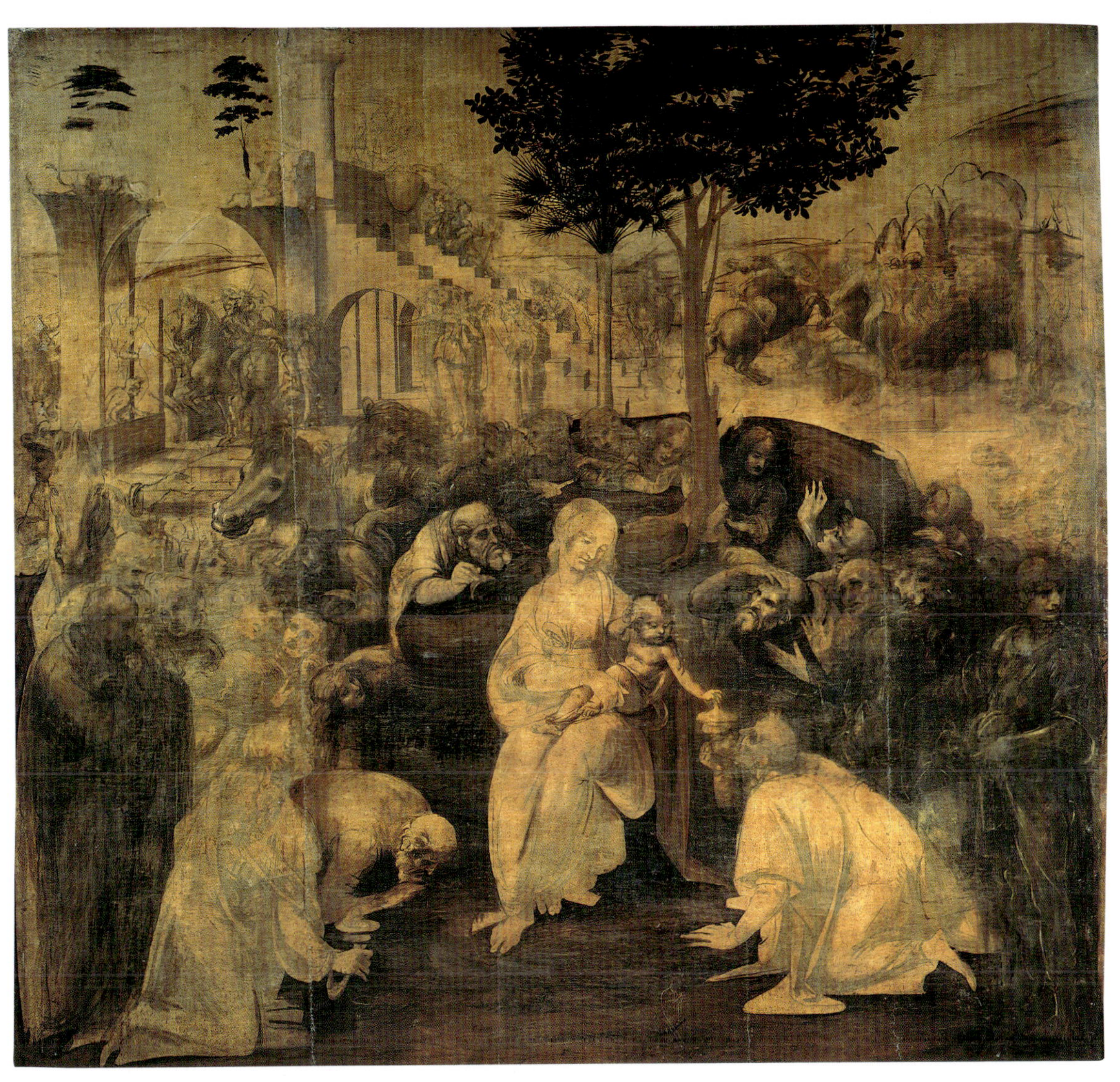

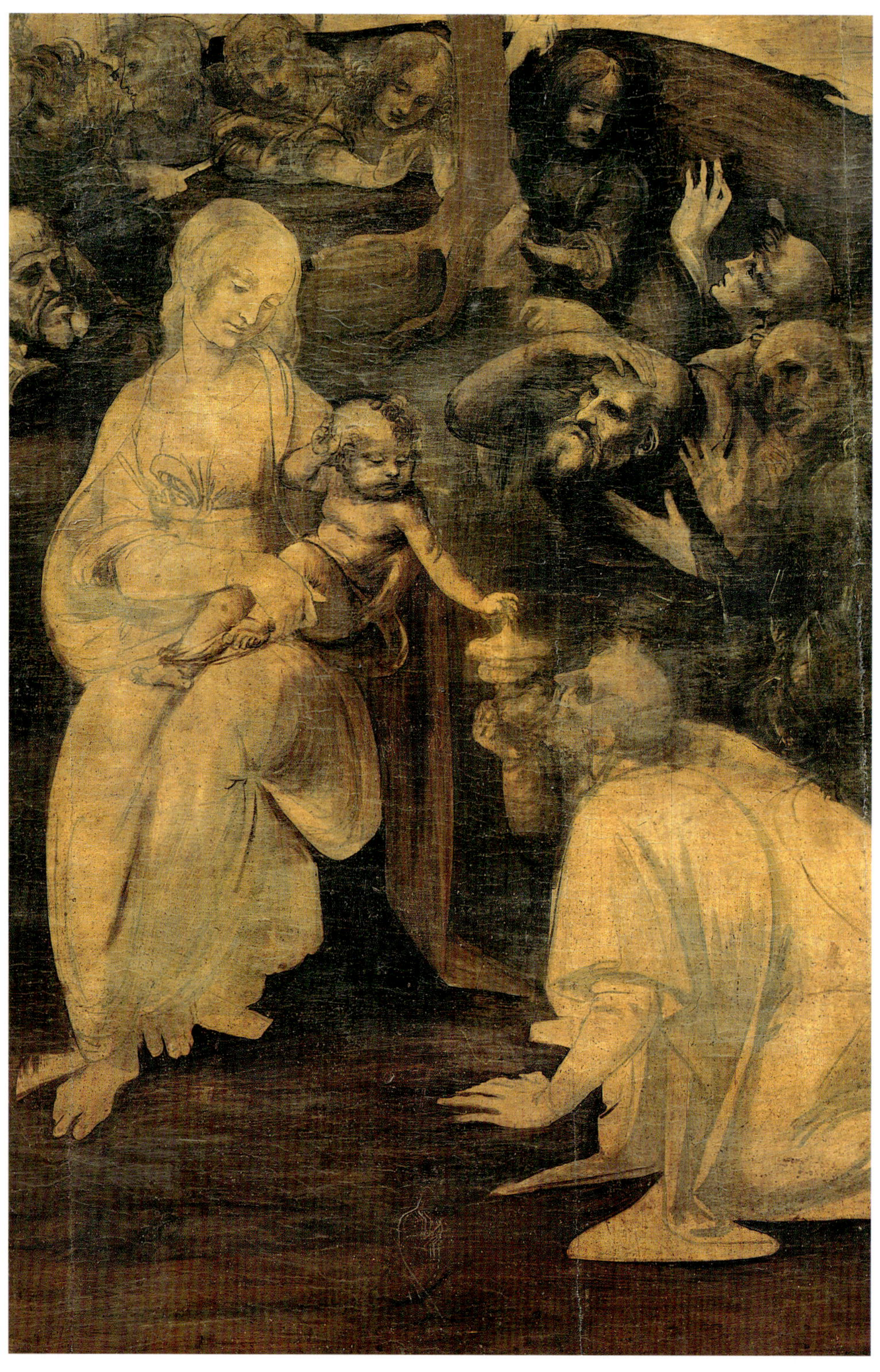

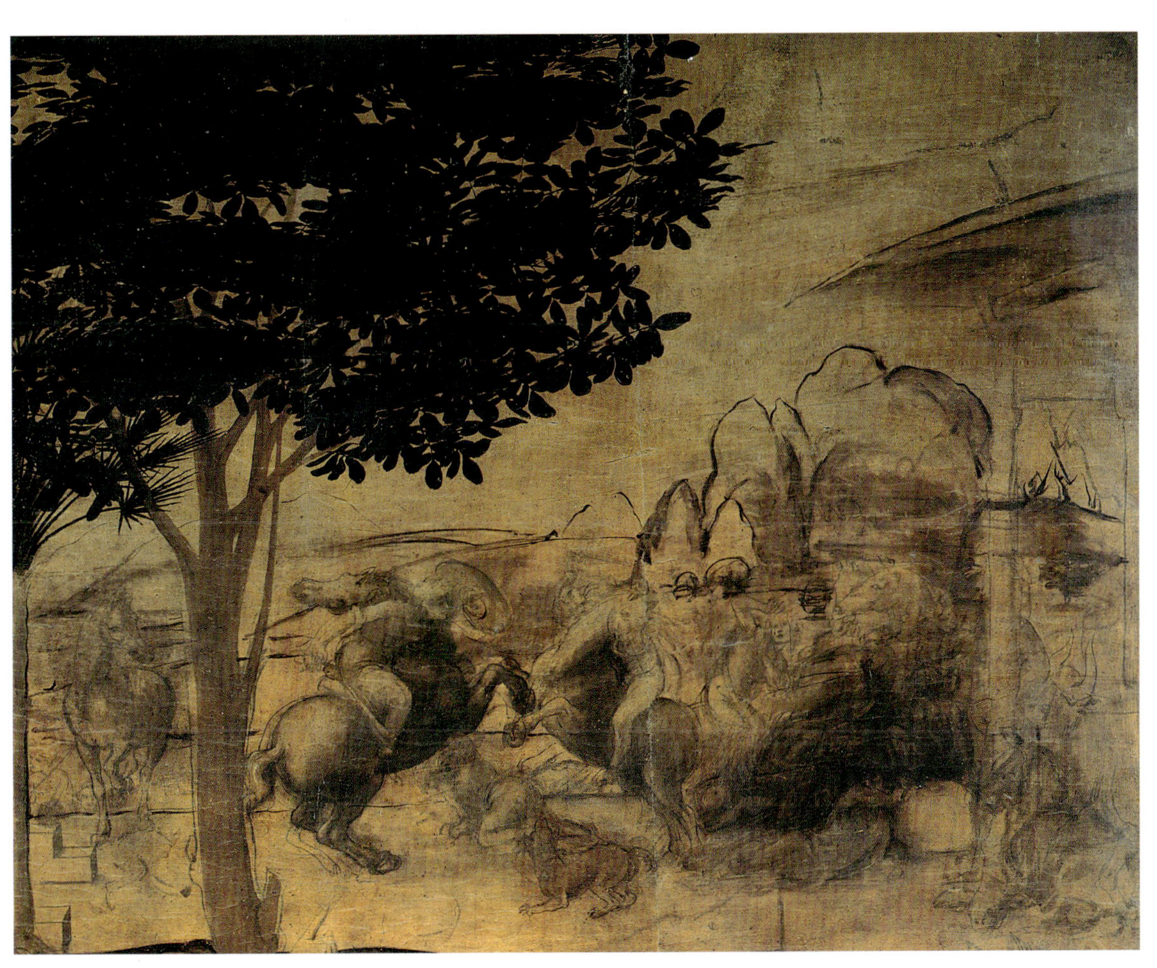

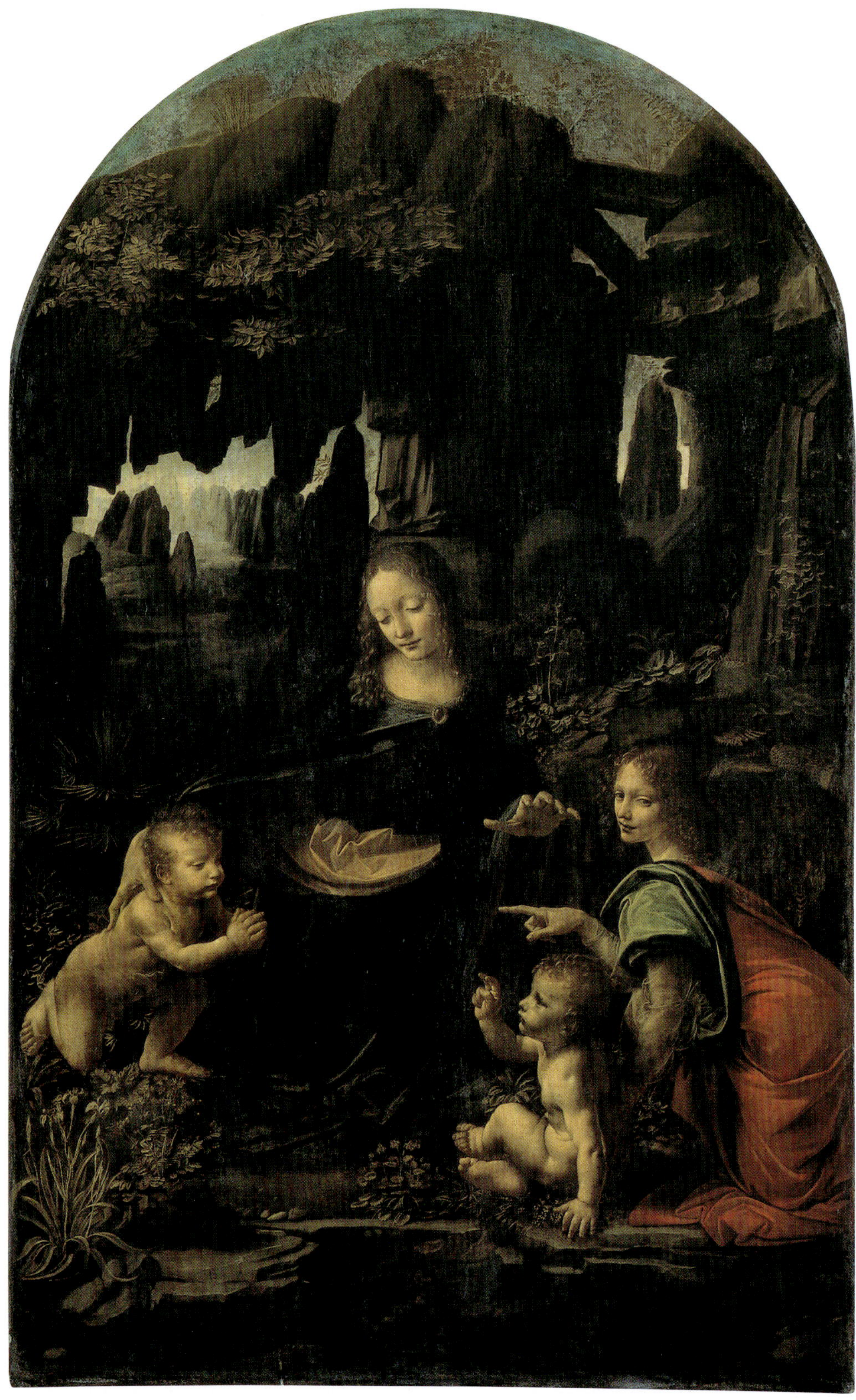

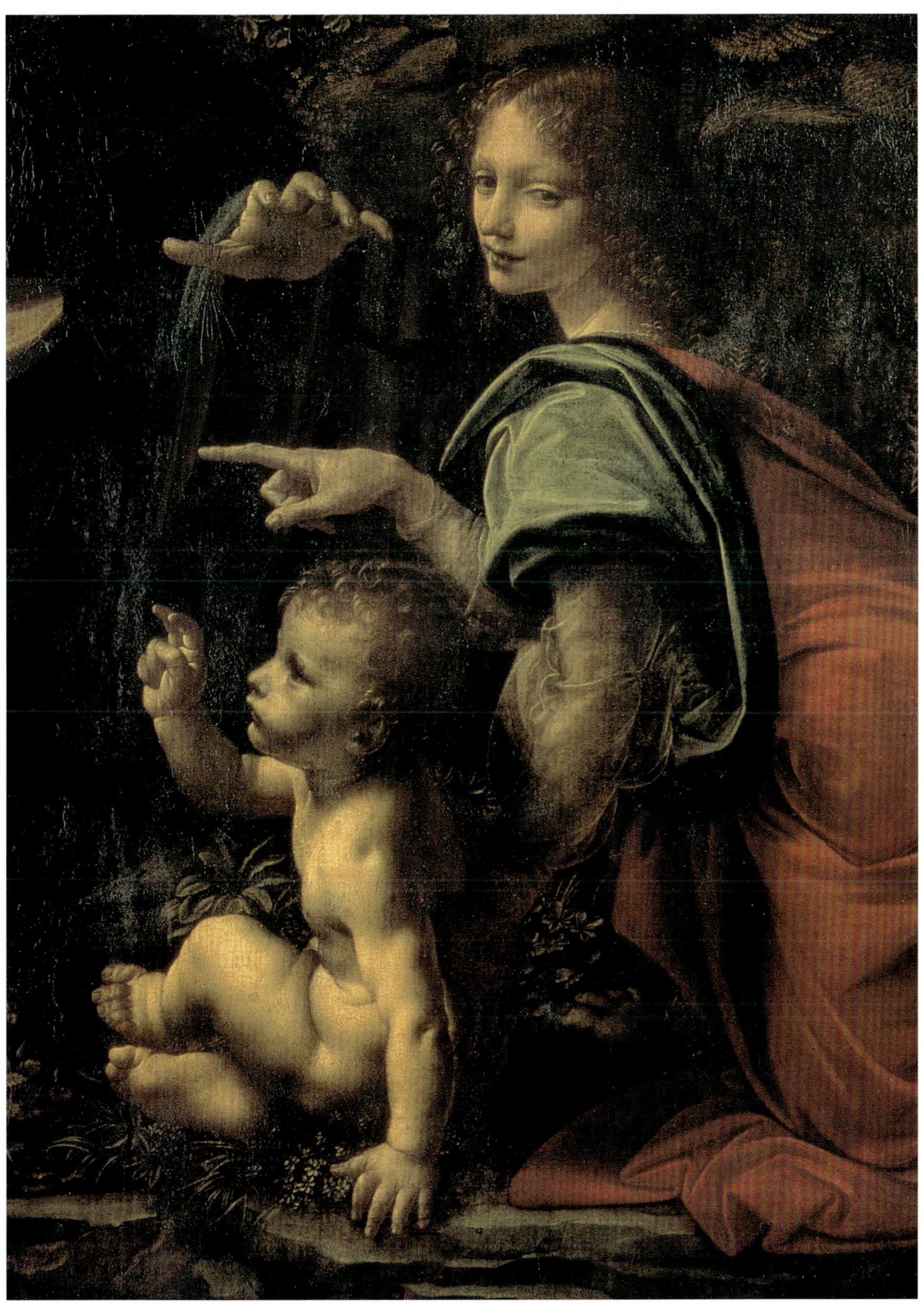

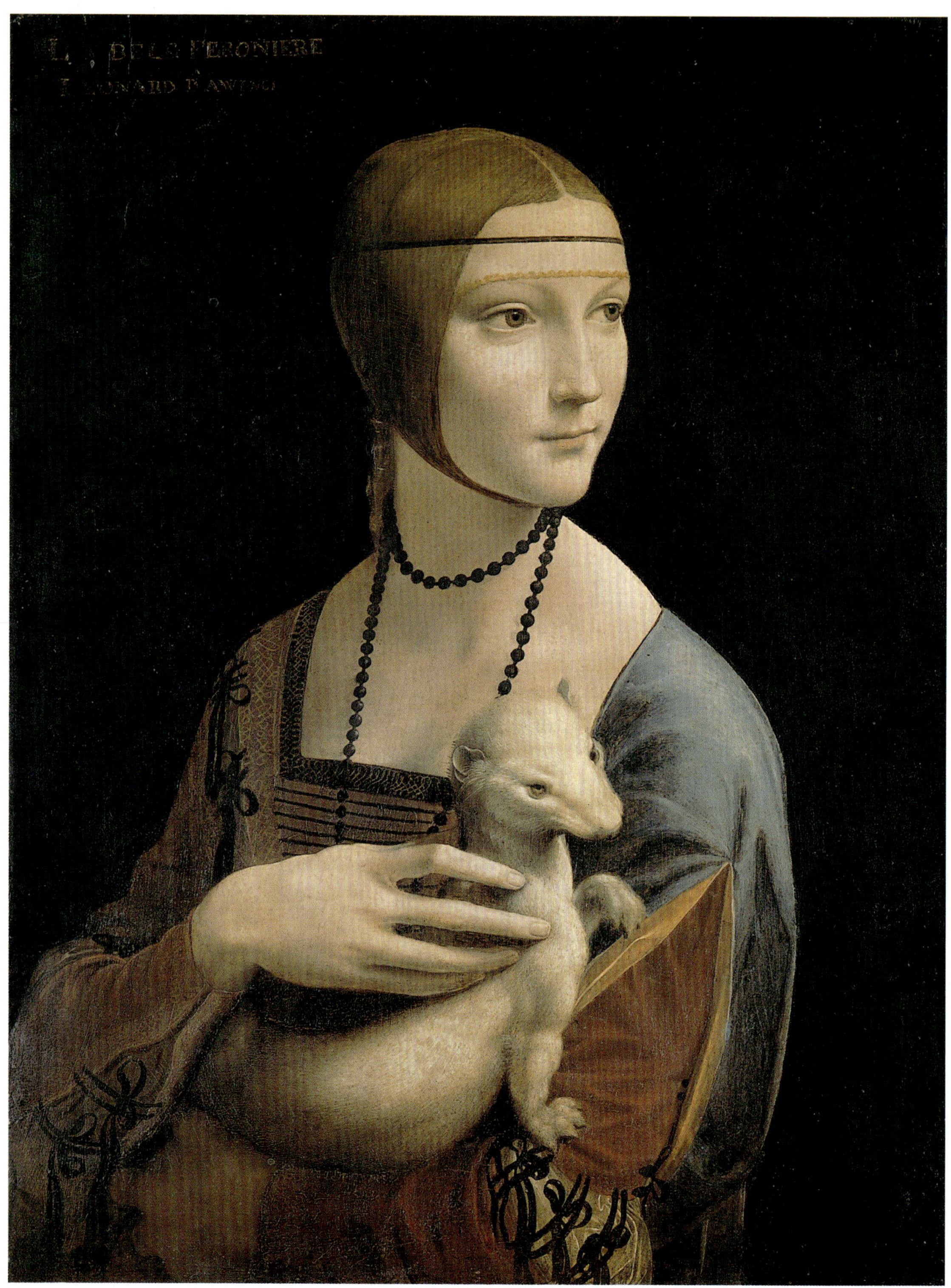
FERONIERE

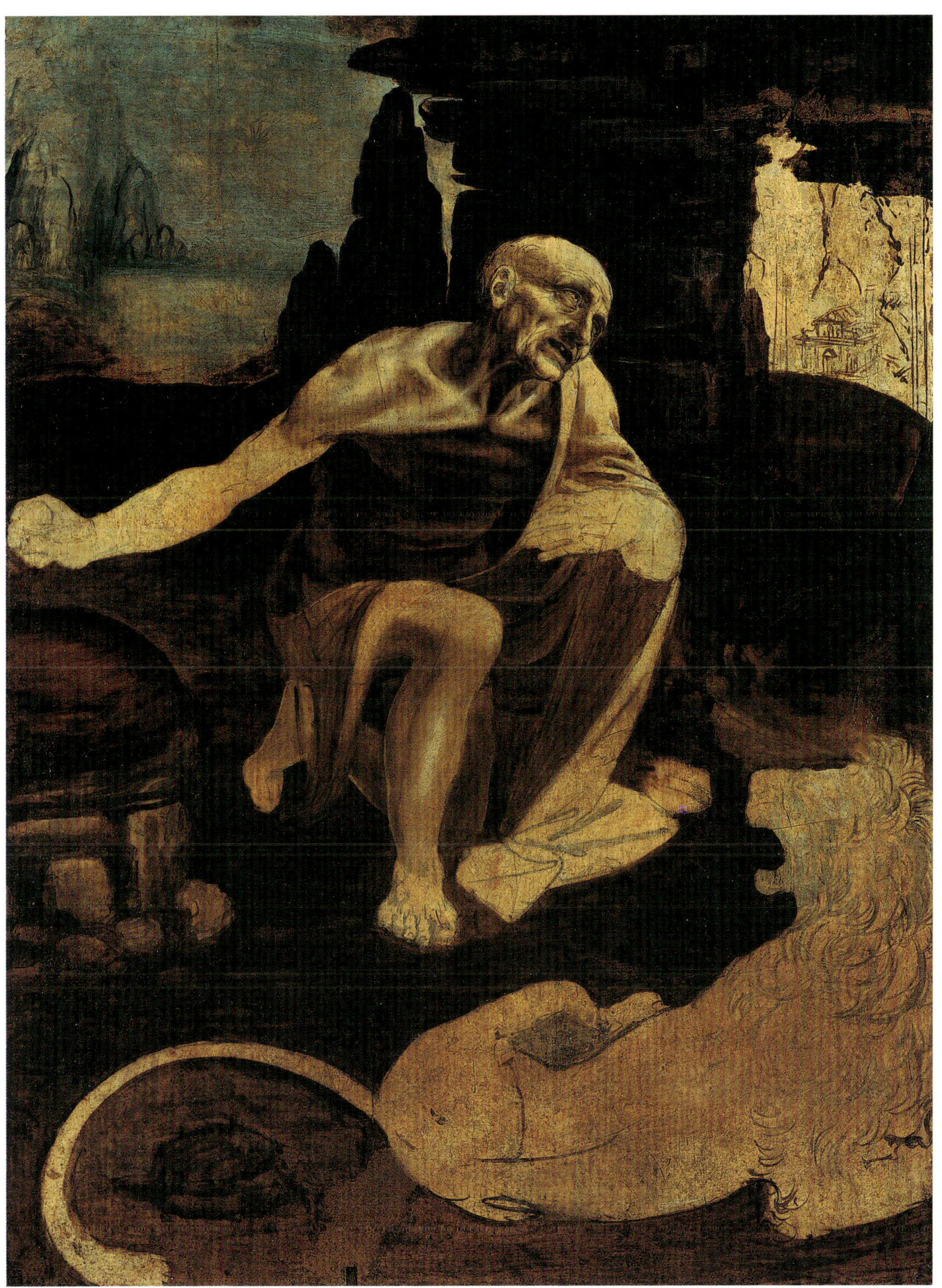

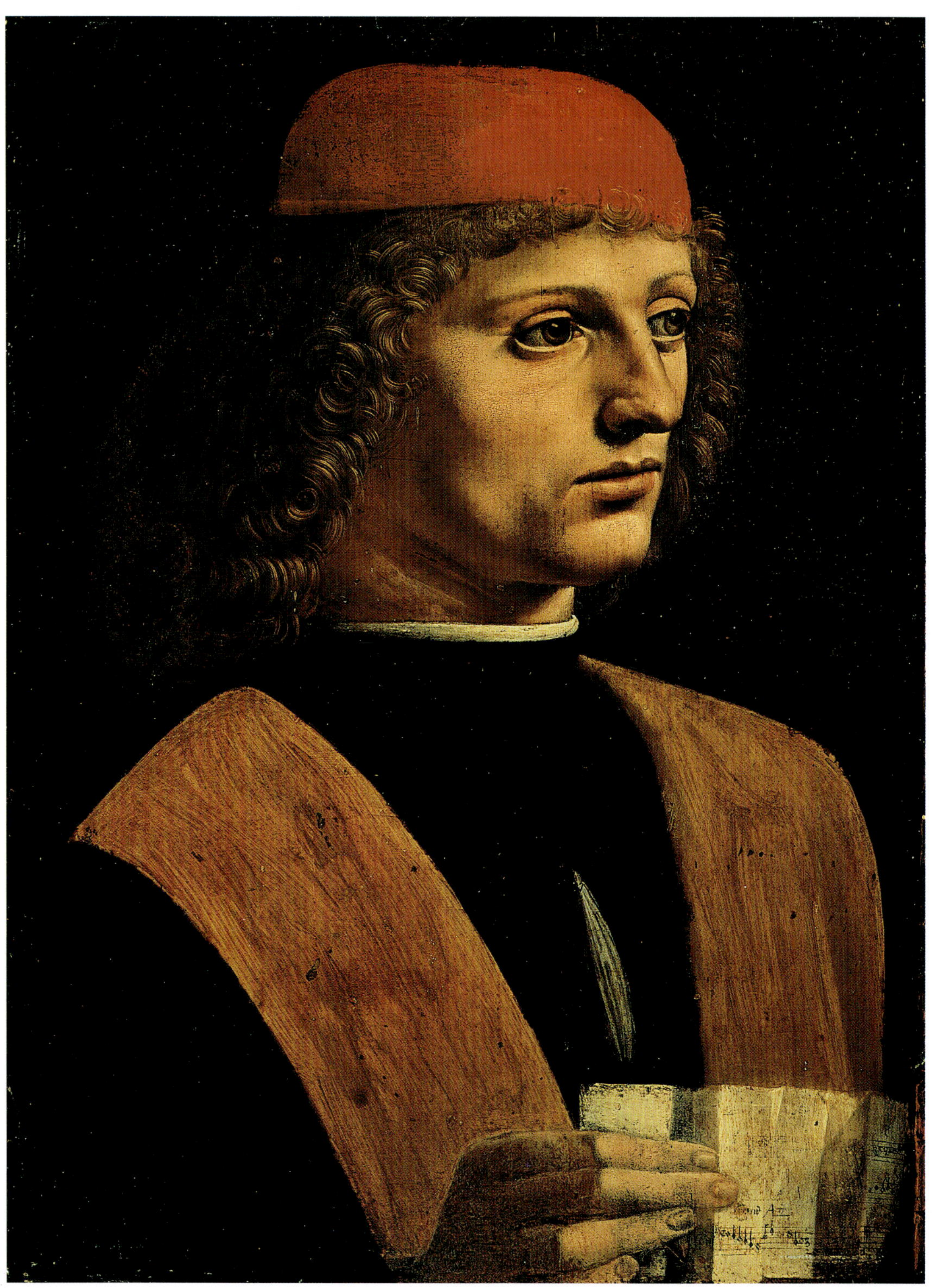

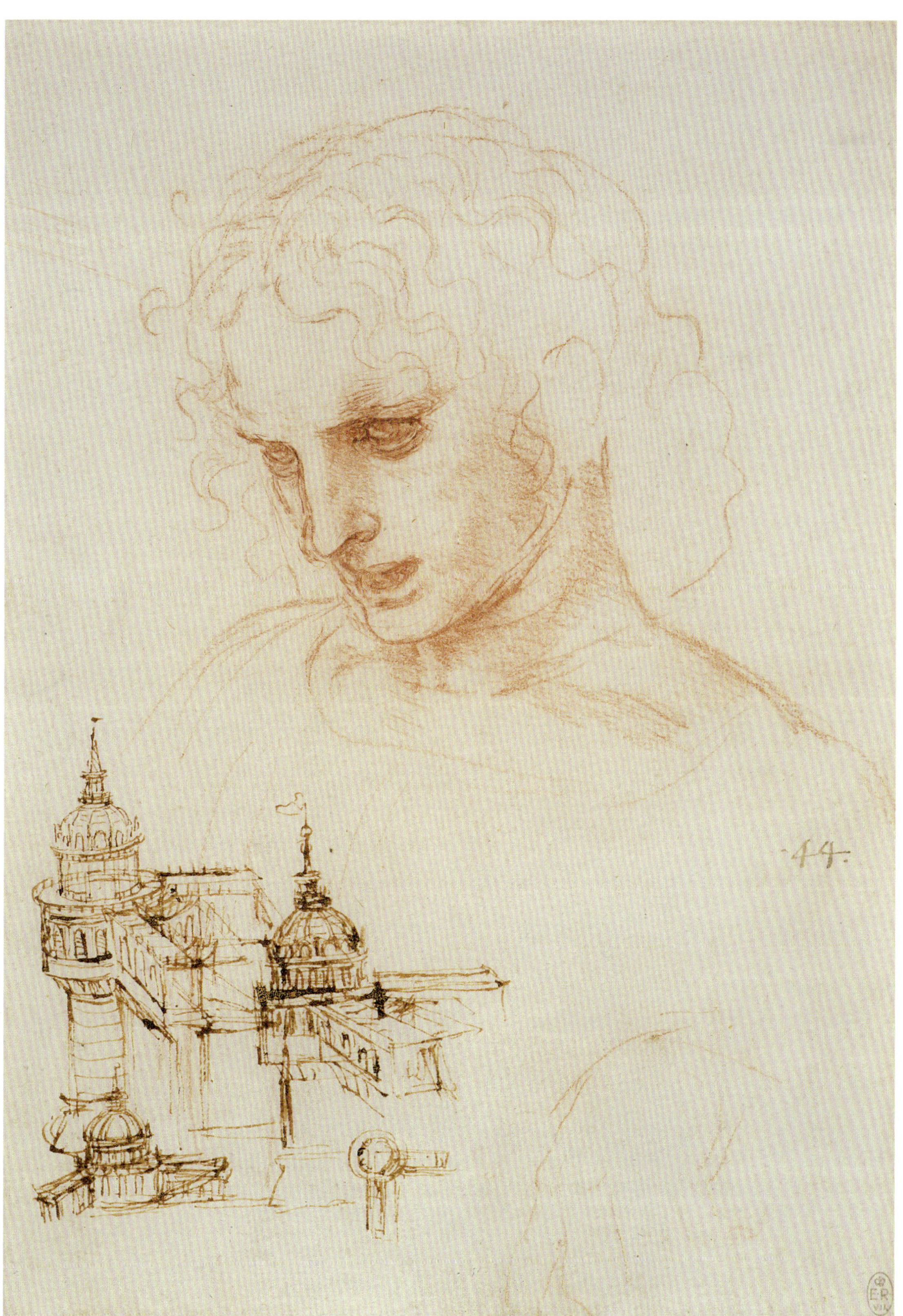

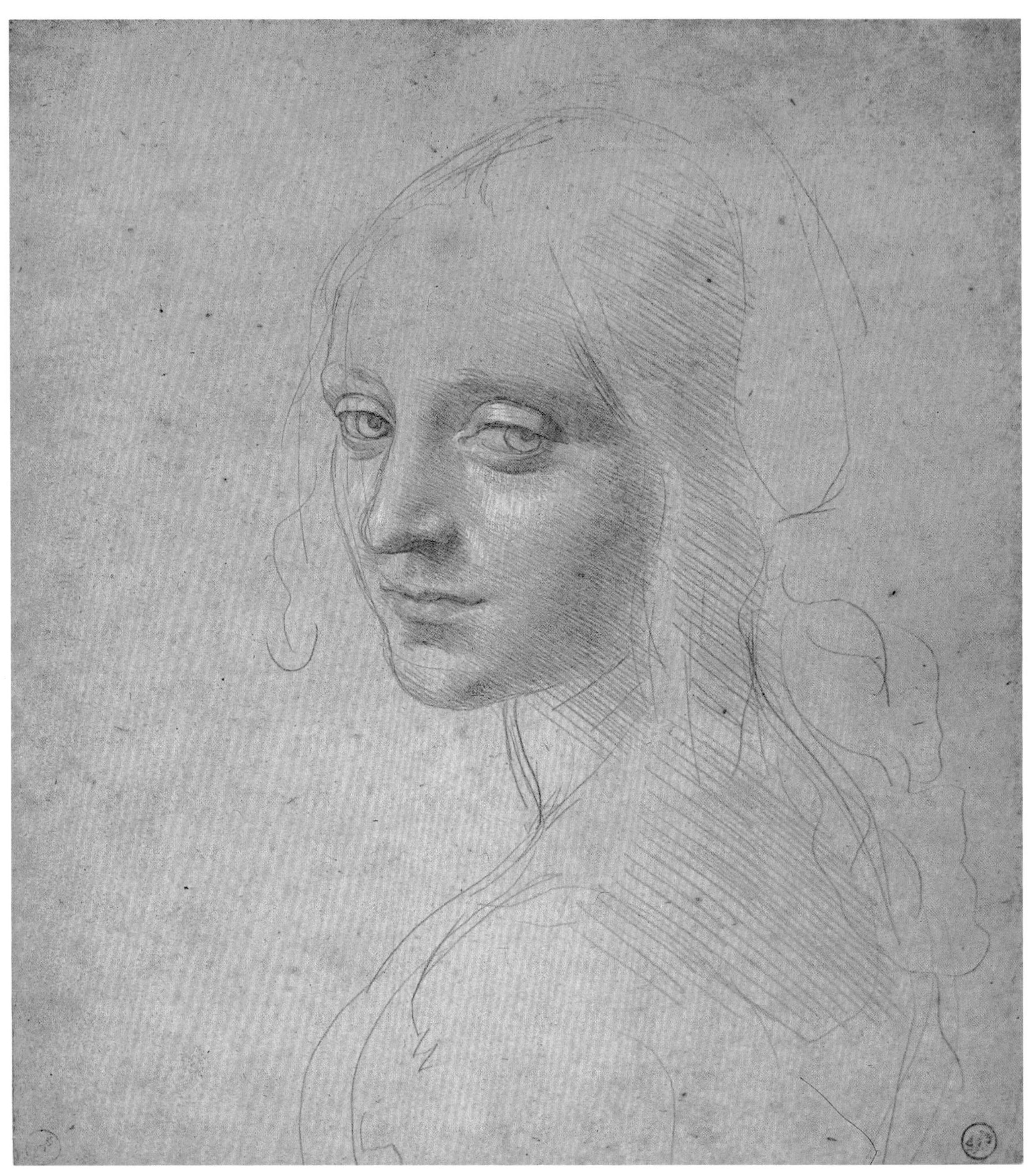

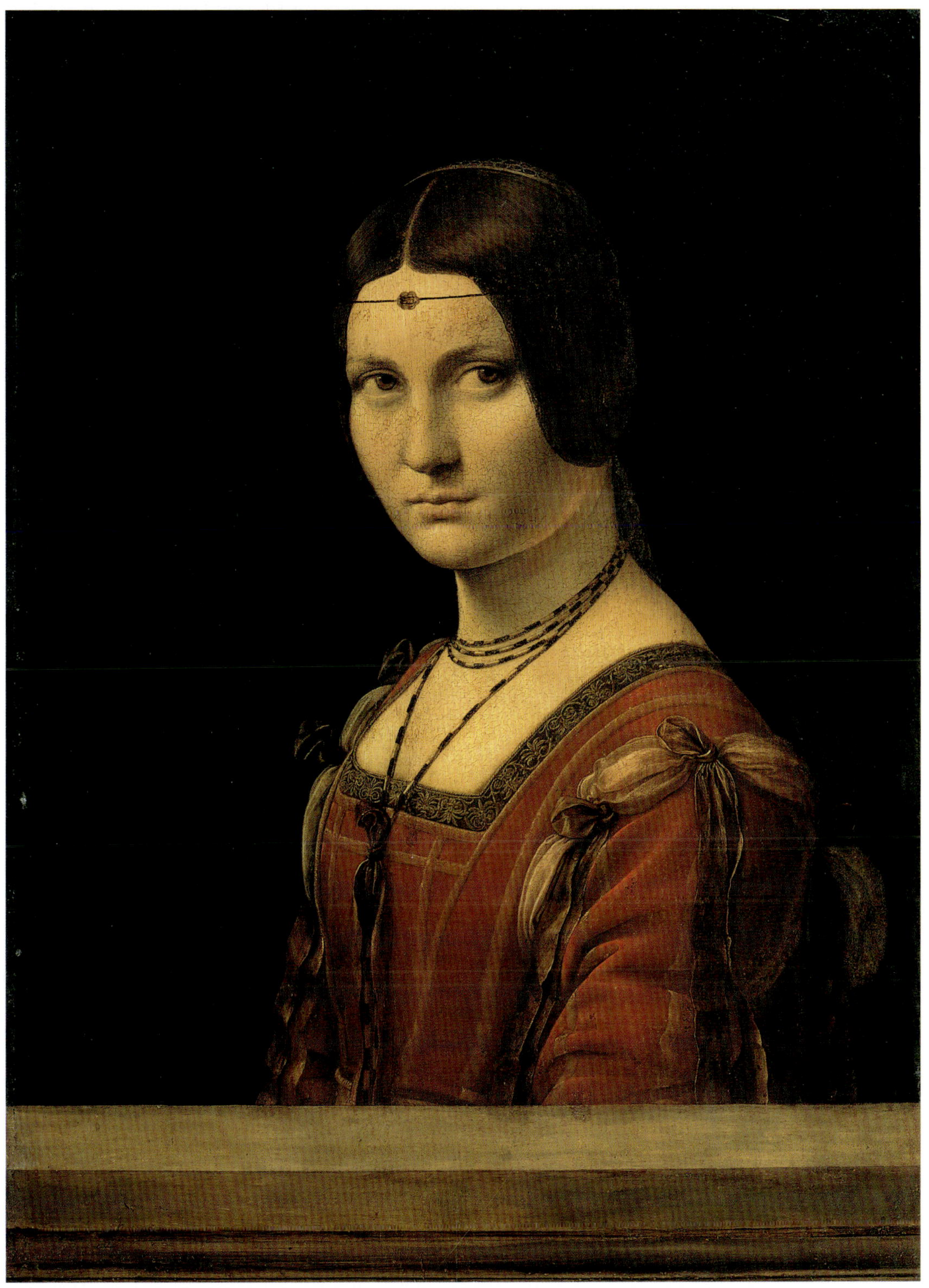

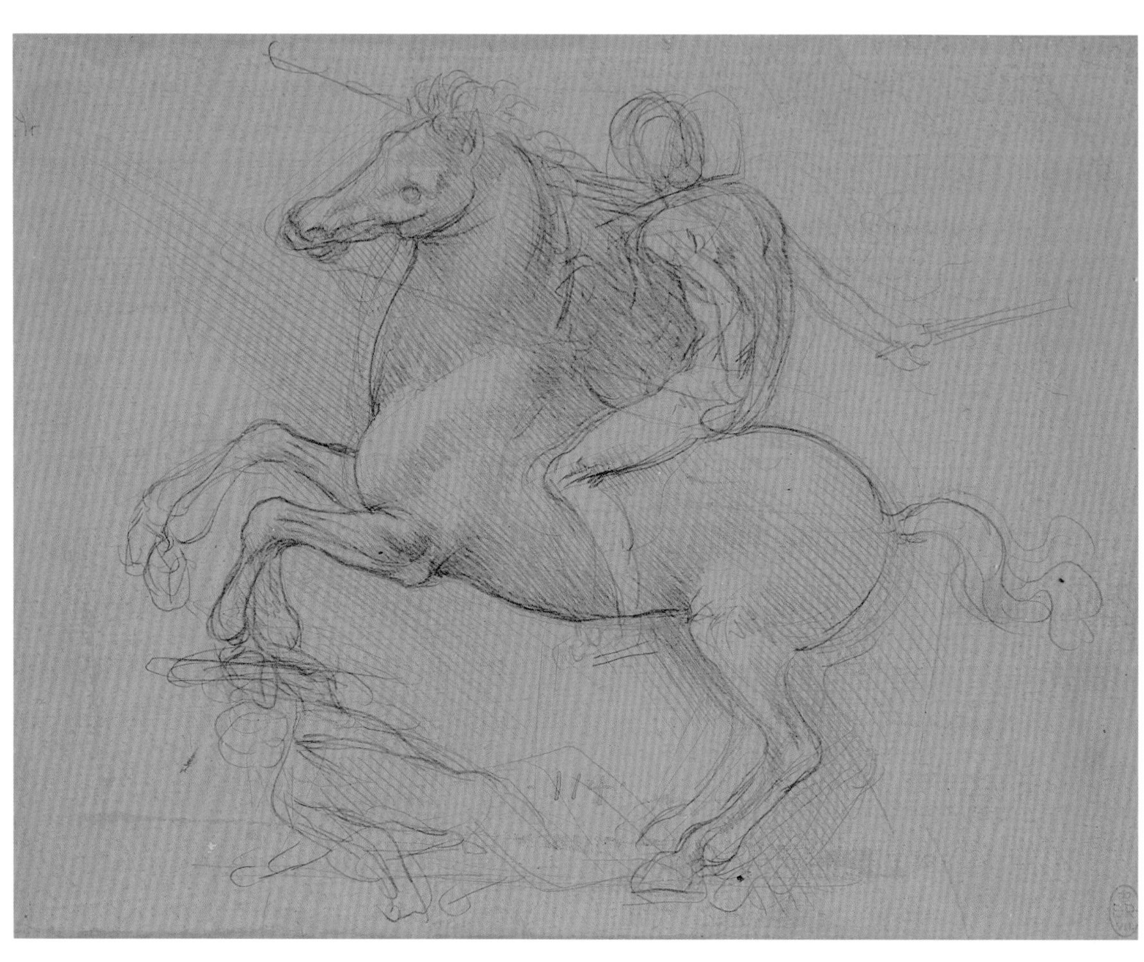

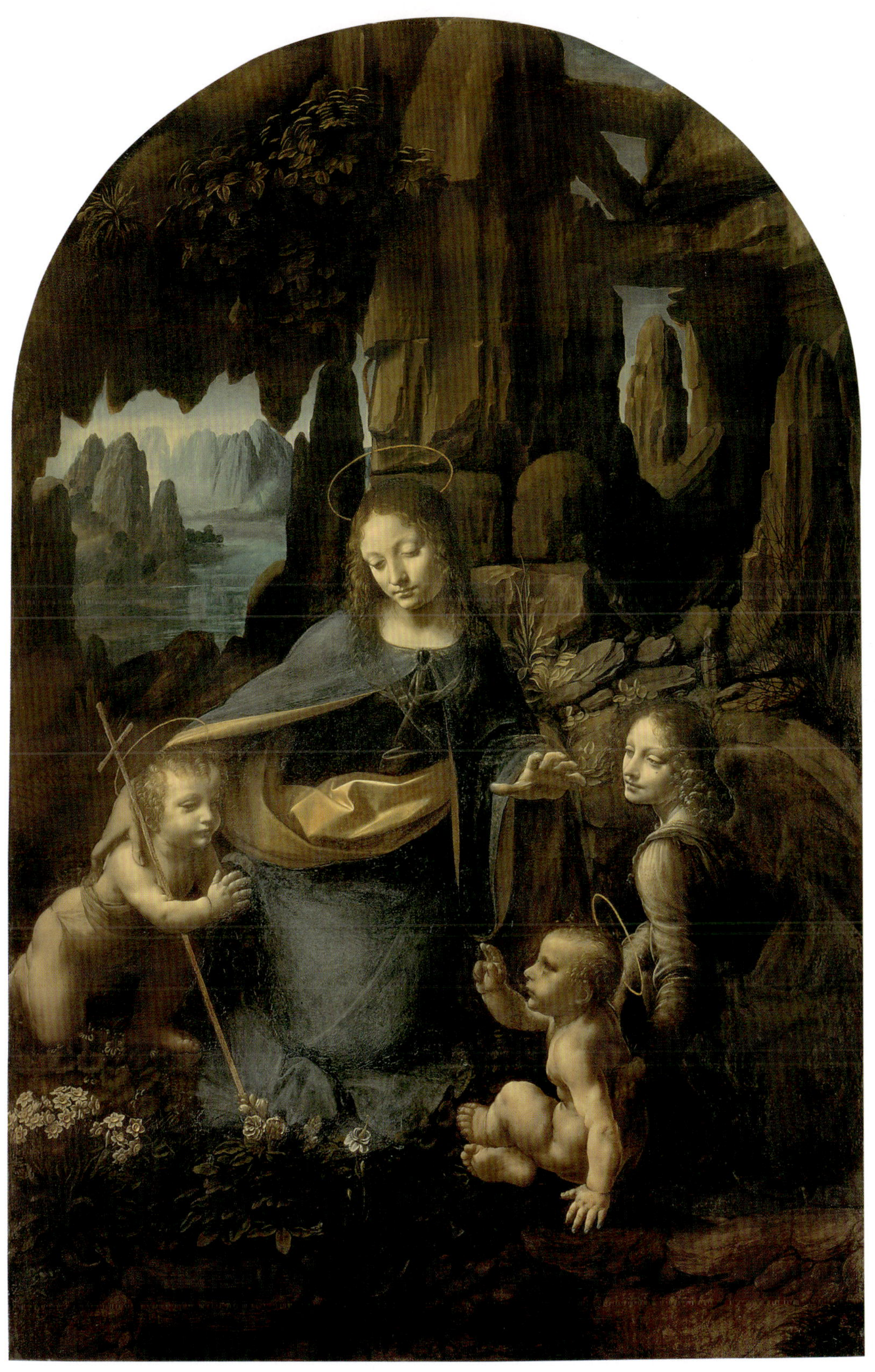

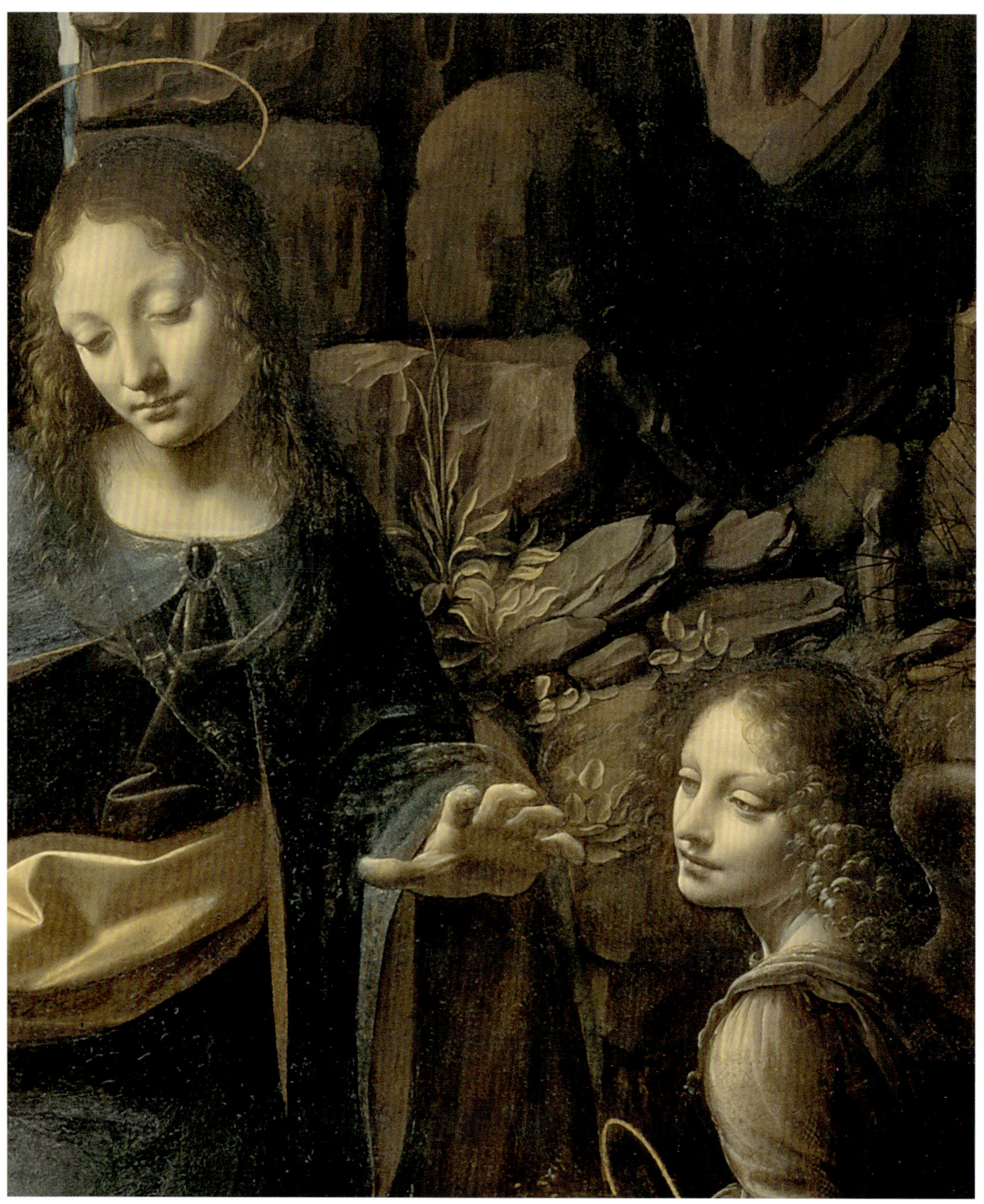

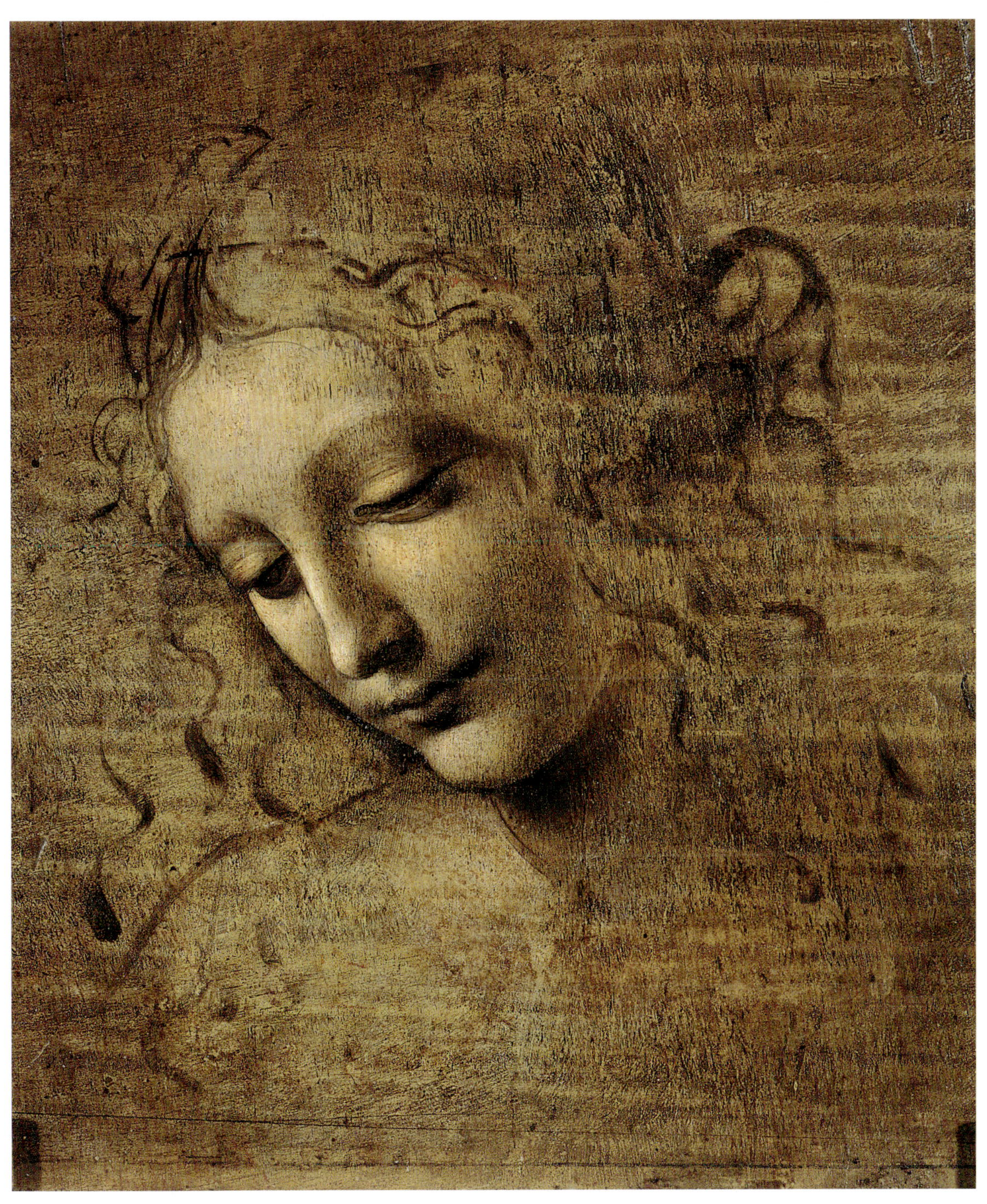

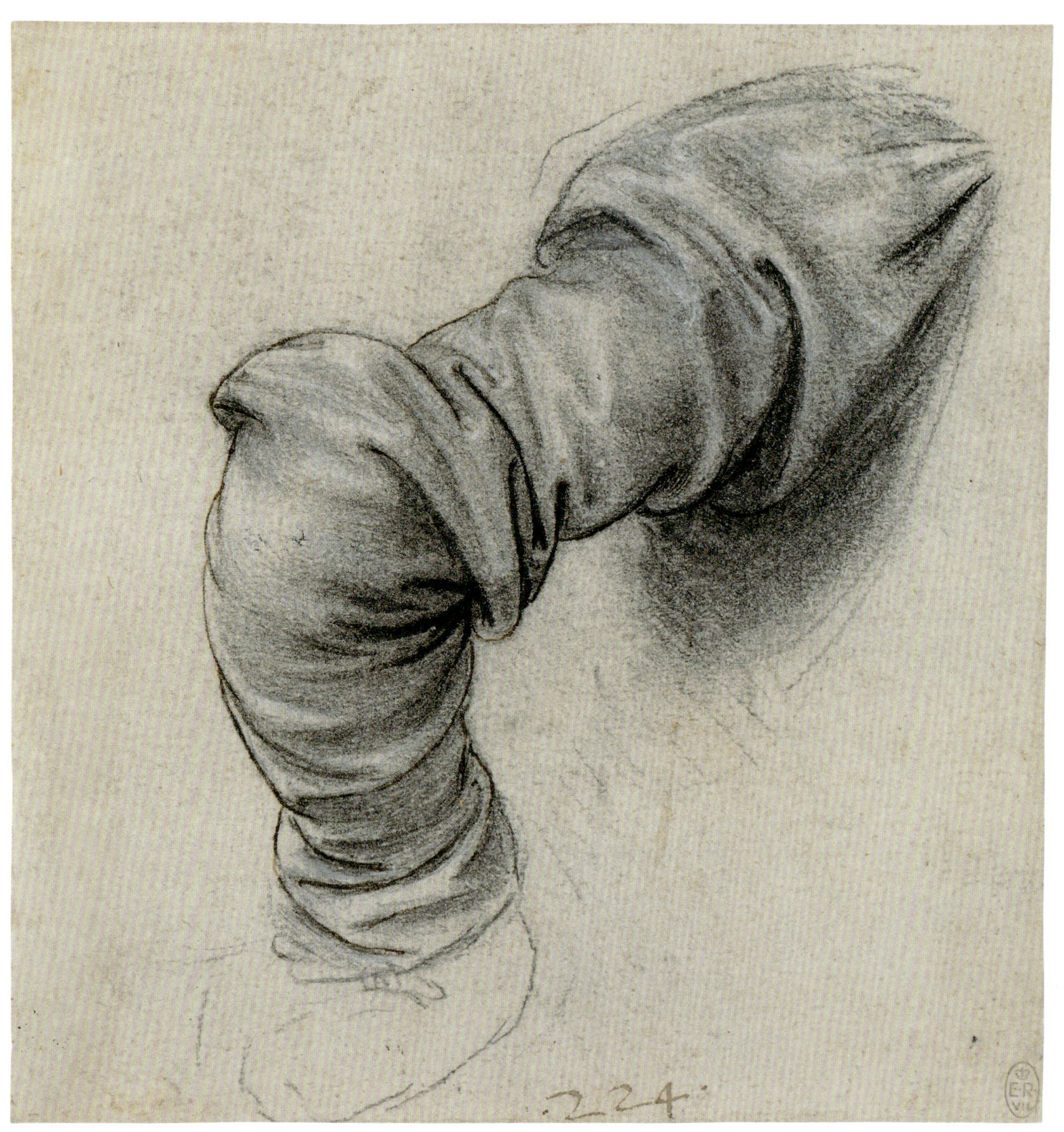

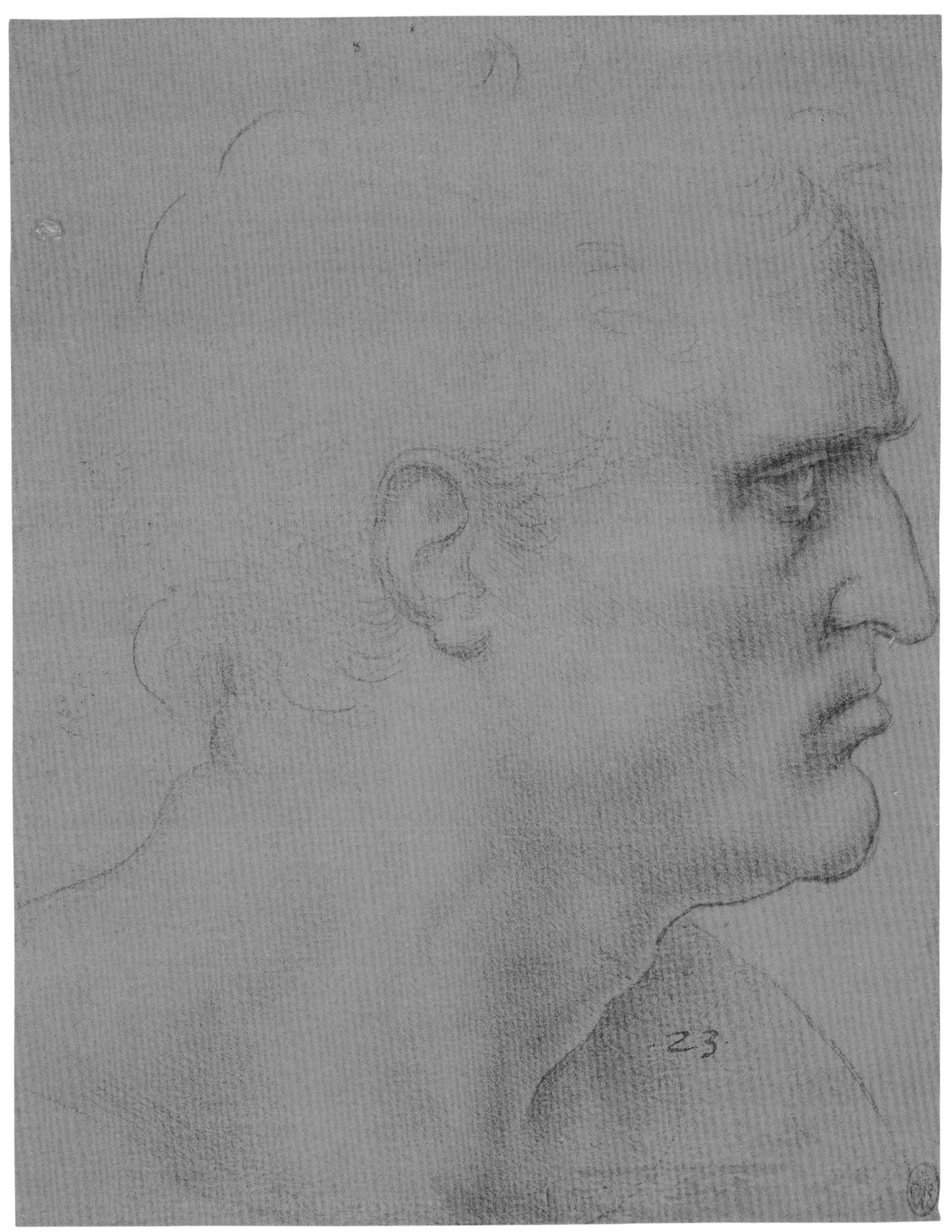
23

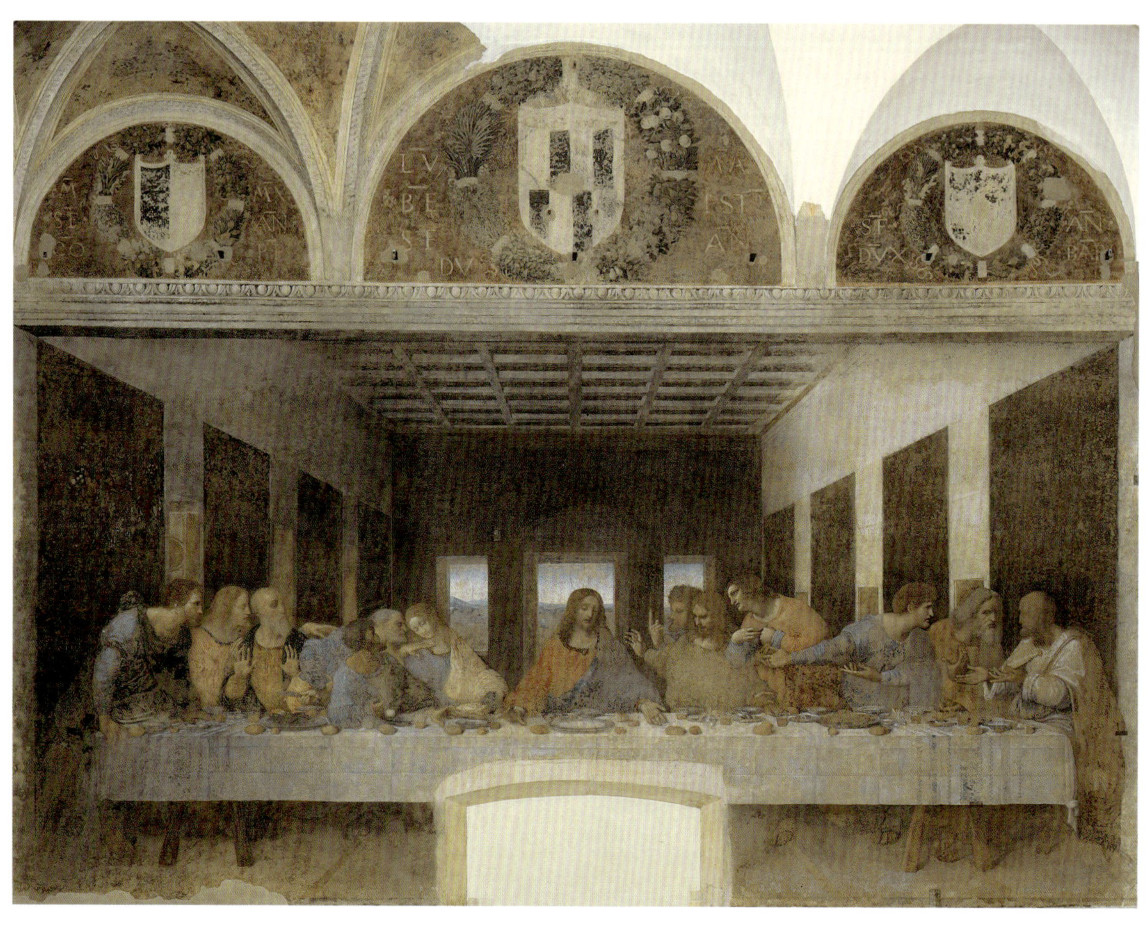

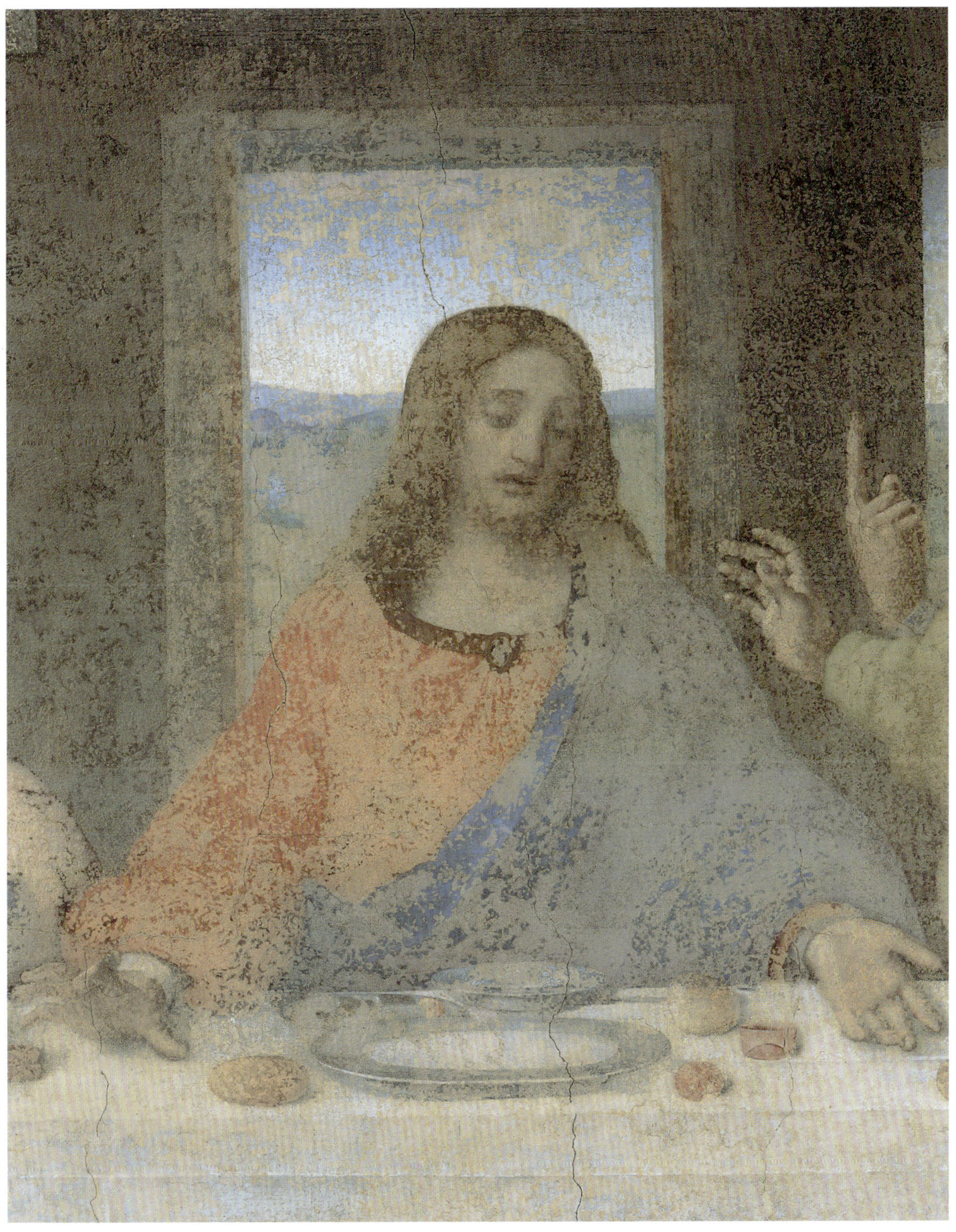

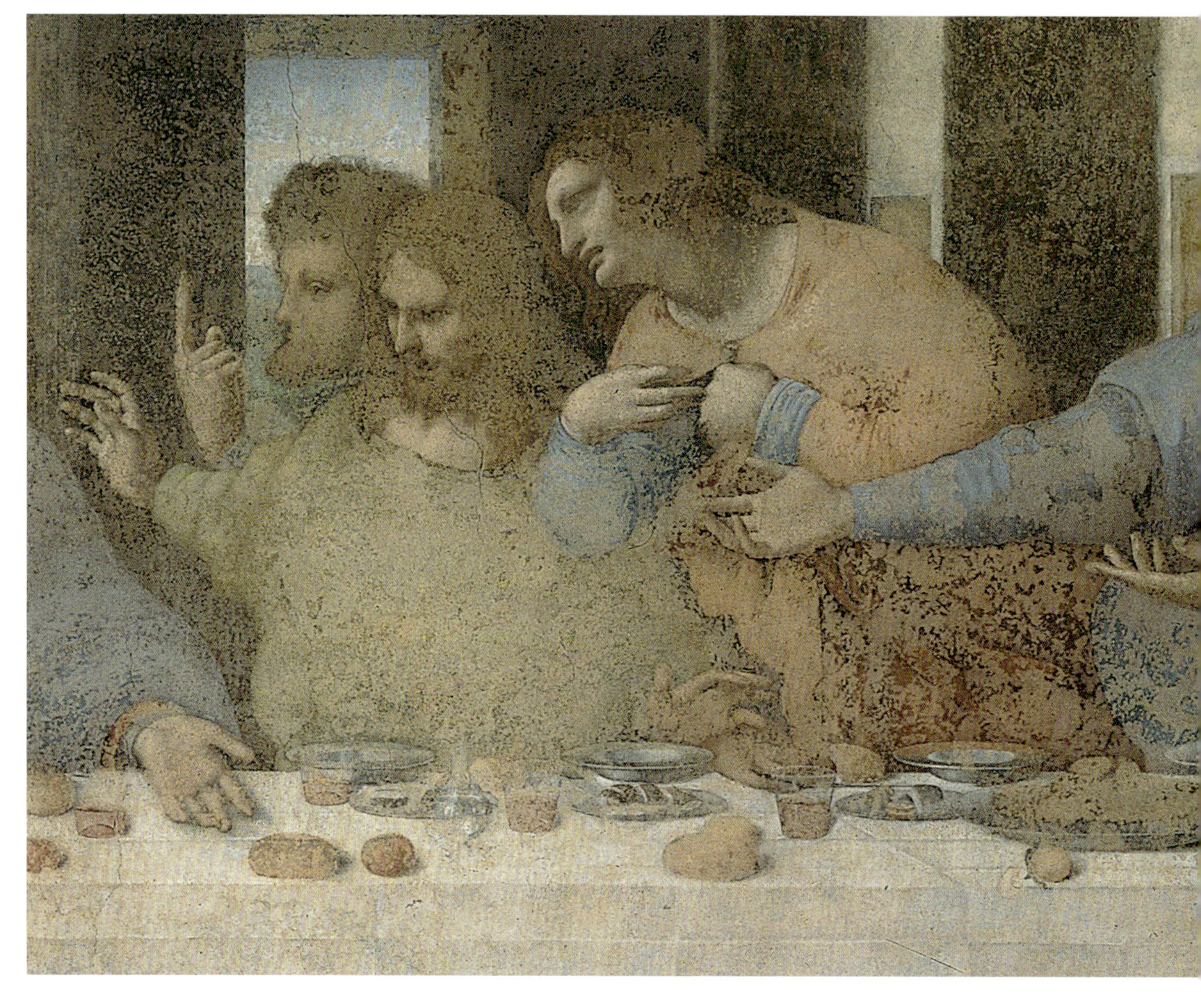

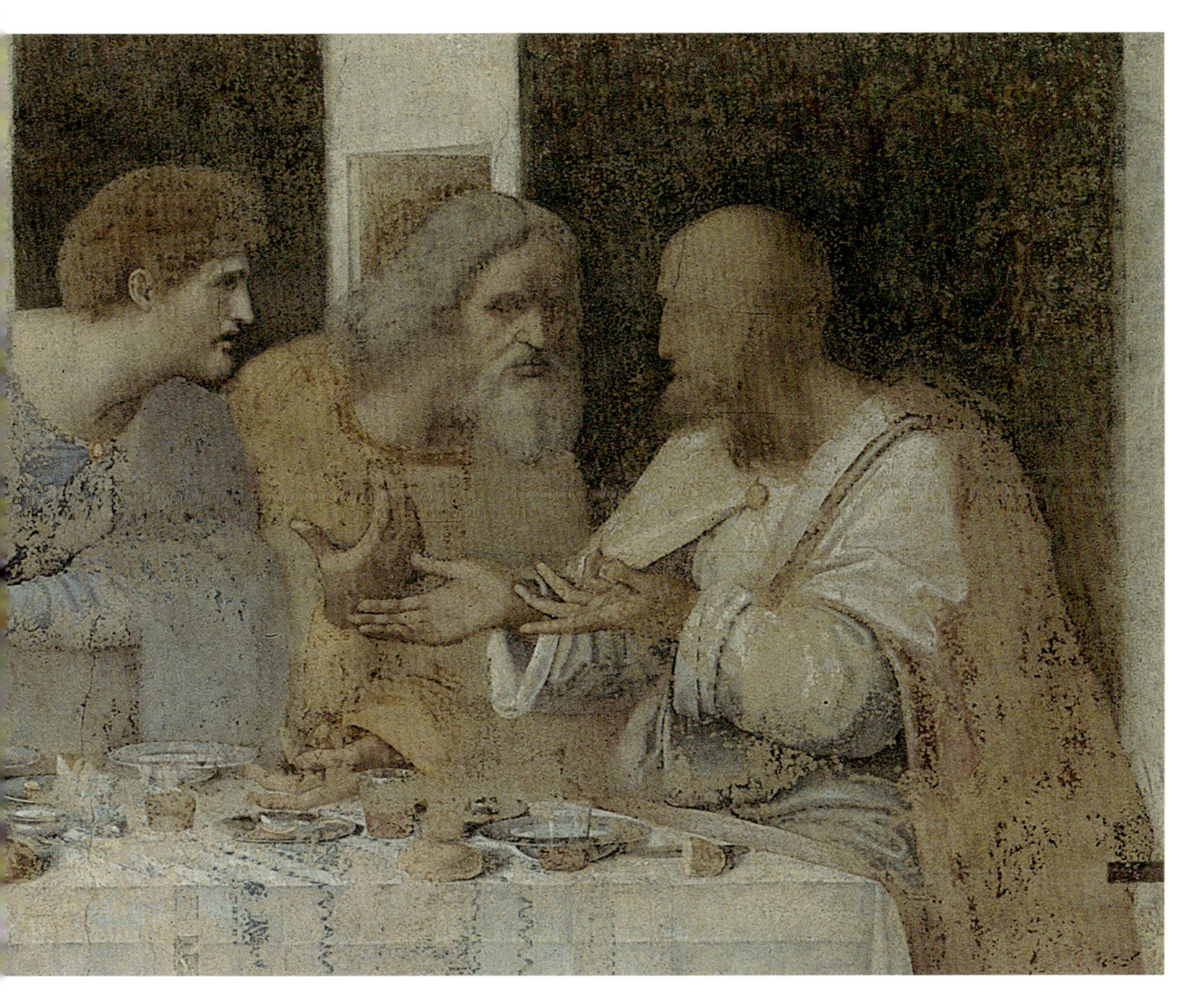

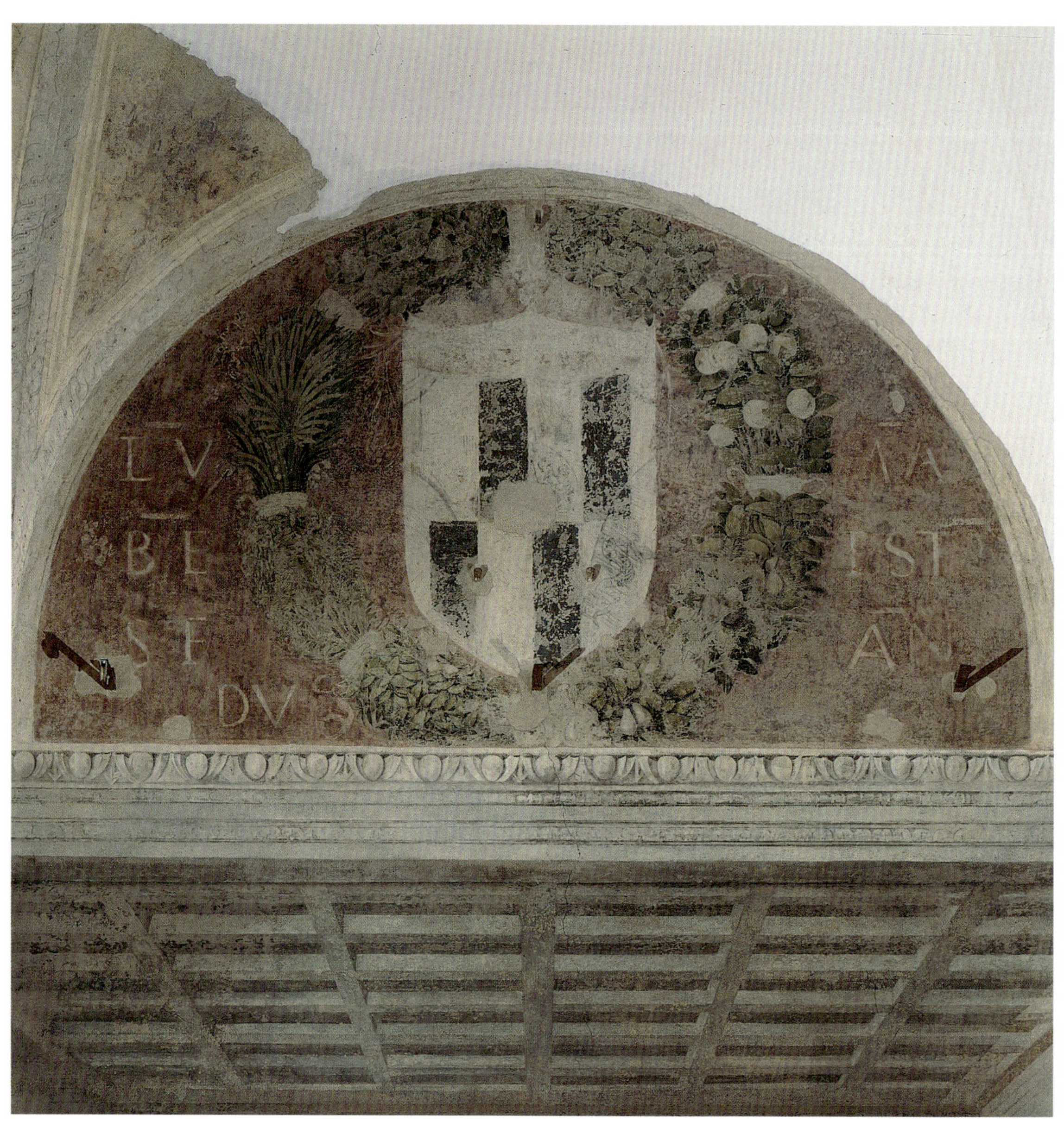
LV
BE
SE
DVS
MA
EST
AN

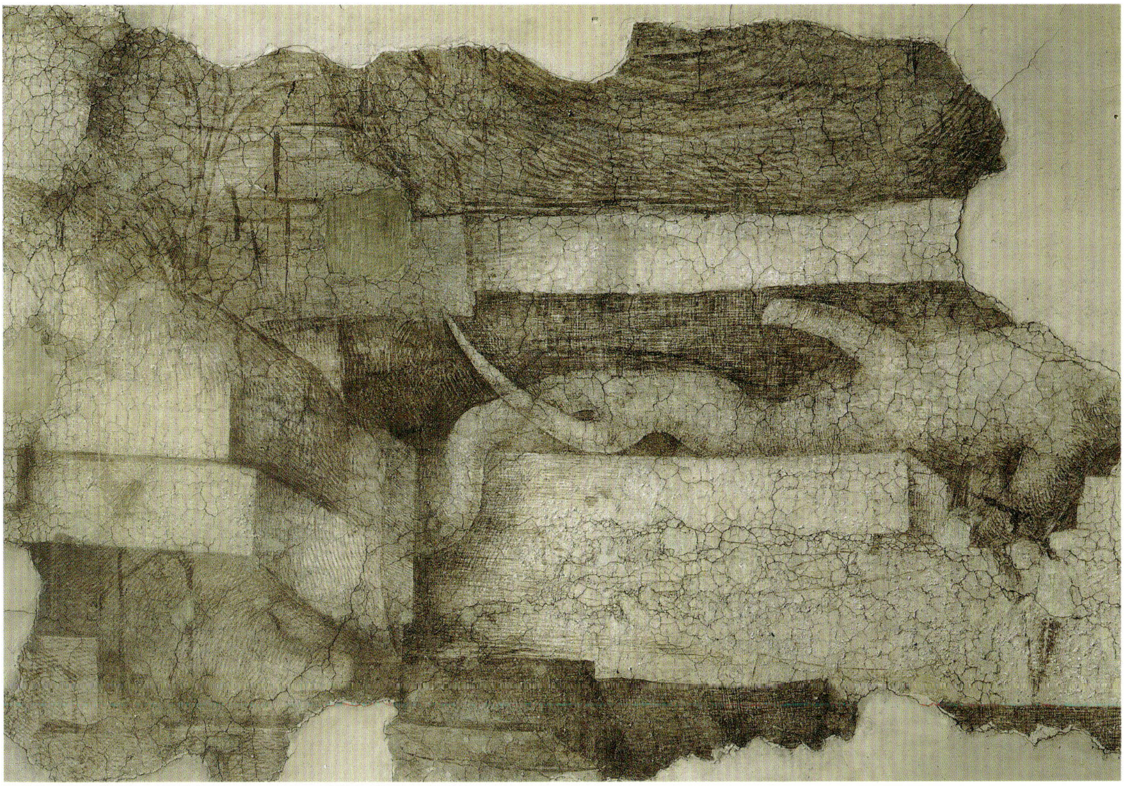

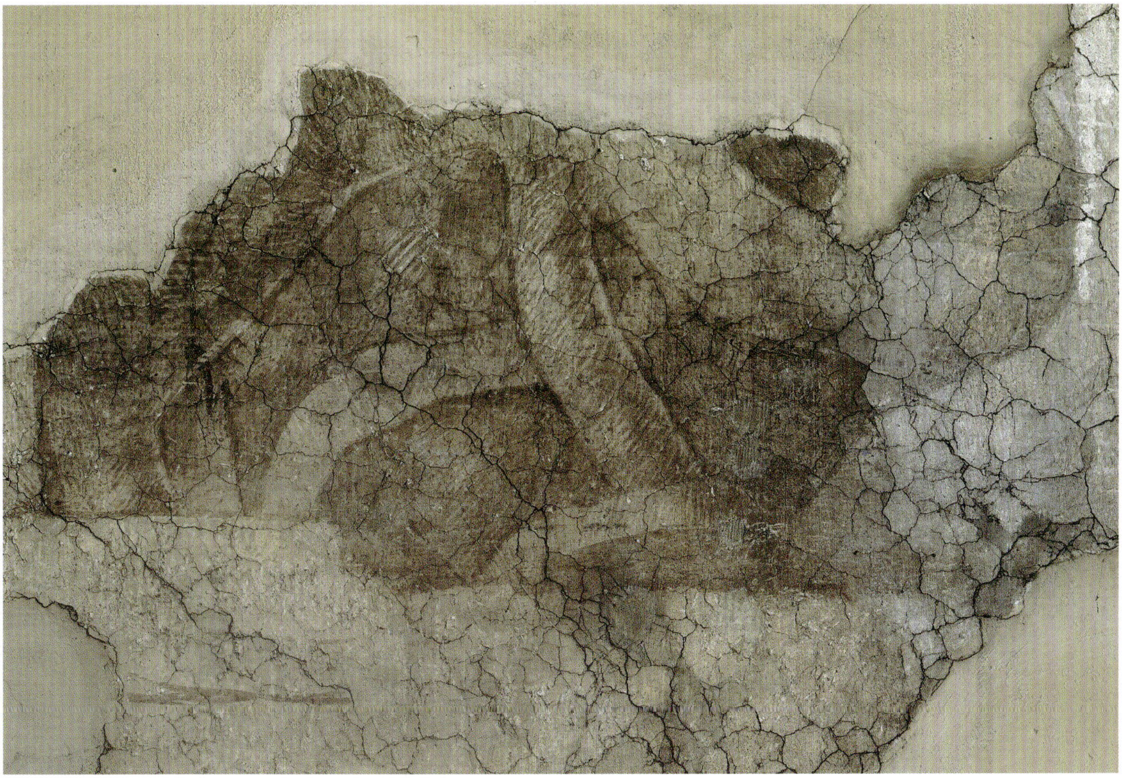

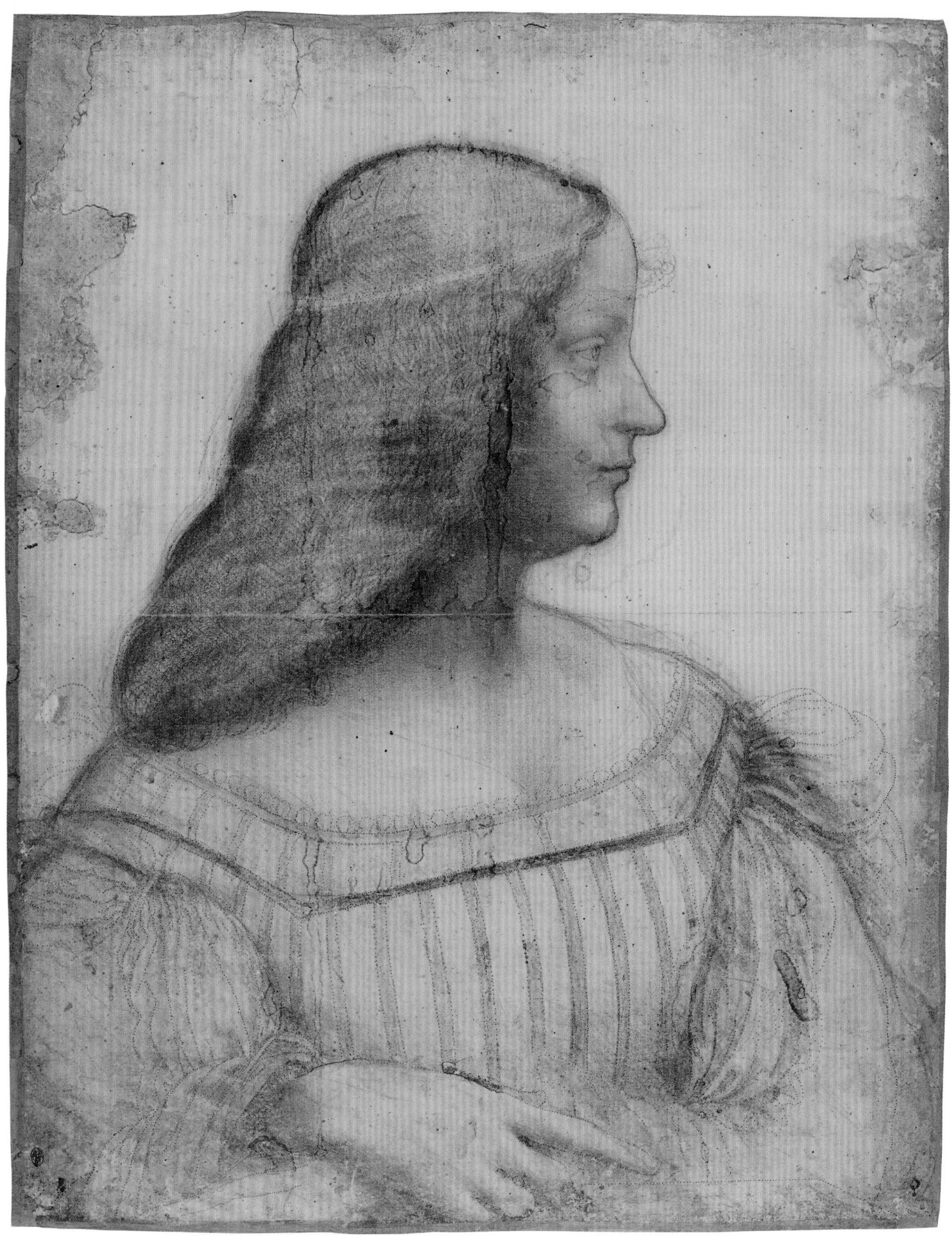

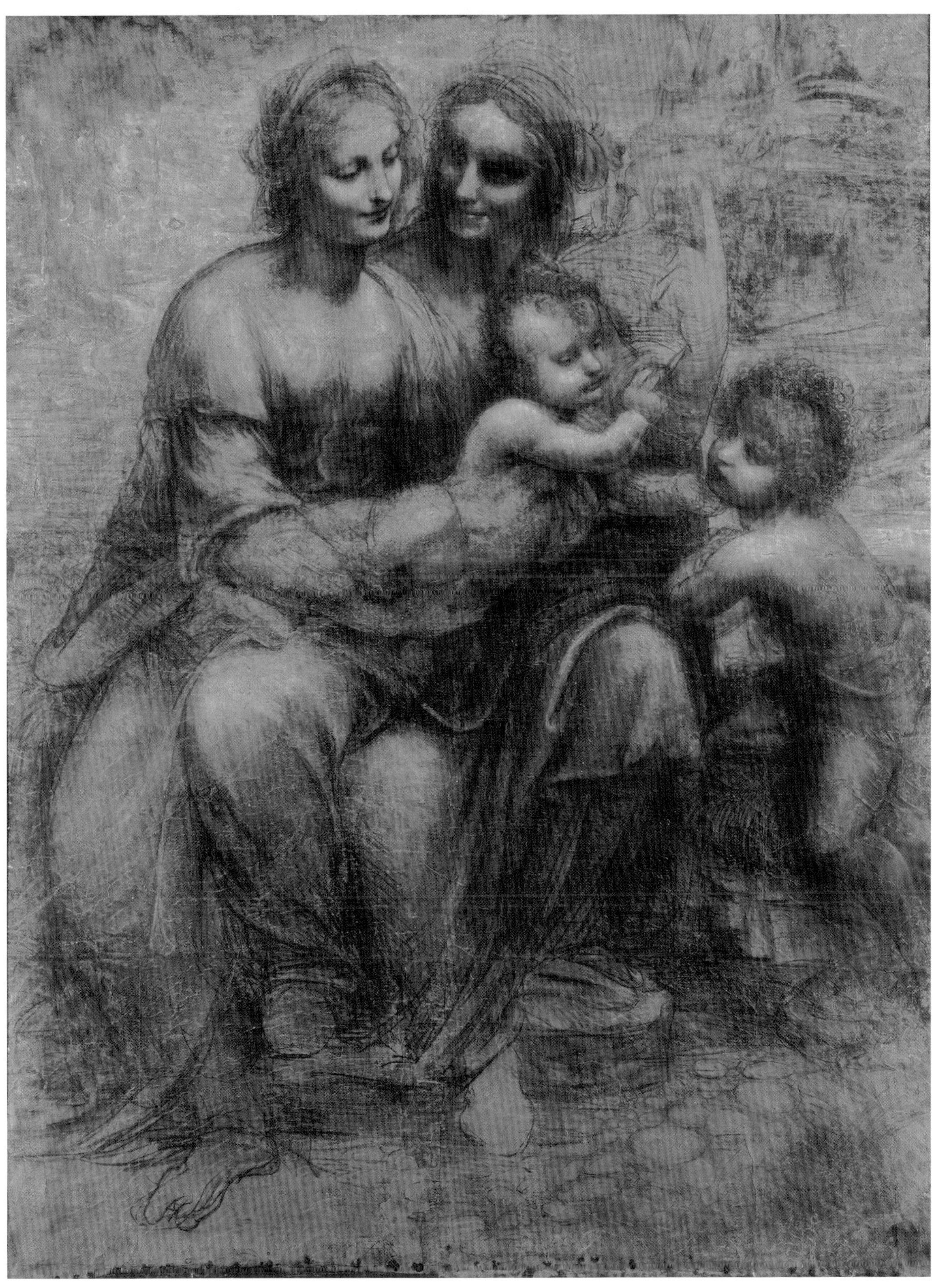

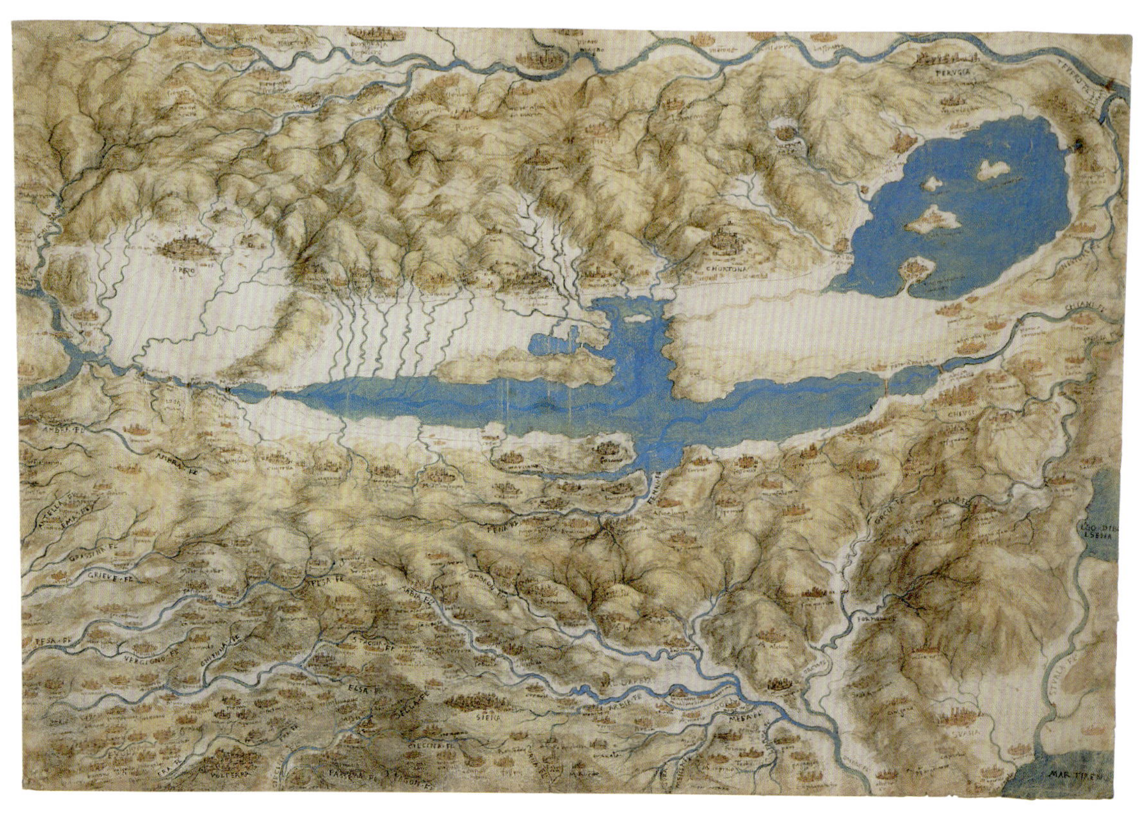
PERUGIA
TEVERO FI
CHIANI FI
CHORTONA
MAR TIREN

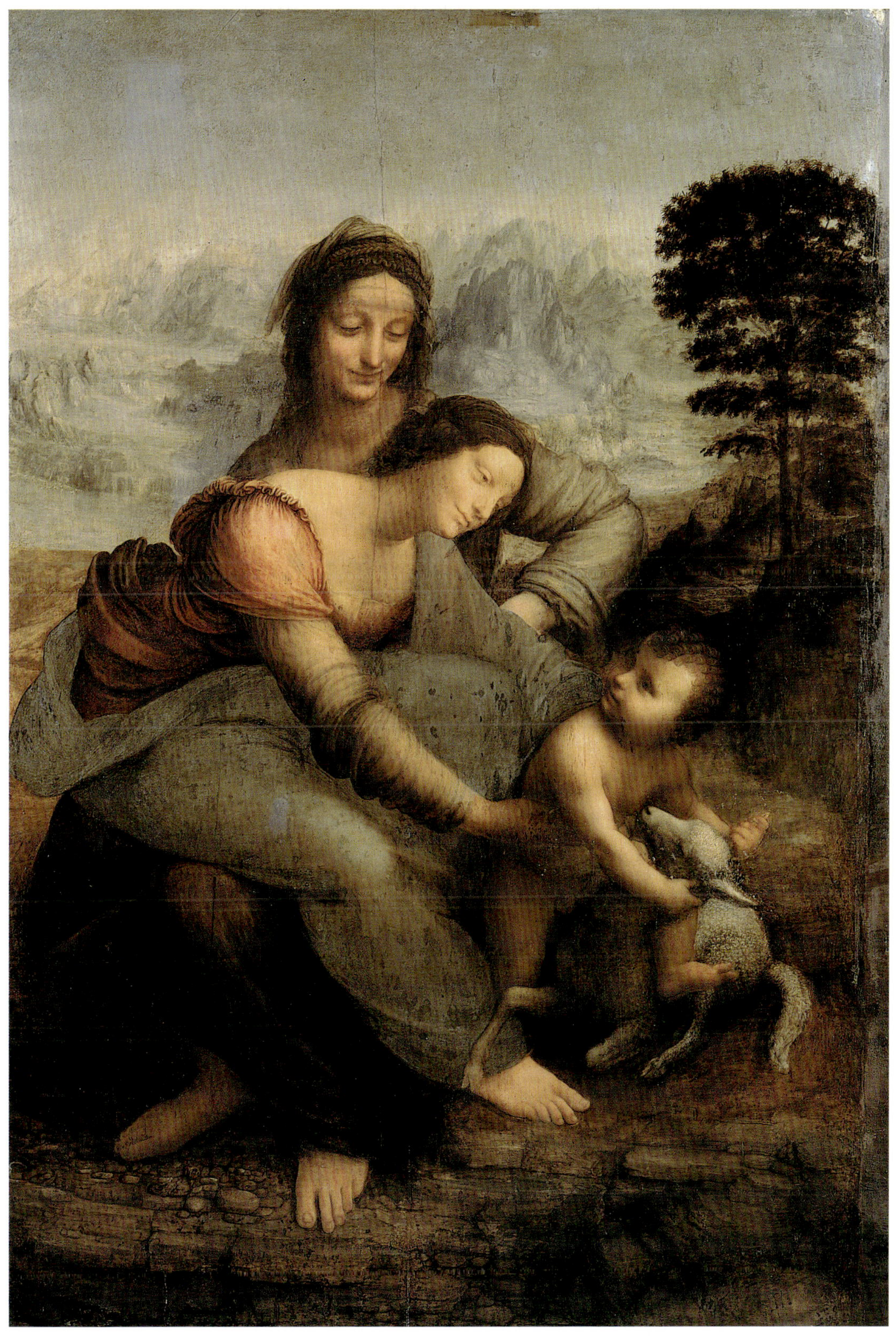

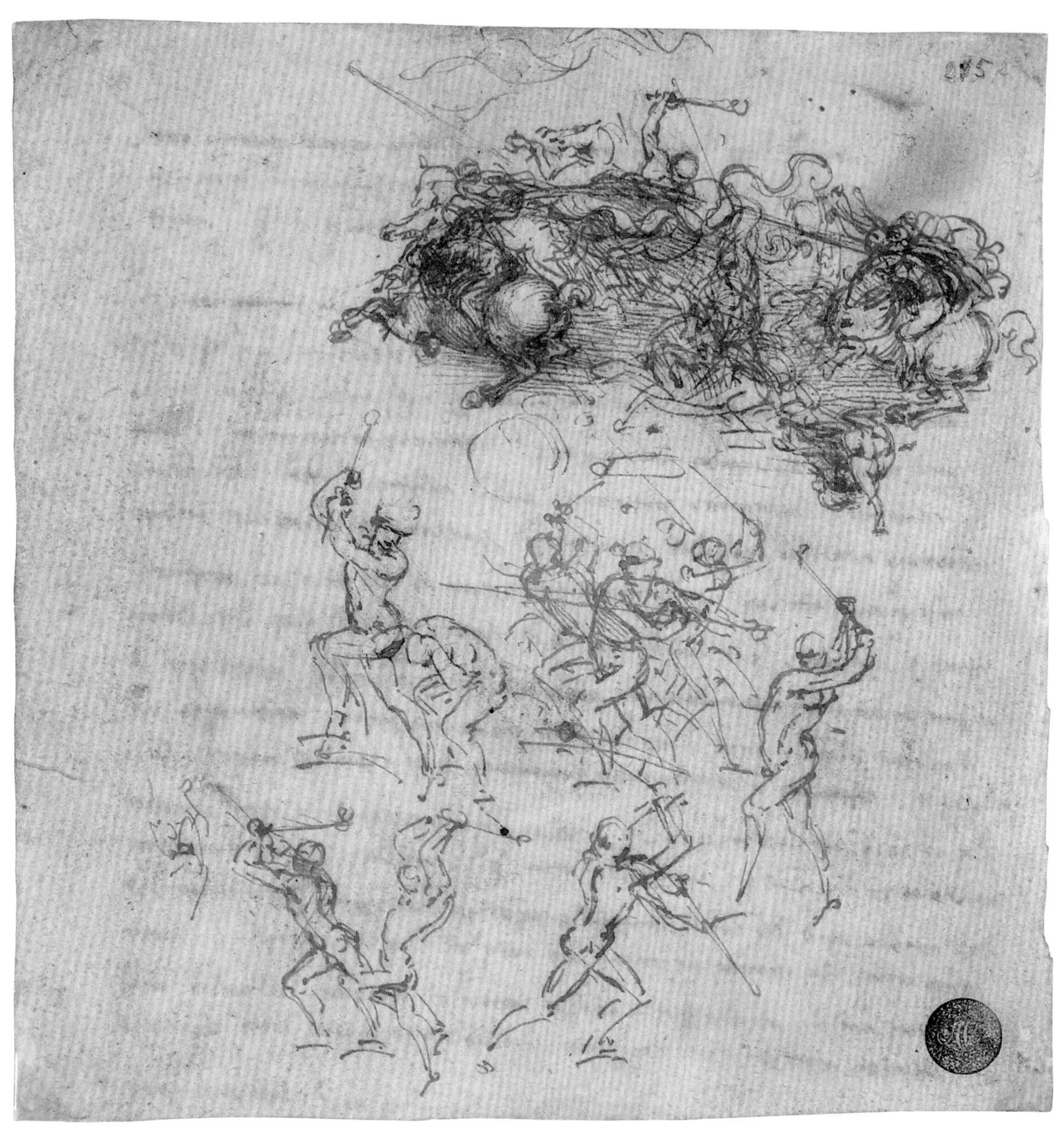

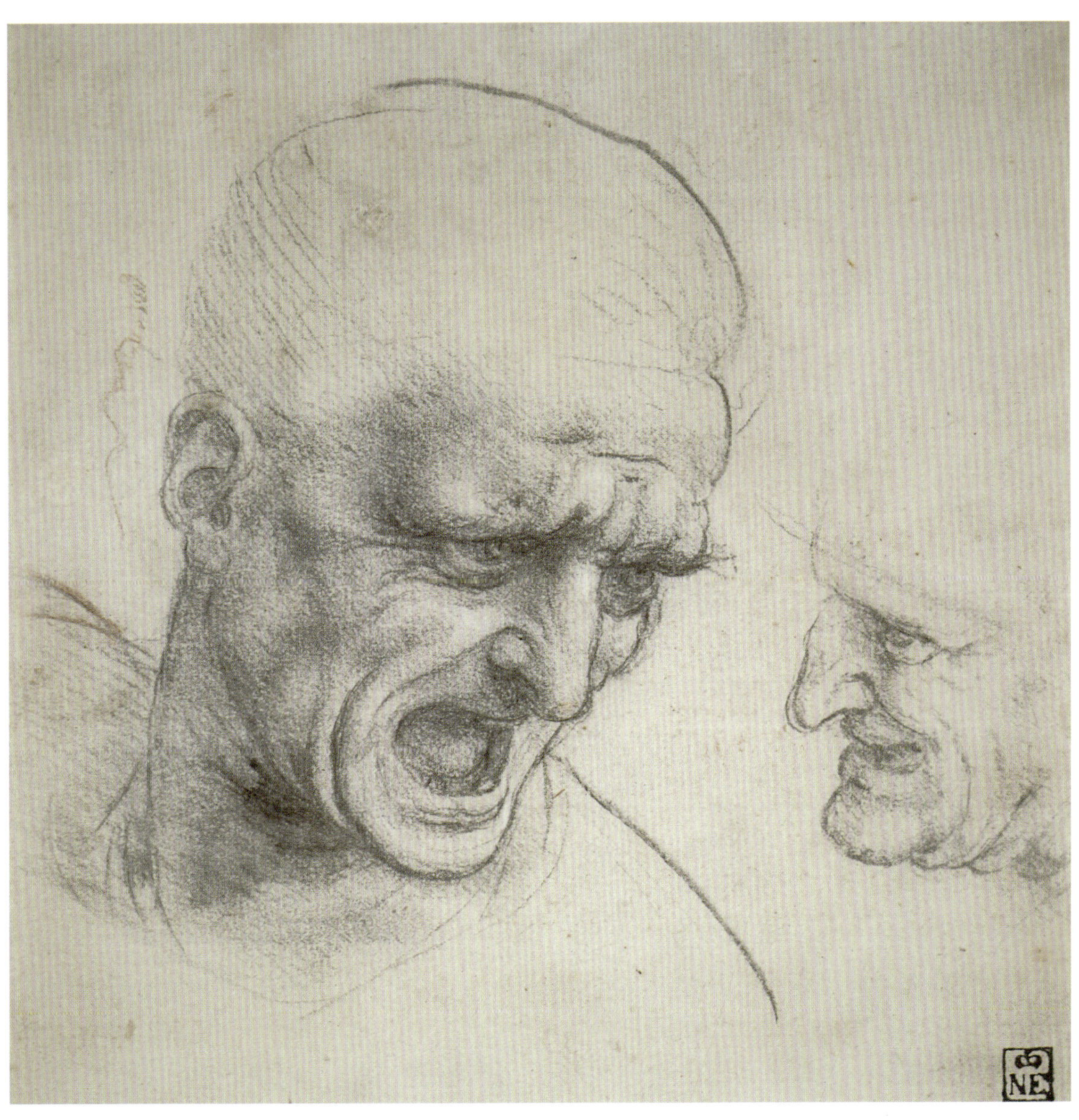

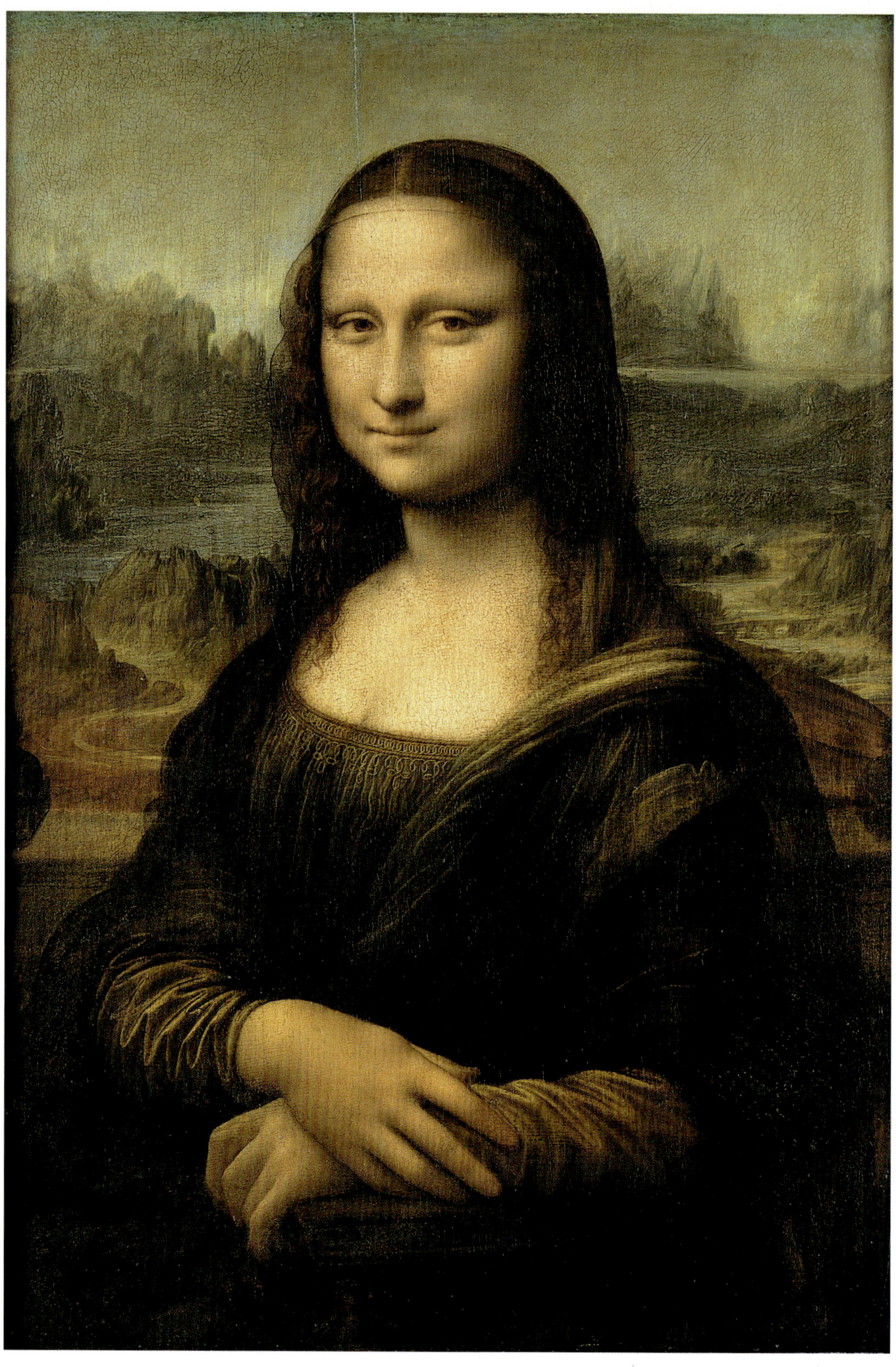

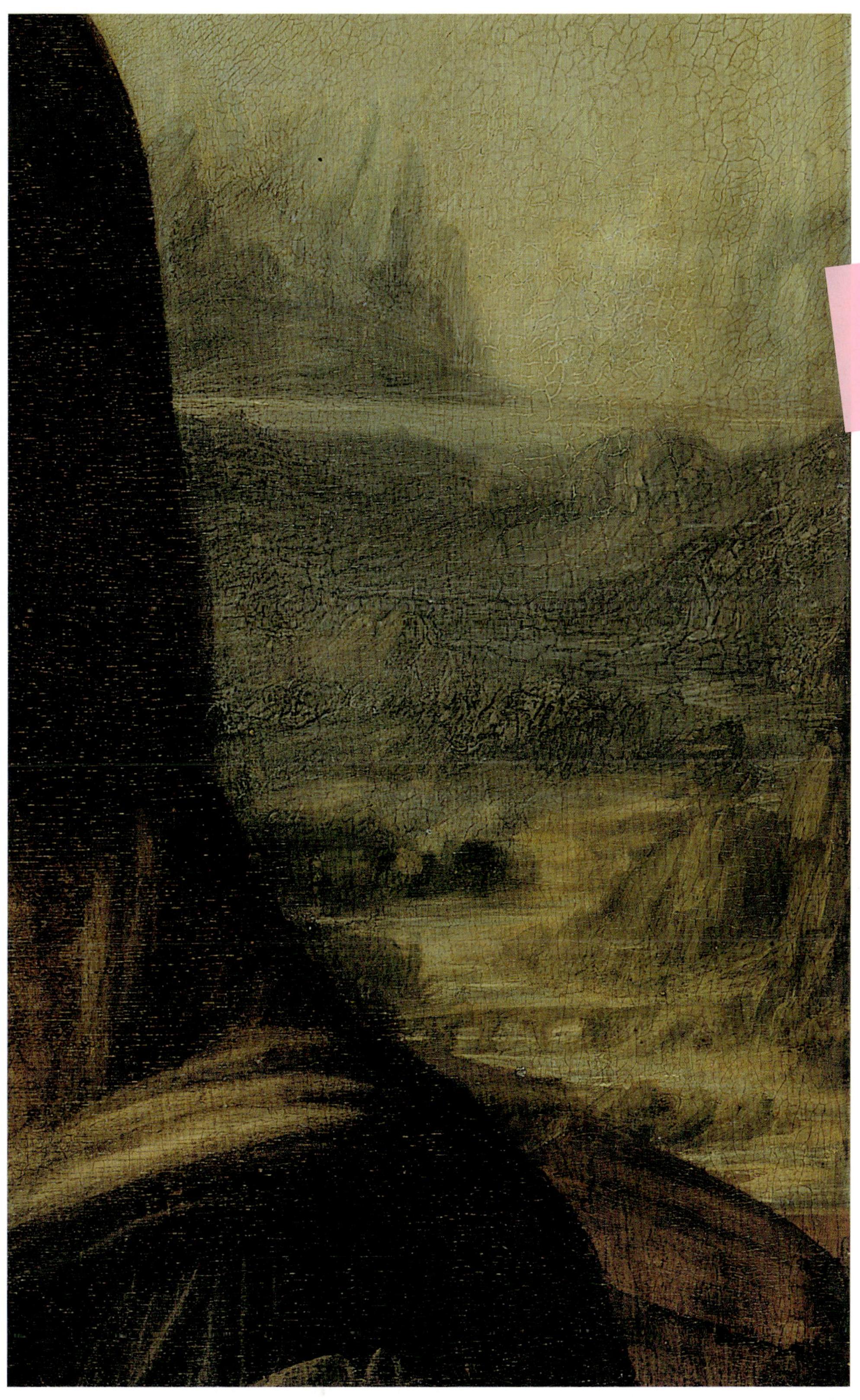

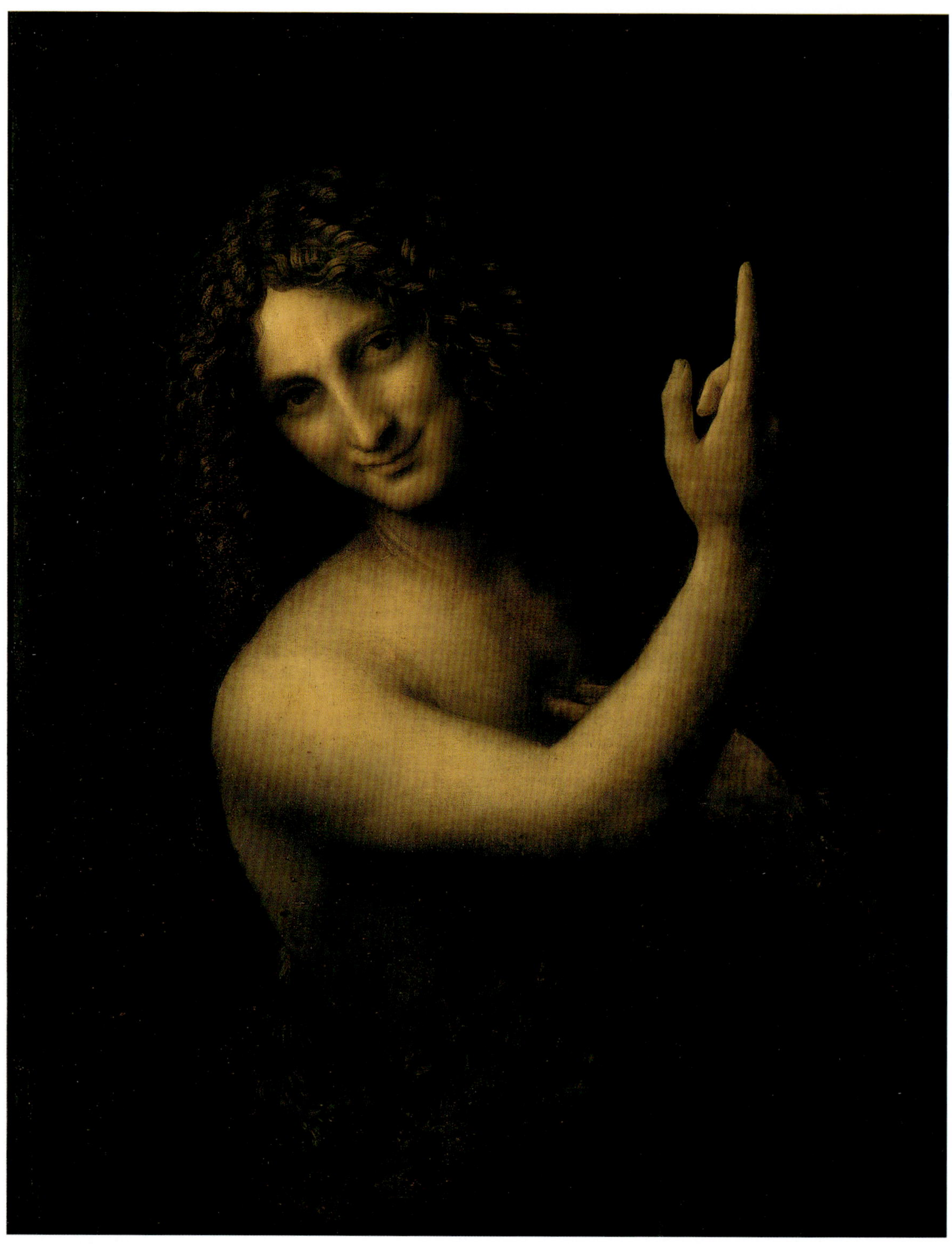

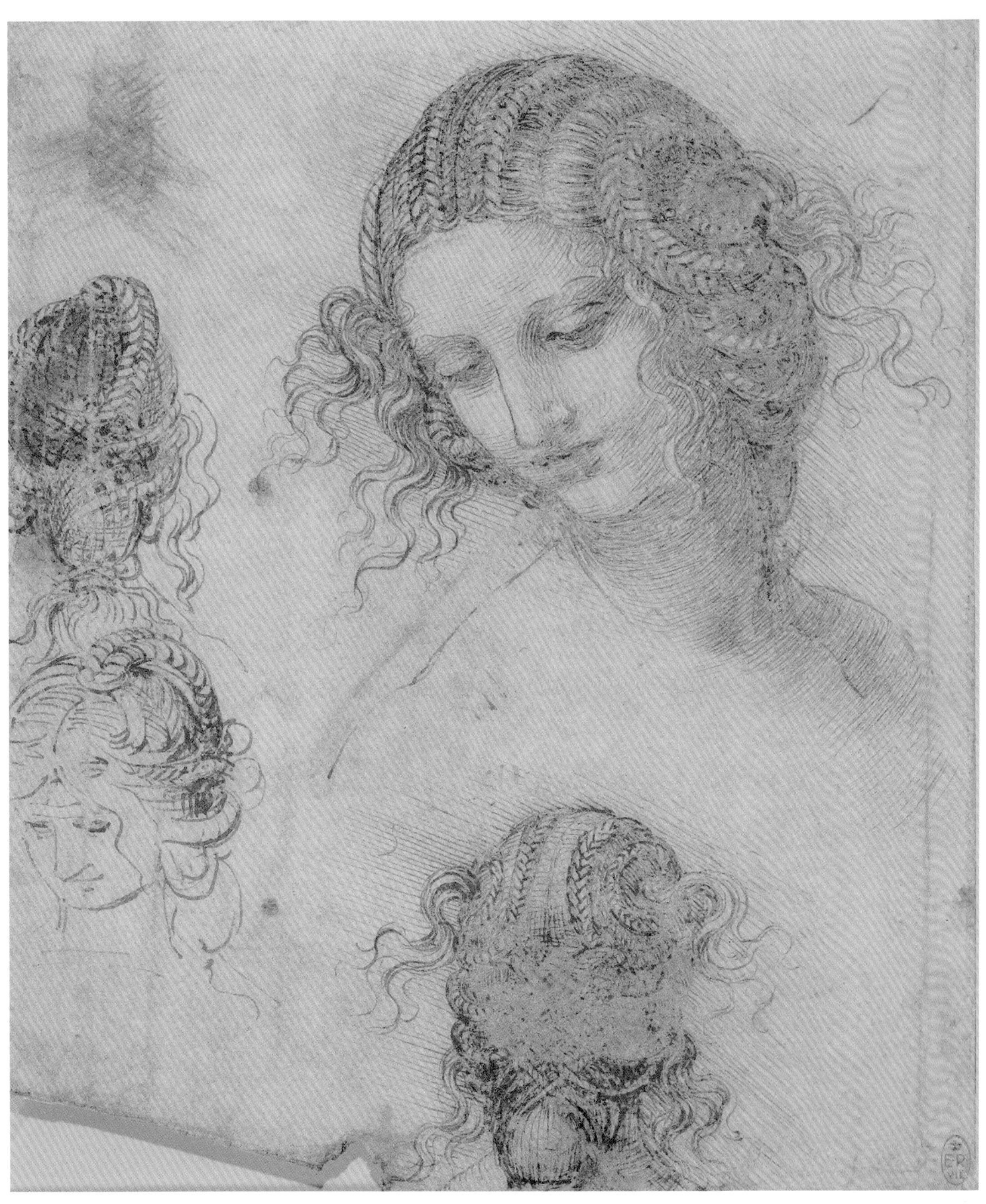

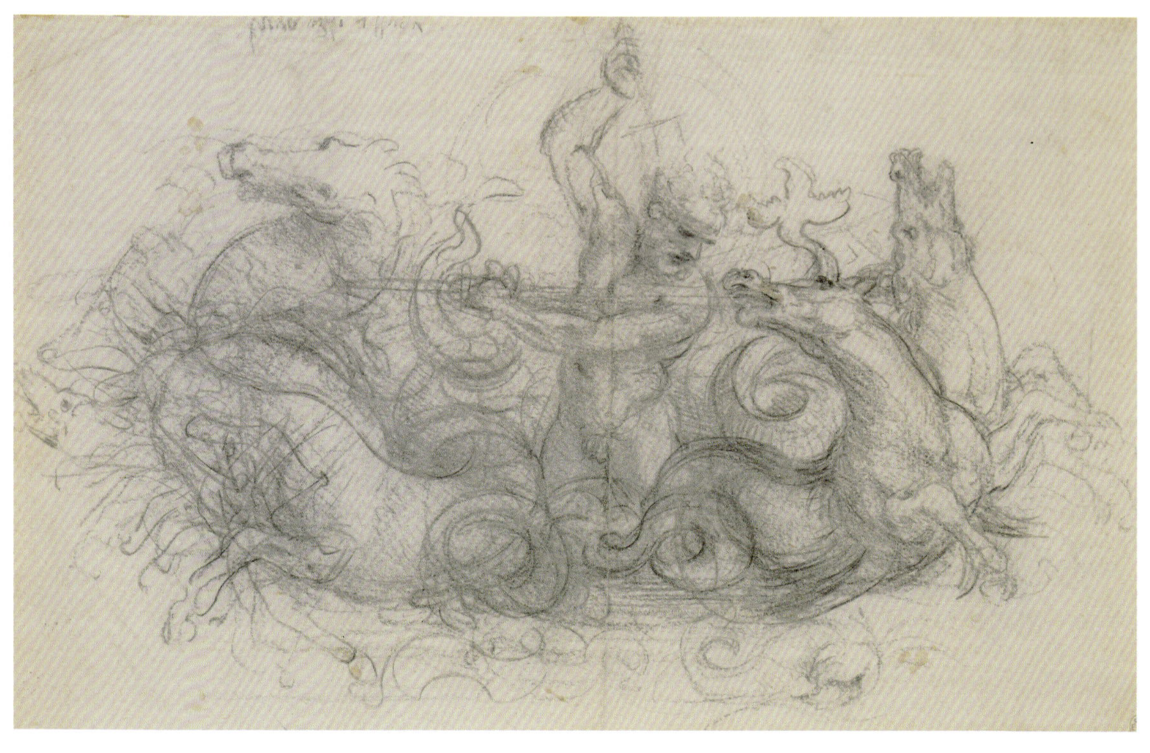

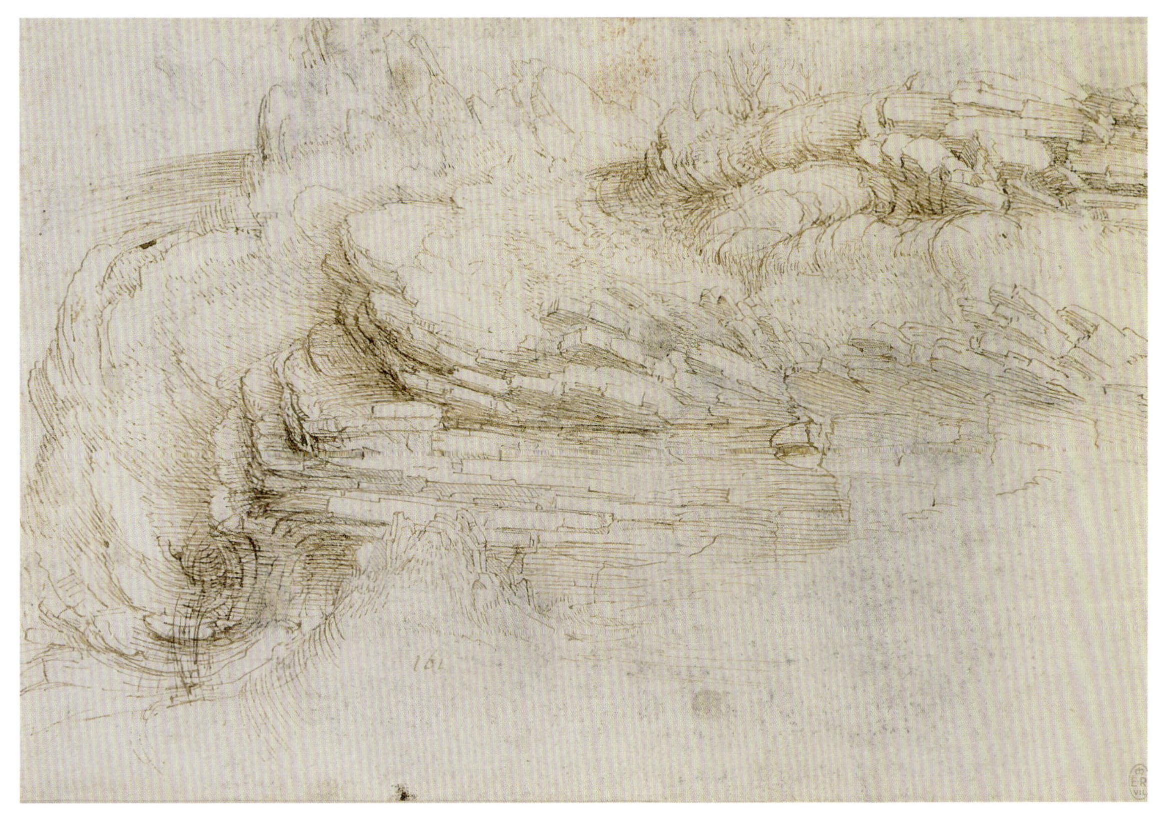

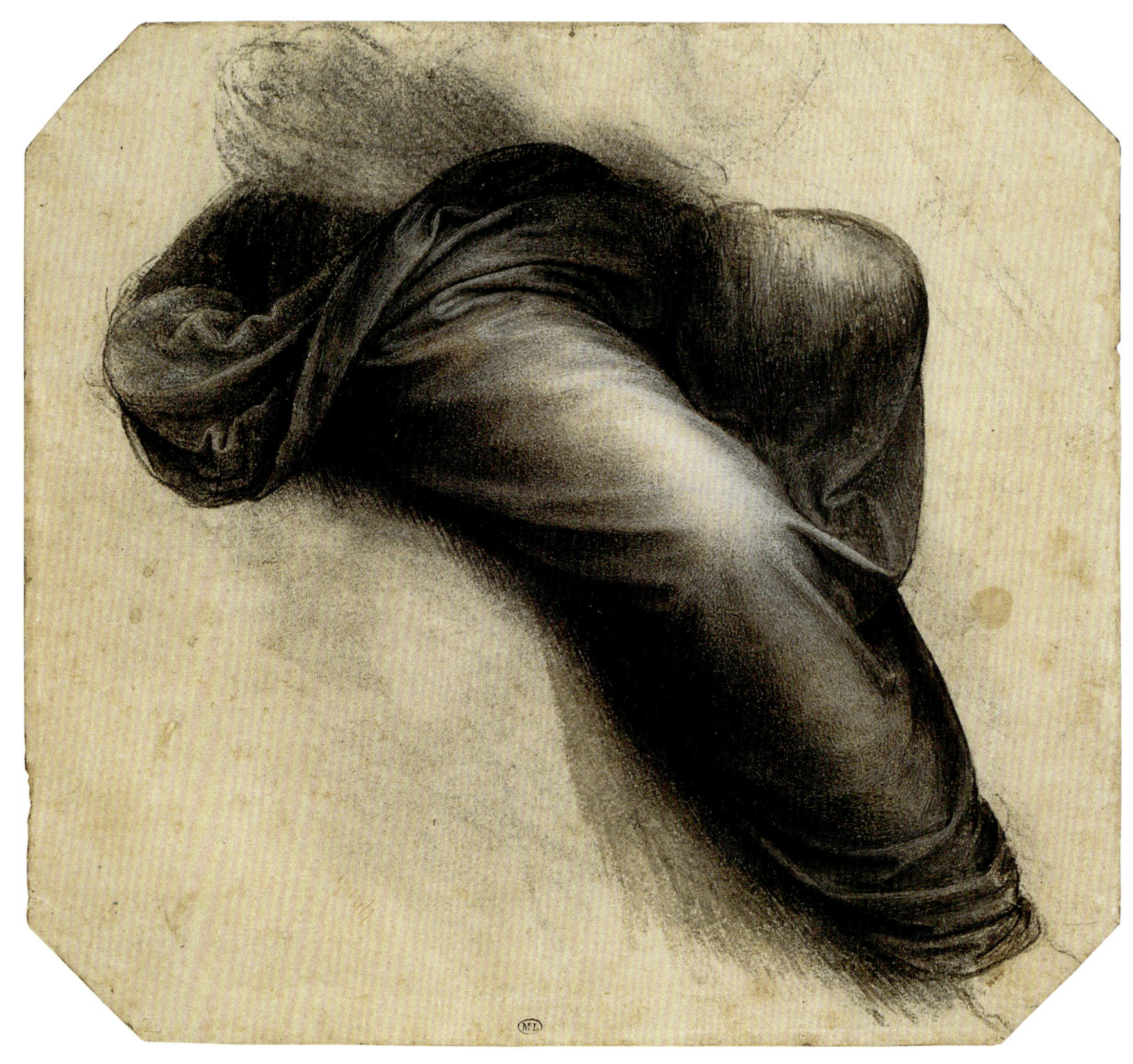

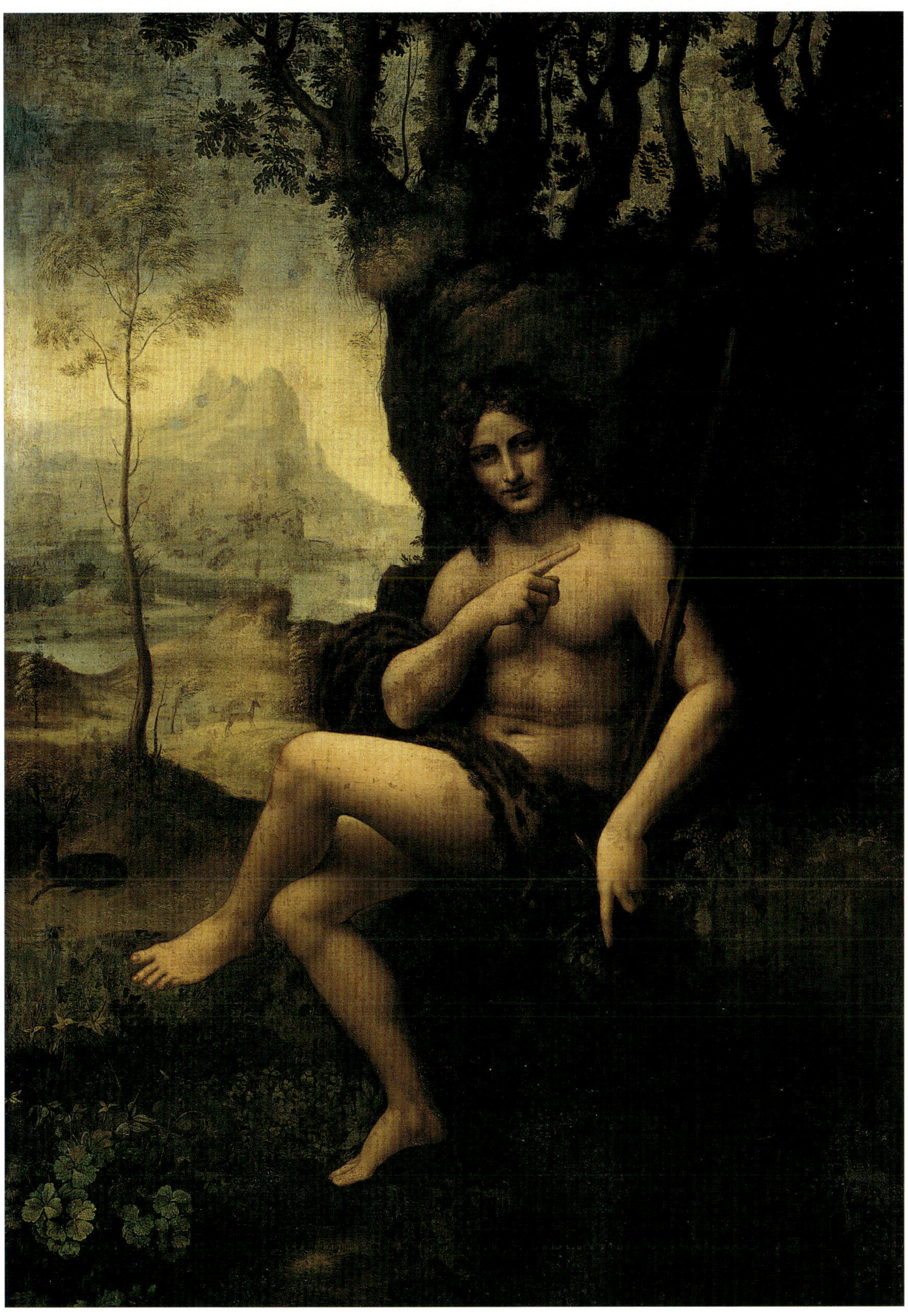

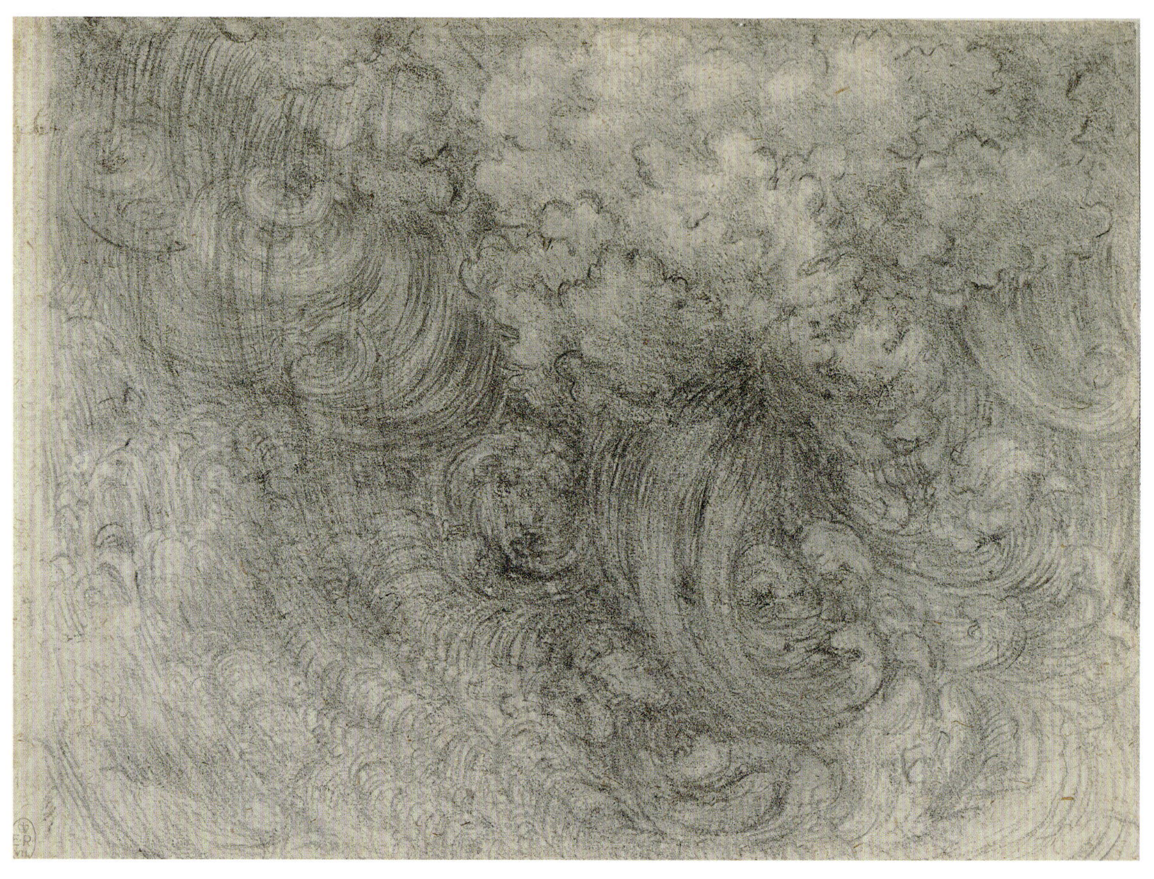

APPENDICES

CHRONOLOGY

1452
15 April. Leonardo is born in Vinci or Anchiano, the illegitimate son of the notary Piero da Vinci and a peasant woman named Caterina.

1457
28 February. In the Vinci family's "portata al catasto" (a sort of income declaration), Leonardo is documented as still living in his father's house in Vinci.

1469
In the "portata al catasto" for this year, Leonardo is documented as being a dependant of his father ser Piero.

1472
Leonardo is enrolled in the painters' guild at the Compagnia di San Luca in Florence.

1473
5 August. Date of the drawing 8P recto in the Uffizi.

1475–76
Date of Bernardo Bembo's first ambassadorship to Florence, and the probable occasion on which Leonardo was commissioned to paint the *Ginevra de' Benci*, now in the National Gallery, Washington, D. C.

1476
9 April and 7 June. Leonardo is named with Iacopo Saltarelli and Bartolomeo di Pasquino (goldsmith), Baccino (a doublet maker) and Lionardo Tornabuoni in an anonymous sodomy report from which he is absolved *cum conditione*. The report specifies that Leonardo "is with Andrea del Verrocchio".

1478
10 January. The Signoria commissions the altarpiece of the San Bernardo chapel in the Palazzo Vecchio from Leonardo for which he receives an advance payment of 25 florins on 16 March. Towards the end of the year he begins two Madonnas, one of which could be the *Benois Madonna* in Saint Petersburg ("[...]ber 1478 I began the two Virgin Marys"; 446 Er, Uffizi).

1479
4 February. Giovanni Bentivoglio, the lord of Bologna, asks Lorenzo il Magnifico to accept the return to Florence of "Paulo de Leonardo da Vinci", who is imprisoned in Bologna for "mala vita". Paolo is a master of marquetry and evidently a pupil or collaborator of Leonardo (certainly not his son, as has nonsensically been presumed).

1481
March. Leonardo begins painting an altarpiece of the *Adoration of the Magi* for the Augustinians in San Donato a Scopeto near Florence. He has two and a half years at most to complete the work in exchange for which he will receive a third part of a property in Valdelsa (which, however, the monks reserve the right to repurchase within three years for 300 florins). Leonardo is obliged to pay for the materials himself, and in addition contribute 150 florins to the dowry for the daughter of Salvestro di Giovanni, but this sum is advanced by the monks "because he says he does not have the means to pay, and time was elapsing and it was prejudicial to us".
July. Leonardo receives payment in kind in exchange for the decoration of the San Donato clock. In August and September he receives supplies of corn, wine and painting materials from the Augustinians in Scopeto.

1483
25 April. With Evangelista and Ambrogio de Predis, in Milan he signs the contract for the pictorial decoration of the ancona dedicated to the Immaculate Conception, which is commissioned by the brothers of the Scuola dell'Immacolata Concezione for the church of San Francesco Grande. The agreement stipulates the painting of pictorial section of the wooden ancona made by Giacomo Del Maino and the

painting of a panel of the Madonna and Child with angels, and two smaller ones with two angels each, respectively musicians and singers, in exchange for 800 imperial lire. The agreement leads to the painting of the *Virgin of the Rocks*.

1487–88

30 July 1487–11 January 1488. The *lignamario* Bernardino de Abiate receives payments from the Veneranda Fabbrica del Duomo di Milano for a wooden model of the crossing tower (tiburium) made to Leonardo's design. Competing in the competition for the crossing tower (which will be won by Giovanni Antonio Amadeo), Leonardo drafts a letter to the *fabbricieri* (*Codex Atlanticus*, fol. 730r): "So as not to be long-winded, I will first explain the plan made by the first architect of the cathedral and I will show you clearly what his intention was, basing my argument on what was effectively carried out; and if I succeed in explaining it, you will easily understand that the model I have prepared has the same symmetry, correspondence and conformity to the building already begun."

1489

"On the 2nd day of April 1489 book entitled on the human figure" (RL 19059r, Windsor Castle). On 28 April he receives 103 lire, 12 *soldi* from Marchesino Stanga, the ducal secretary.
22 July. The Florentine orator in Milan, Pietro Alamanni, writes to Lorenzo de' Medici for Ludovico Sforza (il Moro), who has ordered a model for an equestrian monument to Francesco Sforza from Leonardo, and "he would like to make something of superlative quality" and "he desires you to send him a master or two suitable for such a work: and though he has commissioned this thing from Leonardo da Vinci, it does not seem to me that he hopes very much that he [Leonardo] will be able to complete it". Lorenzo replies on 8 August saying that "here [in Florence] I can find no master who satisfies me".
1 September. In the dedication to the *Epistolae ad magnum Trivultium cum tribus orationibus et uno dialogo* (though only published in 1506), the Milanese poet Piattino Piatti declares his friendship with Leonardo. Piattino dedicates several verses, published in 1502, to the statue of Francesco Sforza.
23 December. Leonardo and the de Predis brothers receive a payment of 730 lire from the "scolari" of the Immacolata Concezione.
31 December. With other artists, including Bartolomeo Suardi (who for the first time in known documentation is referred to as "Bramantino"), Leonardo appears in the accounts of Santa Maria presso San Satiro, Milan.

1490

13 January. In honour of Gian Galeazzo Sforza and Isabella of Aragon, a "paradisiacal" festival is held in Milan castle, supervised by Leonardo and with a libretto by Bernardo Bellincioni.
"On the 23rd day of April 1490 I began this book and restarted the horse" [i.e., the equestrian statue of Francesco Sforza]: MS C, fol. 15v.
10 May. He has his model for the cathedral's crossing tower returned. Ruined during the discussions, its return is promised "at any moment". For the model Leonardo is paid 12 imperial lire on 17 May by the *fabbricieri*.
8 June. Ludovico Sforza decides to send Leonardo and Amadeo to the Sienese architect Francesco di Giorgio Martini in Pavia, to have his opinion on the cathedral there. Two days later Leonardo says he is available, unlike Amadeo, who is busy in Como. On 21 June the *fabbricieri* of the cathedral in Pavia pay the accommodation expenses of Francesco di Giorgio and Leonardo to the innkeeper Giovanni Agostino de Berneriis. While in Pavia, Leonardo also makes a survey of the castle.
In MS C, fol. 15v, on the date 22 July, we see the annotation referring to the entry into the workshop of the ten-year-old Gian Giacomo Caprotti, "thief liar persistent glutton", who, nicknamed Salai, is destined to spend the rest of his life with Leonardo. On 7 September Salai steals the silver "graffio" from Marco d'Oggiono, who is documented for the first time with Leonardo, likewise Giovanni Antonio Boltraffio, whose own silverpoint was to meet the same end on 2 April 1491.

1491
26 January. Leonardo is present in the house of Galeazzo da Sanseverino, the son-in-law of Ludovico il Moro, "to organise the festival of his jousting competition" (MS C. fol. 15v), which is held in honour of the marriage between Ludovico Sforza and Beatrice d'Este.
In an unstated period between 1491 (given the absence of Evangelista, who died in 1490) and 1495 (date that Ludovico Sforza officially becomes duke of Milan), Leonardo and Ambrogio de Predis send an entreaty to Ludovico to ask for an arbitration regarding remuneration for the *Virgin of the Rocks*.

1493
Bernardo Bellincioni's *Rime* are posthumously published (he died in 1492), and likewise the *Coronatione e Sponsalitio de la Serenissima Regina M. Bianca Maria Sforza Augusta* by Baldassarre Taccone, which mark the first mentions of Leonardo in print.
16 July. Leonardo hosts a certain "Catelina", probably his mother (MS Forster III, fol. 88r).
6 October (or perhaps 18 March). Leonardo welcomes a certain Giulio Tedesco in his workshop, who is perhaps a *bombardiere* and expert in casting (MS Forster III, fol. 88r).
"On the 20th day of December 1493 I conclude casting of the horse without its tail and lying on its side" (MS Madrid II, fol. 151v).

1494
Leonardo is in Vigevano, where he takes notes on 2 February and 20 March (MS H, fols 65v and 38r). On 26 June (very probably) his mother Caterina dies (the death certificate tells us that she was living in the parish of Santi Nabore e Felice in the district of Porta Vercellina). On 17 November Ludovico il Moro (now duke, though the title will only be officially conferred upon him by Emperor Maximilian the following year) sends the bronze for the casting of the statue of Francesco Sforza to his brother-in-law, Ercole d'Este, the duke of Ferrara. It is perhaps in this year that Leonardo resolves to go to Louis de Ligny, commander of King Charles VIII of France's army, which is marching towards Naples, to learn Jean Perréal's technique of "coloured pencils".

1495
29 September. With Francesco da Vaprio, Leonardo thinks highly of a "camerollo" decorated by Giovanni Antonio da Como for Andrea da Caravaggio.
14 February. He perhaps decorates the "Camerini" in Milan castle.

1496
8 June. Ludovico Sforza has Pietro Perugino tracked down in Venice to substitute "the painter who was painting the *camerini* [who] today created a certain scandal for which he has absented himself". Perhaps it is at this time that Leonardo offers to execute the doors in Piacenza Cathedral (*Codex Atlanticus*, fol. 887r-v).

1497
29 June. Il Moro orders his secretary Marchesino Stanga "to ask Leonardo Fiorentino that he might finish the work begun in the Refectory of the [church of Santa Maria delle] Grazie, and then to consider the other wall of this Refectory".
8 September and 17 October. Leonardo takes on two collaborators for several months, named respectively Joditti and Benedetto (*Codex Atlanticus*, fol. 189r).

1498
9 February. Dedicatory letter by the Franciscan Luca Pacioli (who arrived in Milan in 1496) in his treatise *De Divina Proportione*, in which he seems to refer to the almost completed *Last Supper* (he also refers to it during the execution of the work). Leonardo is said to have also completed a "worthy book on painting and human movements" and begun "the inestimable work of local movement and percussions and weights and forces, in other words, all accidental weights".
22 March. Letter from the chancellor Gualtiero Bascapè to the duke, in which he states that "no time must be lost on the works in the Grazie".

20, 21, and 23 April. Other letters by Bascapè in which he gives an account of the work undertaken by Leonardo on the "Saletta negra" (lost) and the Sala delle Asse (Castello Sforzesco).
26 April. Isabella d'Este asks Cecilia Gallerani to be loaned the portrait of the lady painted by Leonardo (almost certainly the *Lady with an Ermine*). Cecilia agrees with a letter written on 29 April, and the painting is returned to her on 18 May.
2 October. Leonardo is known to be the owner of a vineyard in Porta Vercellina, given to him by Ludovico Sforza (perhaps in 1497).

1499
26 April. Ratification of the donation of the vineyard.
5–10 September. The French troops of Louis XII, commanded by Gian Giacomo Trivulzio, enter Milan and take the castle.

1500
7 January. Through agents, Leonardo deposits 300 florins at the Ospedale di Santa Maria Nuova in Florence; his accounts with this institution are documented until 1507. In the year 1499 *ab incarnatione* (from 25 March 1499 to 24 March 1500), on an imprecise date, Leonardo is in Florence where he offers an opinion on the structural stability of San Salvatore dell'Osservanza.
13 March. He is in Venice, where he shows the musician Lorenzo Gusnasco da Pavia the cartoon of the portrait of Isabella d'Este. In this period he provides military consultancy to the Republic of Venice on the defence of the Isonzo from invasion by the Turks (*Codex Atlanticus*, fol. 638d-v).
24 April. He is in Florence, where he deposits 50 florins at the Ospedale di Santa Maria Nuova.
11 August. Francesco Malatesta sends Francesco Gonzaga, the *marchese* of Mantua, a drawing by Leonardo of the Florentine villa belonging to Angelo del Tovaglia.

1501
20 March. A brief stay in Rome and Tivoli (*Codex Atlanticus*, fol. 618v).
3 April. The Carmelite Pietro da Novellara informs Isabella d'Este of Leonardo's presence in Florence: "The life of Leonardo is very chaotic and unorganised, and he seems to live from day to day. Since he has been in Florence he has only made a drawing in a cartoon: it is of a Christ-Child of about one year of age, who slipping almost out of the arms of his mother grasps at a lamb and seems to hold it tightly. His mother, who almost rises from Saint Anne's lap, catches at her son to separate him from the lamb (a sacrificial animal) which represents the Passion. Saint Anne, who also rises from her seat, seems to be trying to stop her daughter separating the boy and the lamb, which may signify the Church, which does not want the Passion of Christ to be impeded. These figures are life-size but in a small cartoon because they are all seated or leaning over, and each is in front of the other [...]. This drawing is not yet finished. He has not done others apart from portraits by two of his assistants that he sometimes add touches to. He is very occupied with geometry and has no time for painting."

14 April. Another letter from Novellara to Isabella d'Este: Leonardo promises to work for the *marchesa* after he is freed from this commitments to the king of France (for a version of the *Virgin and Child with Saint Anne*?). He is currently painting a small devotional panel for Florimond Robertet, the secretary to Louis XII: this is the *Madonna dei fusi*, which has either been lost or is perhaps the painting in the Reford Collection, though the extent of Leonardo's involvement in this work is very limited.
31 July. The Mantuan ambassador to Milan, Manfredo Manfredi, informs the *marchesa* that Leonardo has begun to paint for her.
19 September. The duke of Ferrara, Ercole d'Este, asks his ambassador in Milan, Giovanni Valla, to request the permission of Cardinal Georges d'Amboise (Louis XII's lieutenant) to use the "forma" (the casting mould) of Leonardo's Sforza monument in Ferrara, which "every day is breaking up".

26 September. Valla's reply: d'Amboise raises no difficulties but the king must agree to it: the matter does not seem to have been followed up.

1502

12 May. Francesco Malatesta tells Isabella d'Este of Leonardo's opinion of several ancient vases belonging to Lorenzo il Magnifico, which the *marchesa* requested on 3 May.
18 August. Cesare Borgia signs a pass for Leonardo, "our very able and much appreciated Architect and General Engineer for the fortified places and forts of our states" (in the Marches and Romagna).
30 July. Leonardo is in Urbino (MS L, fol. 6r).
1 August. In Pesaro (MS L, cover).
8 August. In Rimini (MS L, fol. 78r).
10–15 August. In Cesena (MS L, fols 46v, 36v).
6 September. In Cesenatico (MS L, fol. 66v).

1503

8 April. In Florence he lends 4 ducats to the miniaturist Attivante di Gabriello. He buys a plot of land that includes a stone quarry near Fiesole.
9 March and 23 June. Further entreaties to Louis XII, by Ambrogio de Predis on the subject of the *Virgin of the Rocks*. Leonardo is out of Milan.
3 July. Offers his help to Sultan Bajazet II to build a bridge in Istanbul.
21–26 July. Completes a tour of inspection for the Florentine Republic of the Verrucola, Cascina, and Pontedera forts, and of the course of the River Arno, in relation to a plan to divert it so that Pisa will be deprived of access to the sea.
18 October. He pays the fee to the Compagnia di San Luca, of which he is evidently a member once again.
24 October. He receives the keys of the Sala del Papa and adjacent rooms in the cloister of Santa Maria Novella, which he uses as a studio to prepare the cartoon for the *Battle of Anghiari*.

1504

25 January. Participates in a debate on the placement of Michelangelo's *David*.
28 February–31 October. Payments for the *Battle of Anghiari*.
4 May. Contract signed between the priors of Libertà, the *gonfaloniere* Piero Soderini and Leonardo for the wall painting of the *Battle of Anghiari* in the Sala del Consiglio Grande in Palazzo Vecchio (Nicolò Machiavelli is also present). In exchange for a monthly salary of 15 large gold florins, Leonardo will have to complete the cartoon by the following 20 April "and it might be that the said Lionardo should begin to paint and colour on the wall of the said Sala that part that he had drawn and furnished in the said cartoon".
14 May. Isabella d'Este writes to Leonardo with extraordinary deference, asking him for "a young Christ of about twelve years of age [...] executed with that most excellent gentleness and suavity that you have as a peculiarity of your art".
9 July. Death of his father, ser Piero da Vinci.
31 October. Another request from Isabella d'Este.
1 November. Leonardo is in Piombino, staying with Iacopo IV Appiani (MS Madrid II, fol. 125r).

1505

28 February and 14 March. Expenses for the scaffolding for the *Battle of Anghiari*.
14 April. He takes in as a pupil and perhaps as a model a certain seventeen-year-old Lorenzo (*Codex on Bird Flight*, fol. 18v).
30 April and 30 August. Payments for the *Battle of Anghiari* to Leonardo, two assistants (Raffaello di Biagio d'Antonio and Ferrando Spagnolo, who is almost certainly Fernando Yañez de Almedina) and to suppliers of materials; Leonardo is also paid for customs' duties for "a bundle of his clothes sent from Rome".

1506

13 February. He nominates Ambrogio de Predis his representative in the suit in Milan against the "scolari" of the Immacolata Concezione. The arbiters to resolve the question are appointed on 4 April and an agreement reached on 27 April. De Predis accepts (on behalf of Leonardo who is still absent from Milan) to complete the *Virgin of*

the Rocks within two years for 200 imperial lire.
30 May. Leonardo obtains permission from the Florentine Signoria to visit Milan for three months, at the end of which he will have to restart work on the *Battle of Anghiari*. It may be in this period that he gives an estimate for the tomb of Gian Giacomo Trivulzio (*Codex Atlanticus*, fol. 492r).
18 and 19 August. Charles d'Amboise, Louis XII's lieutenant in Milan, and Goffredo Carle, the vice-chancellor, write to Florence to ask permission for Leonardo to extend his stay "for at least the whole of the month of September". Permission is granted on 28 August.
9 October. The Signoria in Florence writes to Charles refusing a further extension.
16 December. Letter from Charles d'Amboise to the Signoria, praising Leonardo. It would seem to be a pointer to Leonardo's return to Florence (but it is improbable that it occurred or, if so, it was very short).

1507
12 January. Letter to the Signoria in Florence from the Florentine ambassador Francesco Pandolfini at the French court in Blois: Leonardo is in Milan and Louis XII wants to commission some paintings from him, "Certain panels of Our Lady, and another that I will decide on later. And perhaps I shall have him paint myself".
14 January. Louis XII writes in person to the Signoria: he is about to go to Milan and wants Leonardo to wait for him there as "we have absolute need of master Leonard Avince painter of your city of Florence". Reply to Pandolfini on 22 January in which Leonardo is given permission to remain in Milan, and the Signoria also writes to Leonardo the same day.
26 July. Letter from Louis XII to the Signoria: Leonardo, who, for the first time, is referred to as "nostre paintre et ingenieur ordinaire", will remain in Milan for a legal case regarding a legacy from his uncle Francesco (this is contested by his half-brothers, as Leonardo is an illegitimate son).
3 August. Leonardo and Ambrogio de Predis accept the Dominican Giovanni de Pagnani as the arbiter for the dispute over the *Virgin of the Rocks*.
15 August. Charles d'Amboise writes to Florence to announce Leonardo's return, "to whom with the greatest difficulty we have given permission as he is obliged to paint a panel for his most Christian Majesty" (the king of France).
18 September. He writes to Ippolito d'Este in Ferrara for support in his dispute with his half-brothers.

1508
"Began in the house of Piero di Braccio Martelli on the 22nd day of March 1508" (*Codex Arundel*, fol. 1r).
18 August. Ambrogio de Predis receives permission to remove *The Virgin of the Rocks* from the ancona to have it copied under Leonardo's supervision; earnings will be split between the two painters.
"Began in Milan on the 12th day of September 1508" (MS F, fol. 1r).
23 October. Ambrogio de Predis, on behalf of himself and Leonardo, declares he has received 100 imperial lire for the copy of the *Virgin of the Rocks*.

1509
July 1508–April 1509. Note referring to the payments received from the king of France, in all, 340 *scudi* and 200 francs (*Codex Atlanticus*, fol. 522r).

1510
21 October. He gives his opinion on the design for wooden stalls to the *fabbricieri* of Milan Cathedral.

1510–11
The French court's treasury accounts record the salary paid annually to Leonardo to be 400 Turinese lire.

1513
9 January. He lives in Vaprio d'Adda, in the property of his pupil and friend Francesco

Melzi. He may have left Milan following the restoration of the Sforza in 1512 (RL 19077v, Windsor).
25 March. He is living in Milan at the house of Prevostino Piola, the brother of the stepmother of Bernardino Corio, the historian and functionary of Ludovico il Moro.
"I left Milan for Rome on the 24th day of September 1513 with Giovan Francesco de' Melsi, Salai, Lorenzo and Fanfoia" (MS E, fol. 1v). Lorenzo is assuredly the pupil who entered the workshop in 1505, whereas Fanfoia could be the sculptor Agostino Busti, called Bambaia.
1 December. Expenses for fitting out Leonardo's studio in the Belvedere in the Vatican.

1514
25–27 September. With Giuliano de' Medici's retinue in Parma and perhaps along the banks of the River Po, perhaps as a military engineer (MS E, fols 80r, 96r).
8 October. He becomes a "novizzo" in the confraternity of San Giovanni dei Fiorentini in Rome, but is expelled on 31 December for not having paid his entry fee.

1515
He earns 40 ducats from Giuliano de' Medici, and his collaborator Giorgio Tedesco (a master glass-maker) a further 7 for accompanying Giuliano to Bologna, where he meets the pope, Leo X (Giuliano's brother) in December and the new king of France, François I.

1516
August. Back in Rome, where he takes the measurements of the basilica of San Paolo fuori le Mura.

1517
21 May. He is established in the castle of Cloux in Amboise in the service of François I (*Codex Atlanticus*, fol. 284r).
1 October. Rinaldo Ariosto, the Mantuan ambassador in France, describes a party held in Argentan in which a mechanical lion, probably designed by Leonardo, appears. The party is described again on 3 October in a letter written by the Dominican Francesco Anastasio Turrioni.
10 October. Leonardo receives Cardinal Louis of Aragon at Cloux. Louis's secretary, Antonio de Beatis, describes some manuscripts on the subjects of anatomy, hydraulics and mechanics, plus three paintings: a portrait "of a certain Florentine woman", painted for Giuliano de' Medici (perhaps the so-called *Gioconda nuda*, known from copies and derivations), the *Virgin and Child with Saint Anne* and the half-length *Saint John the Baptist*, now in the Louvre. He also informs us that Leonardo's right hand has been struck by paralysis.
29 December. The same source informs us that "The *Last Supper* is beginning to break up, I do not know if for the damp that attacks the wall or for some other technical error".

1518
The salary for the two-year period 1517–18 is 2,000 *scudi* for Leonardo, 800 for Francesco Melzi, and 100 for Salai, however, according to the accounts of the dukedom of Milan, Salai also receives the extremely high sum of 6,250 imperial lire for having procured several paintings for the king. It seems probable that they are all, or at least in part, works by Leonardo. Furthermore, in Salai's *post mortem* inventory (1525), paintings of unequivocal subject are recorded in Milan ("a *Leda*", "a painting of Saint Anne", and a portrait of a woman "called the Gioconda"); they are of very high value, but these alone do not correspond to the sum paid out in 1518 by François I.

1519
24 April. Leonardo dictates his will. He leaves his drawings and manuscripts to Francesco Melzi, whom he appoints as his executor; he leaves half of the vineyard in Milan to Salai, and half to his servant Battista de Villanis; to his brothers he leaves the cash deposited at the Ospedale di Santa Maria Nuova in Florence.
2 May. Leonardo dies in Cloux Castle.

1 June. Francesco Melzi writes to Leonardo's half-brothers: "I believe you have been informed of the death of master Lionardo, your brother and equally my most excellent father, for whose death it would be impossible for me to express the pain I am suffering: and while my limbs will sustain me, I will be perpetually unhappy, and inevitably so, such was the passionate and most ardent love I bore him. Everyone is sorrowful at the loss of a man so great that nature is not able to produce another. May almighty God grant him eternal peace."

LEONARDO'S MANUSCRIPTS AND EDITIONS OF HIS WRITINGS

Most of Leonardo's manuscripts (no fewer than eighteen and probably more) were left to Francesco Melzi, who died in Vaprio d'Adda in 1570. By means of different routes and events, twelve of these reached the Biblioteca Ambrosiana in Milan between 1609 and 1674, from where they were transferred to Paris in 1795, and where they have since remained (they now belong to the Institut de France). The same fate befell the *Codex Atlanticus*, which was put together by the sculptor Pompeo Leoni in the late Cinquecento from materials taken from other manuscripts that had been split up. The *Codex Atlanticus* was donated to the Ambrosiana in 1637 by Galeazzo Arconati, but removed to France by Napoleon, however, it was returned to Italy following the Congress of Vienna, thanks to the offices of Antonio Canova. Leoni was also responsible for the creation of the *Codex Arundel* and the collection in the Royal Library at Windsor Castle. He too was the owner of the three *Codices Forster* and the two codices rediscovered in Madrid in 1967. The history of the *Codex Leicester* is different: this was the property of Guglielmo Della Porta in Rome in 1537, where it was purchased by Giuseppe Ghezzi in 1690 and sold to Thomas Coke, Lord of Leicester, in 1717. It was bought in 1980 by Armand Hammer and, having been debased to the level of a status symbol for billionaires, again in 1994 by Bill Gates. The codex on the *Flight of Birds*, as it is known, was created by the transfer of material from MS B around 1840 by Guglielmo Libri. It was purchased by Fëdor Sabačnikov and then donated to the House of Savoy in 1893.

Editions (apart from particular exceptions, reference is made to the edition promoted by the Commissione Nazionale per la Pubblicazione dei Manoscritti di Leonardo da Vinci, and it is to this edition that reference should be made for the bibliography of previous editions of the manuscripts):

Codex Atlanticus: *Il Codice Atlantico di Leonardo da Vinci nella Biblioteca Ambrosiana di Milan*, edited by G. Piumati (Milan: Hoepli, 1894–1904), 8 vols.; following restoration and renumbering of the folios, reference is made to Leonardo da Vinci, *Il Codice Atlantico della Biblioteca Ambrosiana di Milan*, edited by A. Marinoni (Florence: Giunti) with 12 vols. of facsimile plates (the overall quality is lower than that of the Piumati edition) published in 1973–75, and 12 volumes of text in 1975–80. Both editions offer diplomatic and critical transcriptions; there is also a smaller version of the Marinoni edition with black-and-white reproductions and the critical (though not always very accurate) transcription alone: Leonardo da Vinci, *Il Codice Atlantico*, presentation by C. Pedretti (Florence: Giunti, 2000), 3 vols. Useful for the chronology and bibliography of the individual folios is C. Pedretti, Leonardo da Vinci, *Codex Atlanticus. A Catalogue of Its Newly Restored Sheets* (New York: Johnson Reprint Corporation, 1978–79), 2 vols.; see also A. Marinoni, *Il Codice Atlantico di Leonardo da Vinci. Indici per materie e alfabetico*, edited by P. C. Marani, Florence: Giunti, 2004.

The complete edition of the manuscripts in the Institut de France (chronology: MS A, ca. 1488–92; MS B, ca. 1485–89.; MS C, ca. 1490–91; MS D, ca. 1508–09; MS E, ca. 1513–14; MS F, ca. 1508; MS G, 1510–15; MS H, composed of three small notebooks bound together, ca. 1493–94; MS I, composed of two small notebooks, ca. 1497; MS K, composed of three notebooks, respectively 1503–05 the first two, and 1506–07 the third; MS L, ca. 1497–1504; MS M, ca. 1495–1500) was the one produced by Augusto Marinoni with a facsimile reproduction: Leonardo da Vinci, *I manoscritti dell'Institut de France* (Florence: Giunti, 1986–90), 12 vols. (MS A 1990; MS B 1990; MS C 1987; MS D 1989, MS E 1989; MS F 1988; MS G 1989; MS H 1986; MS K 1989; MS I 1987; MS L 1987;

MS M 1987). The translation by J. Venerella into English of the mss. in France is currently in progress, published by Ente Raccolta Vinciana di Milano (the following volumes have so far been published: *Manuscript A*, 1999; *Manuscript I*, 2000; *Manuscript C*, 2001; *Manuscript L*, 2001; *Manuscript M*, 2001; *Manuscript F*, 2002; *Manuscript G*, 2002; *Manuscript E*, 2002; *Manuscript H*, 2003; *Manuscript B*, 2003; *Manuscript K*, 2004). *Codex Arundel*: *Il Codice Arundel 263 nel Museo Britannico*, edited by C. Pedretti and C. Vecce (Florence: Giunti, 1998).

Codices Forster (chronology: Forster I, formed by two bundles dated ca. 1505 and ca. 1487–90; Forster II, formed by two bundles dated ca. 1493–97 and ca. 1495; Forster III, ca. 1493–96): *I Codici Forster nel Victoria and Albert Museum di Londra*, edited by A. Marinoni (Florence: Giunti, 1992), 3 vols.
Codex Leicester, 1506–8: *Il codice di Leonardo da Vinci nella Biblioteca di Lord Leicester in Holkham Hall*, edited by G. Calvi (Milan: Cogliati, 1909) (anastatic reprint with an introduction by L. Firpo [Florence: Giunti, 1980]: this is still the best edition); *The Codex Hammer of Leonardo da Vinci*, ed. by C. Pedretti (Florence: Giunti, 1987). The Madrid Codices (chronology; Madrid I, 1490–1508; Madrid II, 1503–05, with a final bundle dated ca. 1490–93): *The Madrid Codices in the Nacional Library Madrid*, edited by L. Reti (New York: McGraw-Hill, 1974), 5 vols.
Codex Trivulzianus, ca. 1487–90: *Il Codice nella Biblioteca Trivulziana di Milan*, edited by A. M. Brizio (Florence: Giunti, 1976); *Il Codice Trivulziano, Codice N 2162 della Biblioteca Trivulziana di Milan*, edited by A. Marinoni, with a note by A. Chastel (Milan: Electa, 1980). Codex on the *Flight of Birds*, ca. 1505: *Il Codice sul volo degli uccelli nella Biblioteca Reale di Torino*, edited by A. Marinoni (Florence: Giunti, 1976). The *Treatise on Painting* (or the *Book of Painting*, its most recent title) is a collection compiled almost certainly by Francesco Melzi, perhaps on the basis of a plan by Leonardo, in which materials have been taken from various manuscripts. Since most of the material has been lost, today it is like a primary source. The first printed edition, based on a fairly short draft, only appeared in 1651 following the interest of Cassiano dal Pozzo and the Fréart brothers. Its engravings were made, though not too faithfully, from sketches by Nicolas Poussin: *Trattato della Pittura di Lionardo da Vinci*, edited by R. Du Fresne (Paris: Giacomo Langlois, 1651). On the vicissitudes and success of this publishing venture, see D. L. Sparti, "Cassiano dal Pozzo, Poussin and Making and Publications of Leonardo's Trattato", in *Journal of the Warburg and Courtauld Institutes*, LXVI, 200, pp. 143-188, and M. Pavesi, "Cassiano dal Pozzo, Nicolas Poussin e la prima edizione a stampa del 'Trattato della Pittura' di Leonardo tra Roma, Milano e Parigi", in *Tracce di letteratura artistica in Lombardia*, edited by A. Rovetta, Bari: Pagina, 2004, pp. 97-133. It was on this edition that later ones were substantially based, sometimes with the collation of other apographs: Naples: F. Ricciardi, 1723 and 1733; Bologna: Istituto delle Scienze, 1786; Florence: Pagani e Graziosi, 1793; and Milan: Società de' Classici Italiani, 1804. The version (which can be traced back to Melzi) of the *Codex Urbinate Latino 1270* in the Vatican Library was first published (with various inaccuracies) in 1817: *Trattato della Pittura di Lionardo da Vinci*, edited by G. Manzi (Rome: Tipografia De Romanis, 1817) (anastatic reprint edited by A. Zevi and published by Savelli, Milan: 1982; on Manzi, see the excellent profile by S. Fabrizio-Costa, *Autour de G. Manzi, éditeur du Traité de la peinture (1817)*, in S. Fabrizio-Costa and J.-P. Le Goff (eds.), "Léonard de Vinci entre France et Italie 'miroir profonde et sombre'", *Actes du Colloque International de l'Université de Caen* (3–4 October 1996) (Caen: Presses Universitarie de Caen, 1999), pp. 193–211. Critical editions are: *Das Buch von der Malerei*, Herausgegeben von H. Ludwig (Vienna: Wilhelm Braumüller, 1882); *Treatise on Painting*, ed. by A. Ph. McMahon, foreword by L. H. Heydenreich, (Princeton: Princeton University Press, 1956); *Libro di Pittura. Codice Urbinate Latino 1270 nella Biblioteca Apostolica Vaticana*,

edited by C. Pedretti and C. Vecce (Florence: Giunti, 1995); an edition exists without the facsimile of the codex (Florence: Giunti, 1996), 2 vols. Two critical editions have also been published of the first part only of the *Treatise*, the so-called *Paragone delle Arti*: *Paragone. A Critical Interpretation with a New Edition of the Text in the Codex Urbinas*, ed. by C. J. Farago (Leiden: Bell, 1992), and *Il Paragone delle Arti*, edited by C. Scarpati (Milan: Vita e Pensiero, 1994).

Another compilation taken by Fra Luigi Maria Arconati (a natural son of Galeazzo) from unpublished materials written by Leonardo was brought together to form the treatise *Del moto e della misura dell'acqua*, edited by F. Cardinali, in E. Manfredi, *Opuscoli idraulici* (Bologna: Cardinali e Frulli, 1826), pp. 271–450; *Del moto e misura delle acque. Appunti raccolti dai manoscritti vinciani da Luigi Maria Arconati* (Bologna: Zanichelli, 1923).

An introductory and easier read on Leonardo's texts is provided by the main anthologies: *The Literary Works of Leonardo da Vinci*, compiled and edited from the original manuscripts by J. P. Richter (London: Sampson Low, Marston, Searle & Rivington, 1883), 2 vols., reprinted by Dover, New York 1970 (expanded second edition edited by I. A. Richter, Oxford University Press, Oxford 1939; reprinted by Phaidon, London 1970). Still the broadest anthology and treated by subject, it is completed with the *Commentary*, also in two volumes, by Carlo Pedretti (Oxford: Oxford University Press, 1977).

Of the many Italian editions, one still available and in many ways unsuperseded is the *Leonardo da Vinci, Scritti scelti*, edited by A. M. Brizio (Turin: Utet, 1952) (expanded second edition, 1966), which for the first time organised the texts principally on a chronological basis and only by theme as a secondary aspect. In doing so, the reader is given a closer idea of the development of Leonardo's thought and literary style. Using the traditional subject-based division of material is *Leonardo da Vinci, Scritti letterari*, edited by A. Marinoni (Milan: Rizzoli, 1952, expanded second edition, 1974); this was the first

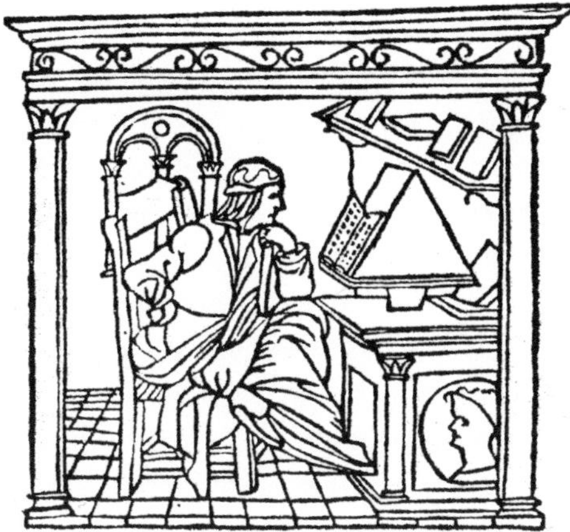

Fig. 9. Frontispiece of the *Rime* by Bernardo Bellincioni, Milan, 15 July 1493, c. 4r (woodcut, 88 x 86 mm)

volume of a planned cheaper edition of "all the writings" but it was never followed up. More recently there have been *Leonardo da Vinci, Scritti*, edited by C. Vecce (Milan: Mursia, 1992) and *Leonardo da Vinci, Scritti artistici e tecnici*, edited by B. Agosti (Milan: Rizzoli 2002), the latter emphasising the critical approach.

An important English anthology is by E. McCurdy, *Leonardo da Vinci's Notebooks*, London: Jonathan Cape, 1938, 2 vols.

Besides this last volume and the editions of the *Treatise on Painting*, with regard to Leonardo's writings on art, see at least *Leonardo on Painting*, edited by M. Kemp and M. Walker (New Haven: Yale University Press, 1989) and in particular the passages by Leonardo in the *Scritti d'arte del Cinquecento*, edited by P. Barocchi (Milan–Naples: Ricciardi, 1971–77), 3 vols.

With regard to philology *strictu sensu*, the fundamental text is by G. Calvi, *I manoscritti di Leonardo da Vinci dal punto di vista cronologico, storico e biografico* (Bologna: Zanichelli, 1925); a new edition has an introduction by A. Marinoni (Busto Arsizio: Bramante, 1982). Also important are C. Pedretti, *Leonardo da Vinci On Painting. A Lost Book (Libro A)*, foreword by K. Clark (Berkeley–Los Angeles: University of California Press, 1964), which is perhaps the most important of the innumerable and very different publications by Pedretti on Leonardo da Vinci.

In this he reconstructs a lost manuscript drafted by Leonardo around 1508; and C. Scarpati, *Leonardo scrittore* (Milan: Vita e Pensiero, 2001).

DOCUMENTS AND LITERARY REFERENCES TO LEONARDO

Leonardo was celebrated in literature from as early as the 1490s: in writings by Bernardo Bellincioni (*Rime*, published posthumously in Milan by F. Mantegazza in 1493, available in the more questionable edition by P. Fanfani [Bologna: Romagnoli, 1876–78], 2 vols., anastatic reprint [Bologna: Commissione per i testi di lingua, 1968]; the woodcut of the frontispiece [fig. 9]—for which the reader should consult U. Rozzo, *Lo studiolo nella xilografia italiana (1479–1558)* [Udine: Forum, 1998]—shows Bellincioni reading in his study and may be based on a sketch by Leonardo derived from memories of the *Madonna Benois* and recent ideas for Saint Peter in the *Last Supper*), Baldassarre Taccone, *Coronatione e Sponsalitio de la Serenissima Regina M. Bianca Maria Sforza Augusta* (Milan: L. Pachel, 1493), and De *Divina Proportione* by Pacioli, printed in Venice by Paganino de Paganini in 1509 (now available in an anastatic version [Turin: Nino Aragno, 1999] but unfortunately with a very poor introduction by P. Thea), and various others.

Works by contemporary authors that mention Leonardo, whether manuscript or printed, that are worthy of a modern edition are: G. Santi, *La vita e le gesta di Federico da Montefeltro duca di Urbino* (ca. 1487–88), edited by L. Michelini Tocci (Vatican City: Biblioteca Apostolica Vaticana, 1985), 2 vols.; P. Gaurico, *De sculptura* (Florence: Giunti, 1504) (the recent edition edited by P. Cutolo [Naples: Edizioni Scientifiche Italiane, 1999] is not up to the version edited by A. Chastel and R. Klein [Geneva: Droz, 1969]); L. Pacioli, *De Viribus Quantitatis*, edited by A. Marinoni and M. Garlaschi Peirani (Milan: Ente Raccolta Vinciana, 1997); N. da Correggio, *Opere,* edited by A. Tissoni Benvenuti (Bari: Laterza, 1969); and *Il Libro di Antonio Billi*, edited by F. Benedettucci (Anzio: De Rubeis, 1991). *Antiquarie Prospetiche Romane*, edited by G. Agosti e D. Isella, Fondazione Pietro Bembo, Parma: Guanda, 2005. During the sixteenth century, in addition to the many quotations taken from Leonardo in *De Architectura* by Vitruvius edited by Cesare Cesariano (Como: Gottardo da Ponte, 1521); in the commentary on Book II and, which remained unknown until recent times, the one on Book X: see C. Cesariano, *Vitruvio De Architectura Libri II-IV. I materiali, i templi, gli ordini*, edited by A. Rovetta (Milan: Vita e Pensiero, 2002) and C. Cesariano, *Volgarizzamento dei libri IX (capitoli 7 e 8) e X di Vitruvio,* De Architectura, *secondo il manoscritto 9/2790 Secciòn de Cortes della Real Academia de la Historia, Madrid*, edited by B. Agosti (Pisa: Scuola Normale Superiore, 1996), references to Leonardo are made in *Il Cortegiano* by Baldassar Castiglione, *Orlando Furioso* by Ludovico Ariosto (in XXXIII, 10 of the 1532 edition), the important references by Paolo Giovio (ca. 1523–27) in *Leonardi Vincii vita* and *Fragmentum trium dialogorum* (texts available in P. Giovio, *Scritti d'arte. Lessico ed ecfrasi*, edited by S. Maffei [Pisa: Scuola Normale Superiore, 1999]), while *Notizia d'opere del disegno* by Marco Antonio Michiel (ca. 1521–43) edited by C. De Benedictis (Florence: Edifir, 2000) (which takes up the text published by T. Frimmel in 1896) will soon be superseded by the edition edited by R. Lauber and being printed by Forum of Udine.

Vasari's *Life* of Leonardo, which was a primary and decisive source for the artist's later fortune, has several variants, including the edition published by Lorenzo Torrentino in 1550 and the one by Giunti in 1568 (on which see A. Conti, "Osservazioni e appunti sulla *Vita* di Leonardo di Giorgio Vasari", in *Kunst des Cinquecento in der Toscana* (Munich: Bruckmann, 1992), pp. 24–36. Both texts are included in G. Vasari, *Le vite de' più eccellenti pittori scultori e architettori nelle redazioni del 1550 e 1568*, edited by R. Bettarini and P. Barocchi (Florence: Sansoni,

1976) vol. IV, pp. 15–38. The other important sixteenth-century source for Leonardo is the Milanese Giovan Paolo Lomazzo, for which refer to his *Scritti sulle arti*, edited by R. P. Ciardi (Florence: Marchi e Bertolli, 1973) vol. I and (Florence: Centro Di, 1974) vol. II, which should be integrated with *Le tavole del Lomazzo (per i settant'anni di Paola Barocchi)*, edited by B. and G. Agosti (Brescia: L'Obliquo, 1997), and the historical framework provided by G. P. Lomazzo and the Facchini della Val di Blenio, *Rabisch*, edited by D. Isella (Turin: Einaudi, 1993).
For other sources—both literary and documentary—that relate to Leonardo's life, see *Leonardo da Vinci. I documenti e le testimonianze letterarie*, edited by E. Villata (Milan: Ente Raccolta Vinciana, 1999) to which should be added the latest discoveries by L. Böninger, "Ein Gerichtsurteil zu einer offenen Geldschuld Leonardo da Vincis aus dem April 1481 (ASF, Mercanzia 7265)", in *Mitteilungen des Kunsthistorisches Institutes in Florenz*, XLIV, 2000, 2/3, pp. 340–41; F. Caglioti, *Donatello e i Medici. Storia del David e della Giuditta* (Florence: Olschki), vol. I, p. 297, note 23, and most importantly J. Shell and G. Sironi, *Un nuovo documento di pagamento per la "Vergine delle Rocce" di Leonardo*, in P. C. Marani (ed.), *"Hostinato rigore". Leonardiana in memoria di Augusto Marinoni* (Milan: Electa, 2000), pp. 27–31. Other new documents are presented in *Leonardo la vera immagine. La vita e i documenti*, edited by V. Arrighi, A. Bellinazzi and E. Villata, exhibition catalogue, Florence, in print. A new and rather interesting document dating from 1579 relating to the *Virgin of the Rocks* is presented by M. C. Passoni, "Nuovi documenti e una proposta di ricostruzione per l'ancona della *Vergine delle Rocce*", in *Nuovi Studi*, 11, forthcoming.

BIOGRAPHIES AND THE LEGEND OF LEONARDO

The best biographies of Leonardo (in the sense that they are strictly accounts of his life to the point of leaving out critical content) are those by E. Solmi, *Leonardo (1452–1519)* (Florence:

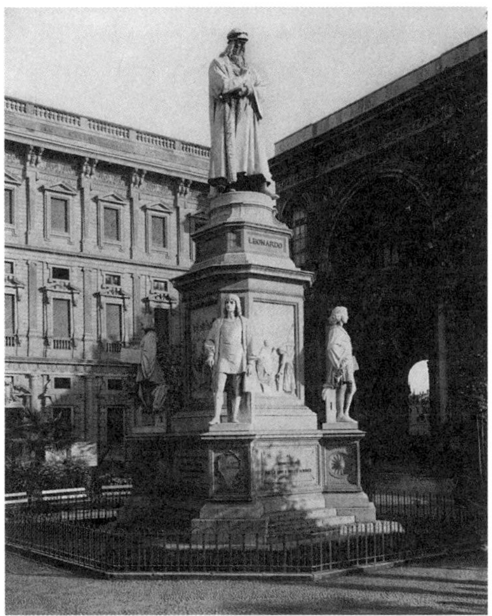

Fig. 10. Pietro Magni, *Monument to Leonardo*, 1872, Piazza della Scala, Milan (Photo: Brogi, late nineteenth century).

Barbera, 1900) (new ed., Milan: Longanesi, 1972) and the recent one by C. Vecce, *Leonardo* (Rome: Salerno, 1998).
There is no real structured work regarding pre-nineteenth-century considerations of the artist, however, the reader might try A. R. Turner, *Inventing Leonardo. Anatomy of a Legend* (New York: Knopf, 1993). At the start of the nineteenth century in Milan, the figure of Leonardo was wrapped up in patriotism, as is seen, for example, in the Milanese edition (1804) of *Trattato della Pittura* (preceded by a very important essay entitled *Memorie storiche su la vita, gli studi, e le opere di Lionardo da Vinci* by Carlo Amoretti, the librarian at the Ambrosiana), the famous book by Giuseppe Bossi, *Del Cenacolo di Leonardo da Vinci Libri Quattro* (Milan: Stamperia Reale, 1810) to commemorate the studies he carried out through the cartoon (now destroyed) of an actual-size copy of the *Last Supper* commissioned by Viceroy Eugenio di Beauharnais and translated into a mosaic by Giuseppe Raffaelli (now in the Minoritenkirche in Vienna). Bossi's book caused a debate to

which even Goethe contributed (*Joseph Bossi über Leonardo da Vinci Abendmahl zu Mailand*, 1817, English translation by G. H. Noeden, *Observations on Leonardo da Vinci's Celebrated Picture of the Last Supper*, London: Bulmer and Nicol, 1821; recently it has been translated into Italian by C. Groff, *Il Cenacolo di Leonardo*, with a contribution by M. Carminati [Milan: Abscondita, 2004]), but which also involved Carlo Verri (*Osservazioni sul volume intitolato Del Cenacolo di Leonardo da Vinci* [...] *scritte per lume dei giovani studiosi del disegno e della pittura* [Milan: Pirotta, 1812]), and against and for Bossi respectively Ugo Foscolo and Vincenzo Monti. On the matter see A. Colombo, "'Titolo nuovo di gallica accortezza'. U. Foscolo e i restauri della Cena di Leonardo", in S. Fabrizio-Costa and J.-P. Le Goff (eds.), *Léonard de Vinci* (op. cit.), pp. 182–92 with bibliographical references. Romantic Neo-Renaissance historicism, employed to disparage the French, encouraged not only the championing by Lombard and Tuscan artists of Leonardo as a leading historical character, but also another restoration (by Stefano Barezzi and Martin Knoller) of the *Last Supper* between 1853 and 1855, sponsored by the Austrian government, and, soon after, the announcement of a competition to produce a statue to Leonardo [fig. 10] (which was won by Pietro Magni but only erected in Piazza della Scala in Milan in 1872 once Italy had been unified).

In parallel the newly restored French monarchy (under Charles X) and then empire (under Napoleon III) rediscovered Leonardo through his link with the sixteenth-century *gloire* of François I, but the fame of the Italian artist later developed around him as an independent figure (the best-known indication of that is the various versions of the *Death of Leonardo* [fig. 11] by Ingres). A fine text for understanding of Leonardo's iconography is R. P. Ciardi and P. Sisi (eds.), *L'immagine di Leonardo. Testimonianze figurative dal XVI al XIX secolo*, exhibition catalogue (Florence: Giunti, 1997); Leonardo's Milanese period is well treated in P. C. Marani, "Il Cenacolo di Leonardo e i suoi restauri nella Milan fra il xv e il xx secolo fra arte e fede, propaganda politica e magnificenza civile", in *I Tatti Studies*, 7, 1997 (but 1998), pp. 191–229. With the first publications of the manuscripts Leonardo's "myth" began to grow at the end of the Ottocento, but on two levels: one is the literary approach which portrayed him as half magician, half dandy (exalted by Baudelaire in France and Walter Pater in England), and the other a positivist slant that considered Leonardo in the light of a scientific prodigy and inventor. Often these two aspects are interwoven and connected in Italy with either clearly nationalistic intent and in France as glorification of "Latin stock". On this see the excellent summary by S. Migliore, *Tra Hermes e Prometeo. Il mito di Leonardo nel decadentismo europeo* (Florence: Olschki, 1994); a less useful text on this matter is E. Franzini's *Il mito di Leonardo. Sulla fenomenologia della creazione artistica* (Milan: Unicopli, 1987). The nationalistic fervour of the Italians continued up until 1939 when Leonardo was defined a "genius of our lineage" in the Leonardo exhibition (described as "abominable" by Longhi) held at the Palazzo dell'Arte in Milan.

At the end of the nineteenth century, two particularly committed monographs appeared in France: the extremely positivist one by G. Séailles, *Léonard de Vinci. Essai de biographie psychologique* (Paris: Perrin, 1892) and the more historicist approach of E. Müntz, *Léonard de Vinci. L'homme l'artist le savant* (Paris: Hachette, 1899). At the start of the eighteenth century, Leonardo was of interest to literati like Paul Valéry, whose essays on Leonardo from the years 1894–1929 are available in Italian: *Scritti su Leonardo*, introduction by E. De Rienzo, transl. by B. Dal Fabbro (Milan: Electa, 1984), and the Russian Dmitri Merezkovsky, who wrote a successful novel in 1900 that was translated into several languages (English title: *Leonardo da Vinci*). The novel was admired by Freud, who was himself the author in 1910 of a famous essay in which he argues for the sublimated homosexuality of Leonardo (English transl. "Leonardo da Vinci and a Memory of His Childhhod", in *The Standard*

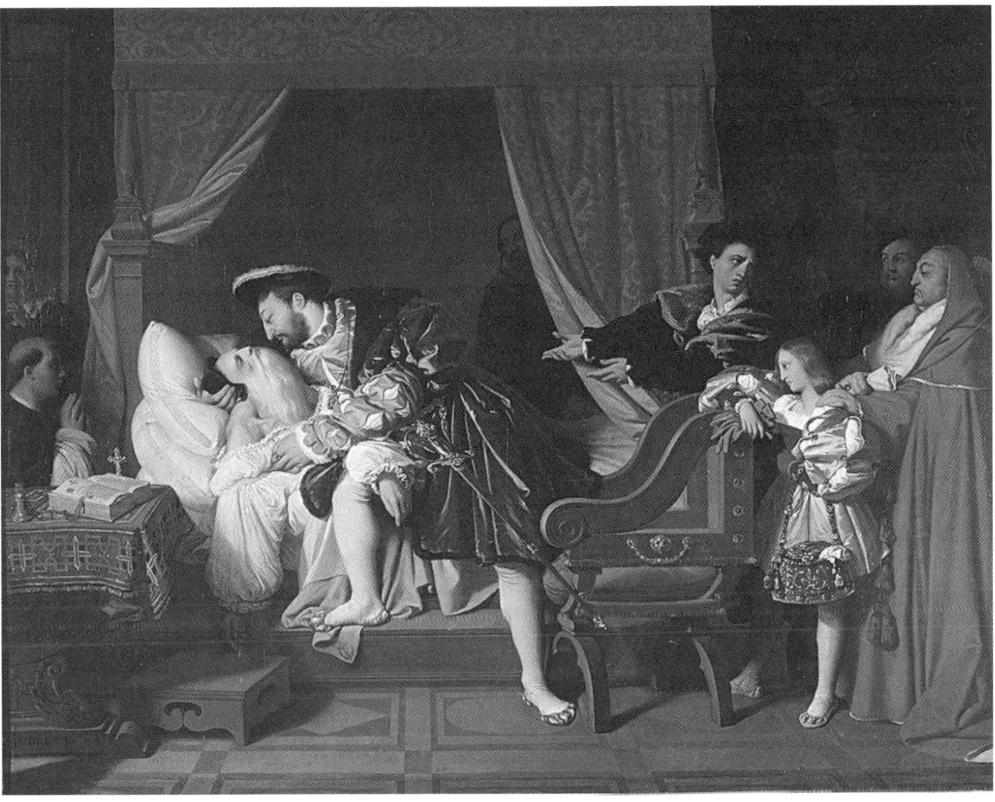

Fig. 11. Jean Auguste Dominique Ingres, *Death of Leonardo*, 1818, oil on canvas, 40 x 50.5 cm, Musée du Petit Palais, Paris.

Edition of the Complete Psychological Works of Sigmund Freud, Translated under the general editorship of J. Strachey in collaboration with A. Freud, assisted by A. Strachey and A. Tyson, 24 vols., London: Hogarth Press, 1953–74, vol. 11, pp. 57–137).

The other face of the studies—that of erudite research—was excellently represented in Italy by Gustavo Uzielli and later by Edmondo Solmi. The celebratory climate inculcated the "rebellion" of Benedetto Croce, who radically depreciated the theoretical value of the *Treatise on Painting* ("Leonardo filosofo", in *Leonardo da Vinci. Conferenze fiorentine* [Milan: Treves, 1910], pp. 225–56, later in B. Croce, *Saggio sullo Hegel seguito da altri scritti di storia della filosofia* [Bari: Laterza, 1948], pp. 207–34), and the young Roberto Longhi who, in his essay-cum attack "Le due Lise" in *La Voce* in 1914 (VI, 1, pp. 21–25; later in *Scritti giovanili* [Florence: Sansoni, 1956], vol. I, t. 1, pp. 129–32), showed himself almost overturning the luxurious prose of Walter Pater (*Studies in the History of the Renaissance* [1873; in *The Renaissance: Studies in Art and History*, ed. by D. L. Hill, Berkeley: University of California Press, 1980]). Longhi's more mature but still problematic consideration of Leonardo can be read in the short, intense and almost troubled pages of "Difficoltà di Leonardo", in *Paragone*, 29, 1952, pp. 10–12 (later in *Cinquecento classico e Cinquecento manieristico* [Florence: Sansoni, 1976], vol. VIII, t. 2, pp. 1–3). This was followed by the new conclusion offered in "Aspetti dell'antica arte lombarda", in *Arte lombarda dai Visconti agli Sforza*, exhibition catalogue (Cinisello Balsamo: Silvana Editoriale, 1958), pp. XVII-XXXVII (later published in *Lavori in Valpadana dal*

Trecento al primo Cinquecento, 1934–1964 [Florence: Sansoni, 1973], vol. VI, pp. 229–48).

LEONARDO THE ARTIST: DISCUSSED GENERALLY AND IN SOME DETAIL

Good and excellent monographs on Leonardo the artist at the start of the century included those by W. Von Seidlitz, *Leonardo da Vinci der Wendepunkt der Renaissance* (Berlin: Bard, 1909), 2 vols., (a second edition was published by Phaidon, Vienna in 1935), which was of impressive erudition; O. Siren, *Leonardo da Vinci: the Artist and the Man*, New Haven-London, Yale University Press-Oxford University Press, 1916 [orig. ed. Stockholm: Bagges, 1911]; L. Venturi, *La critica e l'arte di Leonardo da Vinci* (Bologna: Zanichelli, 1919) with an anastatic reprint by the same publisher in 1988; A. Venturi, *Leonardo da Vinci pittore* (Bologna: Zanichelli, 1920) with an anastatic reprint by the same publisher in 1985; and E. Hildebrandt, *Leonardo da Vinci* (Berlin: Grote, 1927). Others were the book by W. Suida, who made the first analysis of the various artists who adopted Leonardo's style, *Leonardo und sein Kreis* (Munich: Bruckmann, 1929) (It. ed. edited by M. T. Fiorio with transl. by M. Ricci, *Leonardo e i leonardeschi* [Vicenza: Neri Pozza, 2001]), the catalogue raisonné by H. Bodmer, *Leonardo. Des Meisters Gemälde und Zeichnungen* (Stuttgart–Berlin: Deutsches Verlagsantalt, 1931) and most important the short, elegant and fundamental monograph by K. Clark, *Leonardo da Vinci. An Account of his Development as an Artist* (Cambridge: Macmillan, 1939) (new edition edited by M. Kemp and published by Viking, London 1988). Clark's book followed on the heels of his important catalogue of the drawings in Windsor, which set down the fundaments of Leonardo's graphic works based on both technical and stylistic grounds, *A Catalogue of the Drawings of Leonardo da Vinci in the Collection of His Majesty the King at Windsor Castle* (Cambridge: Cambridge University Press, 1935), 2 vols. (2nd ed. revised with the assistance of C. Pedretti and published by Phaidon, London 1968–69, 3 vols.). Based on Clark's classification came the excellent book by A. E. Popham, *The Drawings of Leonardo da Vinci* (London: Jonathan Cape, 1946; new ed., revised and with a new introductory essay by M. Kemp and published by Pimlico, London 1994). Among the many later books worthy of note are the miscellaneous collection *Leonardo. Saggi e ricerche* (Rome: Istituto Poligrafico dello Stato, 1954), which is still one of the most useful texts for the student of Leonardo; and the not quite so important but equally valuable (especially for the essays by M.V. Brugnoli and A. M. Brizio) *The Unknown Leonardo*, edited by L. Reti (New York: McGraw-Hill, 1974). Restricting the field to artististic monographs, in addition to the excellent summaries by A. Ottino della Chiesa, *L'opera completa di Leonardo pittore* (Milan: Rizzoli, 1967) and P. C. Marani, *Leonardo. Catalogo completo dei dipinti* (Florence: Cantini, 1989; and I am pleased to include the compact volume by G. Previtali, *Leonardo* (Milan: Electa, 1960); there are also C. Pedretti, *Leonardo. A Study in Chronology and Style* (London: Thames and Hudson, 1973); C. Gould, *Leonardo. The Artist and the non-Artist* (London: Weidenfeld and Nicholson, 1977); the miscellaneous *Leonardo. La pittura* (Florence: Giunti, 1977; 2nd ed. edited by P. C. Marani, and published by the same company in 1985); M. Rosci, *Leonardo* (Milan: Mondadori, 1979); and M. Kemp, *Leonardo da Vinci. The Marvellous Works of Nature and Man* (London: Dent, 1981). This last work is particularly important for its attempt to consider Leonardo's work as a structured body rather than being divided into "artistic", "scientific" etc. (on the art–science relationship in Leonardo, see the collection of essays also by M. Kemp, *Lezioni dell'occhio. Leonardo da Vinci discepolo dell'esperienza*, transl. by R. and C. Marinoni, P. C. Marani and M. Parizzi [Milan: Vita e Pensiero, 2004], and the very recent *Leonardo*, Oxford: Oxford University Press, 2004). More recently, in addition to the always valuable collection of writings on Leonardo by André Chastel

(*Leonardo da Vinci. Studi e ricerche 1952–1990*, transl. by G. Coccioli [Turin: Einaudi, 1995]), there are the magnificent books by D. Arasse, *Léonard de Vinci. Le rhytme du monde* (Paris: Hazan, 1997: English translation *Leonardo da Vinci*, London: Greenwich, 1999) and, more specifically on the artistic side, P. C. Marani, *Leonardo. Una carriera di pittore* (Milan: Motta, 1999; English translation *Leonardo da Vinci. The Complete Paintings*, New York: Abrams, 2000; a smaller version of this last title is also available). The bulk of the last long monograph by F. Zöllner, *Leonardo da Vinci* (Cologne: Taschen, 2003) is not proportional to its scientific value. On Leonardo's youth there is much to be learnt from D. A. Brown, *Leonardo da Vinci. Origins of a Genius* (New Haven–London: Yale University Press, 1998) though the reader should skip over the section referring to the *Ginevra Benci*. Worthy of a look is A. Natali, *Leonardo. Il giardino di delizie* (Cinisello Balsamo: Silvana Editoriale, 2002). In addition to the sometimes converging hypotheses of Brown and Marani, on the activity of Leonardo in Verrocchio's workshop, see L. Bellosi in *Due collezionisti alla scoperta dell'Italia. Dipinti e sculture del Museo Jacquemart-André di Parigi*, edited by A. Di Lorenzo, exhibition catalogue (Cinisello Balsamo: Silvana Editoriale, 2002), pp. 68–71. Also to be noted are the catalogues of the recent exhibitions on Leonardo in New York and Paris (with use of partly common materials and texts) though it is difficult to agree with all the chronologies and attributions: *Leonardo da Vinci Master Draftsman*, ed. by C. Cappel Bambach (New York–New Haven–London: The Metropolitan Museum–Yale University Press, 2003) and *Léonard de Vinci. Dessins et manuscrits*, edited by F. Viatte and V. Forcione (Paris: Réunion des Musées Nationaux, 2003); the Paris catalogue is the more important of the two due to its explanations about the manuscripts held in the Institut de France.

On the Louvre drawings, useful for the reproductions is: F. Viatte, *Leonardo da Vinci*, Milan: 5 Continents Editions, 2005.

On the subject of Leonardo in Milan and his workshop, note G. Romano, "La Pala Sforzesca", in G. Romano, M. T. Binaghi Olivari, and D. Collura, *Il Maestro della Pala Sforzesca* (Florence: Centro Di, 1978), pp. 6–23; *Zenale e Leonardo. Tradizione e rinnovamento della pittura lombarda*, exhibition catalogue (Milan: Electa, 1982); a good round-up is provided by M. Gregori (ed.) in *Pittura a Milan. Rinascimento e Manierismo* (Milan: Cariplo, 1998) (see in particular the essays by P. Marani and F. Frangi); and finally D. A. Brown, *Leonardo da Vinci. Arte e devozione nelle Madonne dei suoi allievi* (Cinisello Balsamo: Silvana Editoriale, 2003), which should be read selectively with allowance for a poor translation. Soon due to be published is the monumental work by A. Ballarin, *Problemi di leonardismo milanese. Boltraffio prima della pala Casio* (Cittadella: Bertoncello), some of the arguments of which have been made available in university lecture notes, both those relating to Leonardo himself and those to his great and lesser followers. Many of the ideas, plus numerous others, are offered in *Disegni del Rinascimento in Valpadana*, edited by G. Agosti, exhibition catalogue (Florence: Olschki, 2001); with regard to those relating to Leonardo's years in Milan this book agrees to a large extent (on the other hand, the monographs listed above on Leonardo the artist furnish very differing interpretations: many experts date the *Lady with an Ermine* to around 1489–90, and the London *Virgin of the Rocks* to the last decade of the Quattrocento). On the "idealised portraits" of Leonardo and Boltraffio, see D. A. Brown, "Leonardo and the Idealized Portrait in Milan", in *Arte Lombarda*, 67, 1983, pp. 102–16; and E. Rama, "Un tentativo di rilettura della ritrattistica di Boltraffio fra Quattrocento e Cinquecento", in *Arte Lombarda*, 64, 1983, pp. 79–82. On Leonardo's portraiture the reader is referred to J. Shearman, *Only Connect... Art and the Spectator in the Italian Renaissance*, National Gallery of Art, Washington, D.C., 1992. On Leonardo's followers, in addition to Suida's book, which still remains the best, there are *I leonardeschi a Milan. Fortuna e collezionismo*, conference proceedings (Milan, 25–26 September 1990), edited by M.T. Fiorio and P. C. Marani (Milan: Electa, 1991), and *I leonardeschi. L'eredità di Leonardo in Lombardia* (Milan: Skira, 1998; Eng. ed. *The Legacy of Leonardo. Painters in Lombardy 1490-1530*, Milan: Skira 1998), the latter to be read selectively. On Milanese culture during the Renaissance from the standpoint of the history of art, recommended in particular are two works by G. Agosti: *Bambaia e il classicismo lombardo* (Turin: Einaudi, 1990) and *Scrittori che parlano di artisti, tra Quattro e Cinquecento in Lombardia*, in *Quattro pezzi lombardi (per Maria Teresa Binagli)* (Brescia: L'Obliquo, 1998), pp. 39–93. On the culture of the courts, of which Leonardo became a leading figure in Milan, there is no better guide than G. Romano, "Verso la maniera moderna. Da Mantegna a Raffaello", in *Storia dell'arte italiana* (Turin: Einaudi, 1981) vol. 6, t. I, and "Cinquecento e Seicento", pp. 5–83. This involvement as a courtier obliged Leonardo to become also a "man of letters", which was not typical of his culture nor, perhaps, of his nature. This situation has been discussed in masterly fashion (though perhaps with a slight excess of antipathy towards Leonardo) by C. Dionisotti, "Leonardo uomo di lettere", in *Italia medievale e umanistica*, V, 1962, pp. 183–216, republished in *Appunti su arti e lettere* (Milan: Jaca Book, 1995). A serious study on Leonardo's sources—and therefore of the cultural limits and the sometimes moving efforts undertaken to overcome them—can be found in E. Solmi, *Le fonti dei manoscritti di Leonardo da Vinci. Contributi*, a supplement to *Il Giornale Storico della Letteratura Italiana* (Turin: Loescher, 1908) and later published in *Le Fonti dei manoscritti di Leonardo da Vinci e altri studi* (Florence: La Nuova Italia, 1976); A. Marinoni, *Gli appunti grammaticali e lessicali di Leonardo da Vinci*, vol. I, *L'educazione letteraria di Leonardo* (Milan: Castello Sforzesco, 1944), vol. II, *Testo critico* (Milan: Castello Sforzesco, 1952); E. Garin, "Il problema delle fonti del pensiero di Leonardo", in *La cultura filosofica del Rinascimento italiano. Ricerche e documenti* (Florence: Sansoni, 1961; new ed. 1992, pp. 388–401); C. Maccagni, "Riconsiderando il problema delle fonti di Leonardo: l'elenco di libri ai fogli 2 verso-3 recto del Codice 8936 della Biblioteca Nacional di Madrid" (Lettura Vinciana X, 1970), in *Leonardo letto e commentato. Letture vinciane I-XII (1960–1972)*, edited by P. Galluzzi (Florence: Giunti, 1974), pp. 275–307; and A. Marinoni, "La biblioteca di Leonardo", in *Raccolta Vinciana*, XXII, 1987, pp. 291–342. Identification of the *Libro dell'Amadìo* with *La Bella Camilla* is by C. Pedretti, in *La tempesta in biblioteca. Il Paragone delle arti da Urbino a Ischia* (Manziana: Vecchiarelli, 2001). In order to understand the corollary effects of Leonardo's culture and the methodological unity of his studies, leaving aside any artificial division into "subjects", the following are indispensable works: C. Luporini, *La mente di Leonardo* (Florence: Sansoni, 1953; anastatic reprint Florence: Le Lettere, 1997); V. P. Zubov, *Leonardo da Vinci* (1962), English transl. from the Russian by D. H. Kraus (Cambridge, Mass.: Harvard University Press, 1968); and E. Garin, *Scienza e vita civile nel Rinascimento italiano* (Bari: Laterza, 1965). Some valuable points can also be found in the unilateral but engaging work by K. Jaspers, *Lionardo als Philosoph* (Bern: Francke, 1953) (It. ed. edited by F. Masini [Milan: SE, 1988]) and in L. M. Batkin, *Leonardo da Vinci*, It. transl. by G. Mazzinelli (Bari: Laterza, 1988). Also to note is R. Zwijneberg, *The Writings and Drawings of Leonardo da Vinci. Order and Chaos in Early Modern Thought* (Cambridge: Cambridge University Press, 1999). Today superseded but nonetheless historiographically important is the cultural image of Renaissance Florence described by A. Chastel, *Art et Humanisme à Florence au temps de Laurent le Magnifique. Études sur la Renaissance et l'Humanisme platonicien* (Paris: Presses Universitaires de France, 1959; It. transl. by R. Federici, *Arte e umanesimo a Florence al tempo di Lorenzo il Magnifico. Studi sul Rinascimento e sull'umanesimo platonico* [Turin: Einaudi, 1964]); yet the best introduction remains the masterpiece by M. Wackernagel, *Der Lebenstraum des Künstlers in der florentinischer Renaissance. Aufgaben und Auftraggeber, Erkstatt und Kunstmarket* (Leipzig: Seemann, 1938; It. transl. by A. Sbrilli, *Il mondo degli artisti nel Rinascimento fiorentino*, with an introduction by E. Castelnuovo [Rome: La Nuova Italia Scientifica, 1994]).

There are many specific essays in particular works but I will restrict myself to mentioning *Lo sguardo degli angeli* (Cinisello Balsamo: Silvana Editoriale, 1998) and *La montagna e il mare* (Cinisello Balsamo: Silvana Editoriale, 2001), both edited by A. Natali, on the subjects of restoration of the *Baptism of Christ* and the *Annunciation* in the Uffizi; *Leonardo. La dama con l'ermellino*, edited by B. Fabjan and P. C. Marani (Cinisello Balsamo: Silvana Editoriale, 1998), which has a great deal of technical information and discusses the biography of Cecilia Gallerani, though this latter subject is more widely considered in J. Shell and G. Sironi, "Cecilia Gallerani: Leonardo's Lady with an Ermine", in *Artibus et Historiae*, 25, 1992, pp. 47–66; G. Bora, *Due tavole leonardesche. Nuove indagini sul Musico e sul San Giovanni dell'Ambrosiana* (Vicenza: Neri Pozza, 1987; *Fontes Ambrosiani* LXXVIII); P. C. Marani, "Federico Borromeo e i dipinti di Leonardo. Ipotesi sulla provenienza del Musico", in *Borromaica*, 18, 2004, pp. 255–62. P. Brambilla Barcilon and P. C. Marani, *Leonardo. L'Ultima Cena* (Milan: Electa, 1999; Eng. trans. by H. Tighe, *Leonardo. The Last Supper*, Chicago: Chicago University Press, 2001), which was published at the end of the more than twenty-year long restoration of the *Last Supper*, and which is of fundamental importance for the historical and technical information it provides as well as for the high quality of the reproductions. On the *Last Supper* see also L. H. Heydenreich, *Leonardo. The Last Supper* (London: Allen Lane–Penguin Books, 1974); G. Eichholz, *Das Abendmahl Leonardo da Vincis: eine systematische Bildmonographie* (Munich: Scaneg, 1998); and L. Steimberg, *Leonardo's Incessant Last Supper* (New York: Zone Books, 2001), which has more emphasis on the iconography than the history of art. On the popular success of the wall painting, see *Il Genio e le Passioni: Leonardo e il Cenacolo. Precedenti, innovazioni, riflessi di un capolavoro*, edited by P. C. Marani, exhibition catalogue (Milan: Skira, 2001); and C. Scailliérez, *Léonard de Vinci. La Joconde* (Paris: Réunion des Musées Nationaux, 2003).

On Leonardo's studies of optics and their application in his painting, see A. M. Brizio, *Razzi incidenti e razzi refressi* (Lettura Vinciana III, 21 April 1963), in *Leonardo letto e commentato. Letture Vinciane I-XII (1960–1972)*, edited by P. Galluzzi (Florence: Giunti Barbera, 1974), pp. 63–84; J. Ackerman, "Leonardo's Eye", in *Journal of the Warburg and Courtauld Institutes*, XLI, 1978, pp. 108–46; M. Baxandall, *Shadows and Enlightenment* (New Haven–London: Yale University Press, 1995). For the relationship between Leonardo's painting and sculpture, though with the exception of the final attribution to the artist of a terracotta bust taken from others, the reader is referred to M. Kemp, *Leonardo e lo spazio dello scultore* (Lettura Vinciana XXVII, 20 April 1987; Florence: Giunti Barbera, 1988); a balanced analysis of the current situation is provided by P. C. Marani, "Per Leonardo scultore: nuove ipotesi sul bronzo di Budapest, il Monumento Trivulzio e il Rustici", in *Arte Lombarda*, 139, 3, 2003, pp. 154–62; F. Caglioti now also supports the attribution to Leonardo put forward by many scholars in the mid-twentieth century, and recently by Rosci, of the terracotta *Madonna and Laughing Child* in the Victoria and Albert Museum: "Su Matteo Civitali scultore", in *Matteo Civitali e il suo tempo. Pittori, scultori e orafi a Lucca nel tardo Quattrocento*, catalogue of the exhibition in Lucca (Cinisello Balsamo: Silvana Editoriale, 2004, pp. 29–77), particularly p. 72.

Naturally this bibliography is very selective and reflects the preferences of the writer, however, the reader will find all the necessary references therein for further research. Also omitted have been the many books and papers written on Leonardo the "architect", "engineer", "botanist", etc. In conclusion, the reader is reminded of the monumental *Bibliotheca Leonardiana (1493–1989)*, edited by M. Guerrini (Milan: Editrice Bibliografica, 1990), 3 vols., and the collection of essays and bibliographical updates found in the volumes (now at vol. XXX) of the *Raccolta Vinciana*, founded in 1905 by Luca Beltrami. Compared to the early twentieth-century sober presentation of this gazette, the guise of the ephemeral periodical *Achademia Leonardi Vinci* published by Giunti, of which ten issues appeared between 1988 and 1997, seemed luxurious, even overly so. Today there is also the CD-rom published by BIL (Bibliografia Internazionale Leonardiana), updated in May 2003, edited by the Biblioteca Leonardiana of Vinci and by the Cribecu, Scuola Normale Superiore di Pisa. These can refer any reader to more detailed sources.

PHOTO CREDITS

Agenzia fotografica Luisa Ricciarini, Milan [pls. 28, 29, 30, 31]

Bridgeman/Archivi Alinari, Florence [pls. 23, 24, 34]

© 2005 Board of Trustees, National Gallery of Art, Washington [pls. 1, 4, 5]

© 1990, Foto Scala, Florence [pls. 2, 3, 6, 7-9, 16, 18, 37]

Gabinetto fotografico della Soprintendenza Speciale per il Polo Museale Fiorentino, Florence [fig. 2]

© Photo RMN, Paris : Daniel Arnaudet, Michèle Bellot, Jean-Gilles Berizzi, Gérard Blot, Christian Jean, Thierry Le Mage, Hervé Lewandowski, Jacques L'Hoir, Jean Popovich, Jean Schormans [pls. 14, 15, 21, 33, 36, 39, 40, 41, 45, 46; figs. 1, 7, 11]

© Photoservice Electa, Milan [pls. 11, 12, 13, 17, 20, 25, 32]

Rheinisches Bildarchiv Köln, Cologne [pl. 10]

The Royal Collection © 2005, Her Majesty Queen Elizabeth II [pls. 19, 22, 26, 27, 35, 42, 43, 44, 47; figs. 3, 4, 5, 6, 8; page 2]

Szépmüvészeti Múzeum, Budapest [pl. 38]

The Ministero per i Beni e le Attività Culturali kindly gave permission to reproduce the following illustrations from Italian sources [pls. 2, 8, 9, 11, 12, 13, 25, 37]

[1]
Frédéric Elsig
Painting in France in the 15th Century

[2]
Fabrizio D'Amico
Morandi

[3]
Antonio Pinelli
David

[4]
Vincenzo Farinella
Raphael

[5]
Alessandro Angelini
Baroque Sculpture in Rome

[6]
Aldo Galli
The Pollaiuolo

[7]
Edoardo Villata
Leonardo da Vinci

[8]
Giovanni Lista
Arte Povera

[7] Edoardo Villata (Rome, 1971) teaches the History of Lombard Art at the Università Cattolica in Milan. The author of essays in reviews, miscellaneous books and exhibition catalogues, he published the books *Leonardo da Vinci. I documenti e le testimonianze contemporanee* (Milan 1999), *Macrino d'Alba* (Savigliano 2000) and *Gaudenzio Ferrari, Gerolamo Giovenone. Un avvio e un percorso* (Turin 2004, with Simone Baiocco).